*Studies in Writing & Rhetoric*

D1571347

## Studies in Writing & Rhetoric

In 1980 the Conference on College Composition and Communication established the Studies in Writing & Rhetoric (SWR) series as a forum for monograph-length arguments or presentations that engage general compositionists. SWR encourages extended essays or research reports addressing any issue in composition and rhetoric from any theoretical or research per-spective as long as the general significance to the field is clear. Previous SWR publications serve as models for prospective authors; in addition, contributors may propose alternate formats and agendas that inform or extend the field's current debates.

SWR is particularly interested in projects that connect the specific research site or theoretical framework to contemporary classroom and in-sti-tutional contexts of direct concern to compositionists across the nation. Such connections may come from several approaches, including cultural, theoretical, field-based, gendered, historical, and interdisciplinary. SWR especially encourages monographs by scholars early in their careers, by estab-lished scholars who wish to share an insight or exhortation with the field, and by scholars of color.

The SWR series editor and editorial board members are committed to working closely with prospective authors and offering significant developmental advice for encouraged manuscripts and prospectuses. Editorships rotate every five years. Prospective authors intending to submit a prospectus during the 2002 to 2007 editorial appointment should obtain submission guidelines from Robert Brooke, SWR editor, University of Nebraska–Lincoln, Department of English, P.O. Box 880337, 202 Andrews Hall, Lincoln, NE 68588-0337.

General inquiries may also be addressed to Sponsoring Editor, Studies in Writing & Rhetoric, Southern Illinois University Press, 1915 University Press Dr., MC 6806, Carbondale, IL 62901.

*Rural Literacies*

# Rural Literacies

Kim Donehower,
Charlotte Hogg,
and Eileen E. Schell

SOUTHERN ILLINOIS UNIVERSITY PRESS

*Carbondale*

10  09  08  07      4  3  2  1

Publication partially funded by a subvention grant from The Conference on College
Composition and Communication of the National Council of Teachers of English.

Library of Congress Cataloging-in-Publication Data
Donehower, Kim.
  Rural literacies / Kim Donehower, Charlotte Hogg, and Eileen E. Schell.
      p. cm. — (Studies in writing & rhetoric)
  Includes bibliographical references and index.
  ISBN-13: 978-0-8093-2749-2 (pbk. : alk. paper)
  ISBN-10: 0-8093-2749-X (pbk. : alk. paper)
  1. English language—Rhetoric—Study and teaching (Higher)—United States.
2. Academic writing—Study and teaching (Higher)—United States. 3. Rural
population—Education—United States. 4. Country life—United States. I. Hogg,
Charlotte, [date] II. Schell, Eileen E. III. Title.

PE1405.U6D66 2007
808'.0420711—dc22                                                    2006032147

Printed on recycled paper. ♻

The paper used in this publication meets the minimum requirements of American
National Standard for Information Sciences—Permanence of Paper for Printed  Library
Materials, ANSI Z39.48-1992. ∞

Kim Donehower dedicates this book to the memory of her grandmother Cordia Parks Moore.

Charlotte Hogg dedicates this book to the women of Paxton, Nebraska.

Eileen E. Schell dedicates this book to her grandmother A. Elizabeth Schell; to her late father, Robert E. Schell, a farmer until his death in 1984; and to her mother, Neva D. Schell, and her brother, Michael Robert Schell, both farmers until 2001.

# Contents

# Preface

When we began this book, the immediate (and at that time tentative) title of the first draft of the prospectus was *Rural Literacies*. As much as we wondered whether the word "rural" in the title could potentially limit our audience due to the very assumptions we sought to challenge, we were just as committed to emphasizing it. This tension became a central issue in these pages: rural literacies are not something for only rural people to pay attention to; rural should not be seen in opposition to urban but as part of a complex global economic and social network. To understand these connections, we must examine the specifics—material, social, agricultural, historical, and cultural—of rural lives and literacies. We must also challenge the commonplace assumptions about rural people and rural places that deem them lacking in opportunities for literacy work and community engagement. Our project analyzes rural communities and rural people's lives as rich sites for literacy and rhetorical research and for social action.

Before this project, we each individually researched aspects of rural literacies largely because of the lack of engagement with rural contexts in the field's existing literacy and rhetorical research; however, we didn't know each other personally. Then Robert Brooke, editor for the Studies in Writing and Rhetoric series, heard us each present papers on rural issues but on separate panels at the Thomas R. Watson Conference in Louisville, Kentucky, in 2002 and encouraged us to work together on a book project on rural literacies. A few phone calls in May 2003 affirmed our mutual interest in collaborating on such a project. The vast majority of the drafting of this book was done via e-mail and by telephone; we met at the 2004 Conference on College Composition and Communication in San Antonio and for an extended writing retreat in the rural North Carolina community where Kim's family hails from, flying in from North Dakota, New York, and Texas. Amid phone calls, through notes in each other's drafts, and over meals during our brief trips together, we pieced together our senses of ourselves as rural-identified—and found them both similar and distinctive as we disrupted the monolithic terms "rural" and "literacies" in our text. Eileen grew up on a third-generation family farm near Cashmere, Washington, that passed on to her brother, the fourth generation, until the farm ceased operations in 2001; Charlotte lived from the ages of eleven through eighteen in Paxton, a village in western Nebraska where her dad grew up; and Kim was reared near the rural North Carolina town where her mother was raised. Each of us existed within a backdrop that both called to mind and challenged clichéd and problematic images and narratives of rural: the "rosy" past of the independent family farm, the lack of the "empty" Great Plains, and the lag of the economy and "culture" in Appalachia.

Our book was written and arranged to productively reflect the similarities and differences of the rural families, places, and regions we come from—the rural West, the Great Plains, the rural South—and of the different types of research we do: qualitative research and rhetorical analysis. We collaboratively wrote chapters 1 and 5. Our individual chapters also signal our collaboration in that we gave each other's work written and verbal feedback and made occasional edits through multiple and evolving drafts as we fully realized our project. While we composed our chapters to cumulatively build our central argument, our goal was to demonstrate through the theoretical frameworks, methodologies, and tones of the individually authored chapters just a few of the ways rural literacies can be explored and analyzed as an area of research and in the writing classroom.

As is often the case with collaborative projects, we believe this text reaps the riches—in ways a single-authored text could not—of our distinct but overlapping areas of interest and expertise: literacy studies, critical literacy studies, qualitative research, rhetorical history and analysis, globalization studies, feminist theory, pedagogical theory and practice, and, of course, our investment in rural students, citizens, and communities. As we argue throughout the coming pages, collaborative literate action, on a much larger scale and in a variety of venues, is the best hope of ensuring a sustainable future for rural communities—collaborative action undertaken by a variety of stakeholders, rural, urban, and suburban, on issues of common concern, such as sustainable systems of education, economic development, and environmental policies. Such collaborative action is made possible through understanding how different groups can identify and work with one another across lines of difference—region, community, class, race, gender—and by problematizing the kinds of cultural rhetorics perpetuated in the popular media (such as red state versus blue state rhetorics) that divide rural areas from the rest of the United States. We hope our collaboration may serve as a model of such work.

# Acknowledgments

**R**ural Literacies would not be possible without Robert Brooke, who brought the three of us together to write this book. After hearing us speak at the Thomas R. Watson Conference, he encouraged us to work together to address the topic of rural literacies. From our first phone call in May 2003, we found an unexpected bond and collegiality borne out of a common background in rural places, communities, schools, and families. Our collaboration brought us in touch with not only each other but also the places our families hail from: Hot Springs, North Carolina; Cashmere, Washington; Paxton, Nebraska. In particular, we would like to thank Kim's aunt Marilee Moore, who generously provided us with her house in Hot Springs for a week so we could finish the draft of this book. That time writing together on the front porch and soaking in the nearby hot springs will never be forgotten. Generous thanks to Farm Aid and Paul Natkin for permission to print the Farm Aid opening Web page, which appears in chapter 3.

I (Kim Donehower) wish first to acknowledge the generosity of my informants in North Carolina, North Dakota, and Minnesota. Given the history of stereotypes of rural literacies, it is no small matter of trust to submit to an interview by an academic on this topic. I also thank my parents, Bill and Wanda Donehower, for their constant support and love, and my extended family, especially the Moores of Hot Springs, for inspiring me to take up this subject. Charlotte and Eileen have been the best collaborators I could have ever hoped to work with on this project. I have learned so much from their work and from their insight into mine. Deborah Brandt, in both her scholarly work and in her friendship, has been a vital source of encouragement since my days as a graduate student. Thanks also to Jean Lutes for first getting Deb and me together to talk literacy. At the University of Minnesota, Robin Brown and Ellen Stekert helped me to see that the last word on Appalachian literacy had by no means been said and that my work could be both necessary and compelling. Chris Anson, with much grace and good humor, guided my dissertation work in a specialty I was still discovering. Beth Daniell, Peter Mortensen, and Kathy Sohn have offered much encouragement and support since my days in graduate school. I wish to thank Scott Stevens and Rick Hansen, colleagues at California State University, Fresno, for their friendship and for sustaining my interest in the field both during and beyond my sojourn there. Thanks also to my colleagues in the English department at the University of North Dakota for giving me a supportive professional home in which to write. My husband, Jack Russell Weinstein, has served as sounding board, editor, cheerleader, on-call philosopher, and role model of a dedicated writer. This book would not exist without him. Last, I thank Mingus and Adina for keeping me company during the sometimes-lonely process of composing.

I (Charlotte Hogg) would like to thank Kim and Eileen for their invaluable feedback and time and for all I learned about writing and rural issues from them. I would also like to express deep thanks to the women from Paxton who participated in my study for their knowledge and trust; they, too, have taught me much. Thanks also to my parents, Bob and Carolyn Hogg, for their unwavering support and love, and a very special thank you to my husband, Chris Garland, who knew just what to do—be it listening, making me laugh, or buoying my confidence—throughout this project.

I (Eileen E. Schell) wish to thank my parents, Robert E. and Neva D. Schell, for giving me a place from which to stand and to see the world: Schell and Schell Orchards, which stood for four generations. I thank the people of Cashmere, Washington, namely my teachers and the town librarian, Sheila Ogle, for opening the world of books and ideas. When I reached college at the University of Washington, Connie Hale, my first-year composition teacher, was the one who convinced me to go on for advanced study in English and writing. I can never thank her enough for her inspirational example. Bill Irmscher, Eugene Smith, and Charles Johnson also helped me find my way in the world of academia. While I was in graduate school at the University of Wisconsin–Milwaukee, Alice Gillam, Chuck Schuster, and Lynn Worsham were the pivotal forces in helping me find a scholarly voice. I thank Lynn in particular for always challenging me to be a better writer, a better scholar, and a better person. At Syracuse University, I would like to thank my colleagues, especially Steve Parks, Scott Lyons, Carol Lipson, and Lois Agnew, and current and former graduate students Tobi Jacobi, Dianna Winslow, Carolyn Ostrander, Jennifer Wingard, Gale Coskan-Johnson and others for listening to my occasional ramblings about rural literacies and the state of the U.S. family farm. Vice Chancellor Deborah Freund and Dean Cathryn Newton and the College of Arts and Sciences at Syracuse University deserve a special thanks for granting me a research leave in spring 2005, which allowed me to work on revisions of the book and to conduct further research on the loss of the small family farm. Kim and Charlotte deserve a huge thanks for being such wonderful collaborators, researchers, and writers. On the home front, my partner, Thomas C. Kerr, and daughter, Autumn E. Kerr, helped me remember that there was a world outside the page. Last, I would like to thank Adrienne Lamberti for her scholarly example and for providing solidarity as a fellow academic "farm kid" who understands intimately the economic and emotional weight of the loss of the family farm.

*Rural Literacies*

# 1 / Constructing Rural Literacies
## Moving Beyond the Rhetorics of Lack, Lag, and the Rosy Past

*Kim Donehower, Charlotte Hogg, and Eileen E. Schell*

The sheer size of rural America argues against a dominant type of rural experience. The United States is the fourth largest nation in land area, and most of its territory is rural. It covers seven time zones from east to west and reaches latitudes north of Sweden and south of Egypt. If rural America were a separate nation, its population would comprise the world's 23rd largest country, following the United Kingdom, France, and Italy.

— Dee Davis and Tim Marema, "A Rural Perspective"

**W**hen you saw the words "rural" and "literacy" together in the title of this book, what came to mind? Visions of a nineteenth-century farm wife reading by candlelight in her claim shanty? Pictures of a quaint one-room schoolhouse? Or were there more contemporary images of idyllic small towns or rural counties populated by farmers and those who work the land for a living? You might recall Sinclair Lewis's portrait of the narrowness of small town life in his novel *Main Street* or the bigotry of the Ku Klux Klan in the rural South as depicted in *Birth of a Nation*. Or perhaps the title led you to expect a Jonathan Kozol–like exposé of the insufficiencies of rural education or an analysis of the "red state"/"blue state" dichotomy promoted by the Right and taken up by the mainstream media in the 2000 and 2004 elections. Maybe you grew up in a rural area or have rural students and came to this book because your experience with rural life and rural literacy do not match the images you find in the media.

We pose these questions to address the multifaceted way in which the word "rural" signifies and brings on a series of images: some positive, some negative, but many highly impressionistic, ahistorical, and seriously out of synch with the current economic realities of rural life.

Ralph Weisheit, David Falcone, and L. Edward Wells characterize the
"rural" definitional problem accurately when they argue that "like
such concepts as 'truth,' 'beauty,' or 'justice,' everyone knows the term
rural, but no one can define the term very precisely" (qtd. in "What
Is Rural?"). Who is included under the rubric of rurality and who
is not? The United States Department of Agriculture acknowledges
the contested nature of the term, remarking that "many people have
definitions for the term rural, but seldom are these definitions in agreement. For some, rural is a subjective state of mind. For others, rural is
an objective quantitative measure" ("What Is Rural?"). As a quantitative
measure, the Department of Commerce's Bureau of Census defines
rural essentially as not urban: "For Census 2000, the Census Bureau
classifies as 'urban' all territory, population, and housing units located
within an urbanized area (UA) or an urban cluster (UC)." Urbanized
areas and clusters include "core census block groups or blocks that
have a population density of at least 1,000 people per square mile
and surrounding census blocks that have an overall density of at least
500 people per square mile" ("Census 2000"). Rural areas, therefore,
include "all territory, population, and housing units located outside
of UAs and UCs." Geographic entities, such as census tracts, counties, metropolitan areas, and the territory outside metropolitan areas,
often are "split" between urban and rural territory, and the population
and housing units they contain are partly classified as urban and
partly classified as rural. For the purposes of this book, we define
"rural" as a quantitative measure, involving statistics on population
and region as described by the U.S. Census; as a geographic term,
denoting particular regions and areas or spaces and places; and as a
cultural term, one that involves the interaction of people in groups
and communities.

Calling someone or someplace rural also sets off a chain of associations and representations that carries complex histories and cultural
narratives. For instance, it is often thought that rural America is largely
a homogeneous place. However, as Dee Davis and Tim Marema's report
"A Rural Perspective" indicates, "the myth of rural homogeneity masks
underlying diversity among the people who have historically lived in
the American countryside." Many ethnic groups' traditions are rooted

in rural areas, including "music, food, visual arts, folk tales, crafts, and other cultural manifestations of distinct rural groups." At the same time, contemporary rural America is still thought of as largely white working- and middle class when, in actuality, "nearly half the nonwhite population that lives in rural America is clustered in areas where minorities make up one-third or more of a county's population." People of color are 25 percent of the overall U.S. population and constitute 17 percent of people living in rural areas. Almost half of the Native American population lives in rural areas: "Rural Native American population clusters are located in the Four Corners region, Oklahoma, the Northern Great Plains, and most of Alaska. Except in Alaska, these clusters are linked to the reservation system." In the South, "the rural counties in which African Americans make up one-third or more of the population are located in the lowland South: the traditional plantation areas of the Mississippi Delta, Deep South, and Mid-Atlantic states." In the Southwest region of the United States, Latino/a people "are located in or adjacent to the Rio Grande Valley from southern Colorado to the Gulf of Mexico, California's Imperial and Central valleys, and the southern High Plains of Texas and New Mexico." People of color grouped in these areas "continue to reflect the unique historical circumstances each group faced as they established themselves in the United States or found themselves there by force or annexation." To acknowledge the diversity and complexity of rural populations is a first step toward moving away from the commonplace myth that rural America is homogeneous.

Like the term "rural," the term "literacy" also sparks a variety of associations and is often defined broadly and diffusely. Literacy has been used in both popular and academic contexts to mean everything from the skills needed to learn to read and write at the barest functional level to the ability to recall and apply vast amounts of knowledge from a variety of fields. Bookstores feature titles purporting to increase our cultural literacy, financial literacy, visual literacy, science literacy, and math literacy. As Deborah Brandt points out in *Literacy in American Lives*, literacy is generally represented as a kind of resource—"economic, political, intellectual, spiritual—which like wealth or education, or trade skill or social connections, is pursued for the opportunities and protections that it potentially grants its seekers" (5). As we use the term in this book, "literacy" describes the skills and practices needed to gain knowledge, evaluate and interpret that knowledge, and apply knowledge to accomplish particular goals. In this sense, "reading" refers to the ability to gather and process knowledge from a variety of "texts"; "writing" means the ability to transform knowledge to achieve a particular purpose, just as writers transform ideas and information to accomplish rhetorical goals.

As we tried to define "rural literacies" for the purposes of this book, it was telling that we could not find a specific definition that we could work within or against in the field of literacy studies. Certainly, there have been many researchers whose work has taken place in rural areas, from Shirley Brice Heath to John Lofty to Andrea Fishman and others, but generally, the rural context—the economic, political, social, cultural, and educational constraints affecting the practice of rural literacies—is not foregrounded in these qualitative studies. For our purposes, we would like to propose a definition that is more appropriate to analyzing the uses of literacy in rural contexts. Rural literacies, then, refers to the particular kinds of literate skills needed to achieve the goals of sustaining life in rural areas—or, to use Brandt's terms, to pursue the opportunities and create the public policies and economic opportunities needed to sustain rural communities.

### Conceptualizing Sustainability

We use the word "sustain" as a conscious reference to "sustainability," a concept we return to throughout this book as we suggest alternate ways of understanding rural literacies. Sustainability has become a word with cachet, particularly in the last two decades, and is at risk of losing its weight and complexity, as articles in the September 2004 *Atlantic Monthly* and elsewhere describe.[1] Often used in ecological contexts, the term has been employed by a variety of other disciplines such as architecture and management (Owens 21).

A common, brief definition of sustainability comes from a 1987 report by the World Commission on Environment and Development (the Brundtland Commission), which describes sustainability as the ability "to meet the needs of the present without compromising the ability of future generations to meet their own needs" (43). The United Nations Conference on Environment and Development (Rio Summit/ Earth Summit) held in 1992 in Rio de Janeiro, Brazil, emphasized a shift toward developing sustainable economies and environmental practices. The Earth Summit resulted in Agenda 21, "a wide-ranging blueprint for action to achieve sustainable development worldwide." Agenda 21 has served as the cornerstone for many global and local discussions of sustainability (United Nations Conference). Adaptations of Agenda 21 have been made specifically as part of a governmental agenda in the United States. The President's Council on Sustainable Development (PCSD), assembled by former president Bill Clinton in June 1993, issued a statement establishing the interdependence of "economic prosperity, environmental protection, and social equity" (President's Council). The PCSD articulated ten goals regarding health and the environment, economic prosperity, equity, conservation of nature, stewardship, sustainable communities, civic engagement, population, international responsibility, and education—goals that seem applicable to all communities.[2] In particular, Goal 6, Sustainable Communities, calls for community members "to create healthy communities where natural and historic resources are preserved, jobs are available, sprawl is contained, neighborhoods are secure, education is lifelong, transportation and health care are accessible, and all citizens have opportunities to improve the quality of their lives." Goal 6, indeed, offers a sense of what sustainability might look like in both rural and urban communities.

In the field of composition studies, ecocompositionists such as Derek Owens have been among the first to take up sustainability as a conceptual framework. Owens has worked to develop a sustainable pedagogy that is based upon his work with urban and suburban composition students at St. John's University in Queens, New York. He contends that "most [definitions of sustainability] are predicated on an ethos of intergenerational justice," suggestive of the well-known Iroquois Confederacy's decision-making practice that considers consequences for the next seven generations (23). He mentions six values connected to sustainability, laid out by W. Edward Stead and Jean Stead: "wholeness, posterity, smallness, community, quality, and spiritual fulfillment" (Owens 27). For the purposes of our discussion and conceptualization of sustainability as an important component of rural literacy and rural life, we draw upon Owens's main definition of sustainability:

> Sustainability is an intergenerational concept that means adjusting our current behavior so that it causes the least amount of harm to future generations. Sustainability is also concerned with intergenerational equity: understanding the links between poverty and ecosystem decline. Sustainability means recognizing the short- and long-term environmental, social, psychological, and economic impact of our conspicuous consumption. It means seeking to make conservation and preservation inevitable effects of our daily lifestyles. It means forsaking a great many of the trappings of our consumerist culture in order to live more simply, thereby diminishing the impact of our ecological footprints. It means looking critically at our contemporary behaviors from the perspective of children living generations hence, and modifying those behaviors accordingly. (xi)[3]

Like Owens, we embrace a multidimensional definition of sustainability, one that is informed by ecological, economic, political, and social factors and the interdependence of these factors. Our view of sustainability, though, emphasizes analyzing the "social sustainability" of rural communities, whereas Owens's work largely addresses urban contexts. In her study of rural Australia, geographer Sharon Pepperdine argues that "social sustainability," or the "well-being of communities," has been a concept that is not well understood or studied, even as it is a concept that "is integral to any assessment of sustainability since it reflects, and impacts upon, ecological and economic sustainability." Pepperdine's research, which is concerned with rural planning and policy development, urges geographers and social scientists to consider social factors often absent in the discourse on sustainability. We find her notion of social sustainability particularly useful for researchers across the disciplines—including the humanities—as she argues that "stakeholder input" provided by local people is necessary in considering the future of any rural area. Our notion of "stakeholder input" is grounded in a view of critical literacy for democratic citizenship where rural people and urban and suburban allies create and engage in opportunities for dialogue and action to influence the policies and practices that affect their communities and lives.

Education, literacy work, and literacy sponsorship are key to such efforts to create dialogue around sustaining communities, a point Owens underscores in his discussion of the report "From Classroom to Community and Beyond: Education for a Sustainable Future," part of the Public Linkage, Dialogue and Education Task Force of the PCSD. The report notes that a key element of education for sustainability is to help people see the relevance of their actions, "learning citizenship skills and understanding that citizens have the power to shape their lives and their communities in light of their vision of a healthy and prosperous future" (qtd. in Owens 35). Henry Giroux, long an advocate of education for citizen-participation, describes the role of academics both inside and outside the classroom in accomplishing this goal. In "Cultural Studies, Public Pedagogy, and the Responsibility of Intellectuals," Giroux argues that "pedagogy" has too long been understood as applying only to classroom contexts, and,

> even when pedagogy is related to issues of democracy, citizenship, and the struggle over the shaping of identities and identifications, it is rarely taken up as part of a broader public politics—as part of a larger attempt to explain how learning takes place outside of schools or what it means to assess the political significance of understanding the broader educational force of culture in the new age of media technology, multimedia, and computer-based information and communication networks. (60)

To engage in public pedagogy, then, means both to teach beyond the classroom and to analyze the pedagogies of those other institutions and groups who shape the public's understanding of social and political issues. These are the goals of this book—to examine the spaces, both inside and outside classrooms, where teaching and learning about rural literacies and rural issues take place and to promote models of citizen participation that will ensure the future of rural communities and spark potential solidarity between rural, urban, and suburban communities.

Key to a revitalized understanding of citizenship and civic education is the notion of global citizenship, which emphasizes the interconnectedness of the local and the global. In "Education for Global Citizenship and Social Responsibility," Julie Andrzejewski and John Alessio define "global citizenship" as "knowledge and skills for social and environmental justice." A central force in global citizenship is critical literacy, as it fosters the skills, attitudes, motivation, and values necessary for effective public participation. Indeed, one can see the centrality of critical literacy in Andrzejewski and Alessio's articulation of the learning objectives for global citizenship in the college or K–12 classroom, which we selectively highlight here:

- Students will be able to examine the meaning of democracy and citizenship from differing points of view[,] including non-dominant, non-western perspectives.
- Students will understand and reflect upon their own lives, careers, and interests in relation to participatory democracy and the general welfare of the global society.
- Students will be familiar with fundamental national and international laws, documents[,] and legal issues pertaining to citizenship, democracy, and human rights.
- Students will be able to compare and evaluate the policies of an institution, community, state[,] or nation in the context of its stated philosophical and cultural values.
- Students will be able to locate information from a variety of sources, identify underlying values[,] and investigate the veracity of the information.

All of these skills have a literacy component to them and involve reading and writing that lead to more active participation in the decisions that help or hinder sustainability.

## The Role of Public Pedagogy

Andrzejewski and Alessio's articulation of learning objectives for global citizenship has a good deal in common with Jacqueline Edmondson's notions of a critical "public pedagogy" for global citizenship in rural contexts. Edmondson's insightful book *Prairie Town: Redefining Rural Life in the Age of Globalization* points readers toward a notion of sustainable rural life that is based upon the idea of a critical, public pedagogy. Edmondson defines critical, public pedagogy as a pedagogy that "links teaching and learning to social empowerment. It allows individuals to imagine a different, more just world and to work toward that vision as it becomes situated within broader struggles for democracy" (33). A critical, public pedagogy in rural contexts involves communities in public dialogues about their future and works against the division and privatization of the needs of individuals and groups. With a critical, public pedagogy, "there must be a commitment to learning about others coupled with a common mission to move forward and actively address and transform shared issues of social justice" (33).

Edmondson draws in part on Giroux, who states that while public pedagogy work can take on many forms, "its deepest impulse is rooted in issues of compassion and social responsibility aimed at deepening and extending the possibilities for critical agency, racial justice, and economic and political democracy" ("Public Pedagogy" 356). Employing the theories of Stuart Hall, Giroux contends that the key to any kind of public pedagogy "is the need to begin at those intersections where people actually live their lives and where meaning is produced, assumed, and contested in the unequal relations of power that construct the mundane acts of everyday relations" (355). In short, "public pedagogy . . . becomes part of a critical practice designed to understand the social context of everyday life as lived relations of power" (355). In rural contexts, a critical, public pedagogy interrogates constructions and representations of rural people and life and examines "the extent to which characterizations of the rural match (or not) observations of demographic, social, and economic conditions" (Edmondson 114); this is a key goal of this book. A critical, public pedagogy also works to foster social change, mobilizing citizens locally to affect "state and federal agendas that work to wrest control away from local peoples" (114). This critical, public pedagogy is multi-pronged, as Edmondson's study shows, and is deeply invested in fostering critical literacies that consider local, national, and global contexts.

Understanding the interconnections between the local and the global is important not only for fostering in our students the literacies they need for global citizenship but also as a way to understand and, where appropriate, resist, critique, and imagine alternatives to the official logic of neoliberalism, the global movement toward increased privatization of public services and toward a market economy dominated by predatory multinational corporations—what many simply call "globalization." The triumphant ascendancy of globalization, much touted by politicians, business leaders, newspaper columnists, TV news anchors, and "fast-cutting globe-hopping ads of dot.coms, financial service companies and hardware giants," has been promoted as a historical inevitability (Szeman 2). As Imre Szeman notes, the logic of globalization has been "accepted pragmatically as the new reality of contemporary existence, or indeed, greeted enthusiastically as a phenomenon that will improve domestic economic conditions while promoting the good life abroad" (2). However, accepting globalization as the inevitable march of progress means ignoring the real problems that accompany such expansion. As mentioned in this chapter and elsewhere, in rural areas in the United States and in many areas across the globe, globalization and the national and international public policies that enable it have often meant the systematic dislocation of people, the loss of local businesses, the loss of sustainable agriculture in favor of factory farming, the creation of environmental problems due to unlimited and unchecked industrial expansion, the location of privatized prisons, and the list goes on. To address these problems head-on, we need a critical, public pedagogy that is cognizant of the rhetorics and pedagogies of the media representations and public policies behind globalization. Giroux notes that Szeman's analysis exemplifies such a critical, public pedagogy.

Szeman argues that we can turn to the anti-globalization/alternative globalization protests staged in Washington, D.C., Seattle, Cologne, London, Prague, Melbourne, and elsewhere as pedagogical models, as these protests created space for alternative pedagogies in the form of "People's Summits, teach-ins, [and] Q & A sessions" (3). At these public pedagogy sessions, citizens exchanged information, created coalitions, and staged debates about their future and their communities' futures "in a world that, for better and for worse, is interconnected as never before" (4). Meanwhile, world leaders and trade representatives made decisions about global economic policy and trade behind police barricades in the sleek conference rooms of international hotels.

The alternative globalization protests also brought together groups of people who normally did not talk or work with one another—Zapatistas, Korean farmers, "environmentalists, labor unions, protesters against genetically modified foods, activists opposed to the practices of organizations like the WTO [World Trade Organization] and World Bank, Sea Turtles, and the Black Bloc" (3). While the mainstream media tended to portray alternative globalization protesters as black-clad, Starbucks-smashing anarchists, the alternative media told a different story—a story of citizens taking to the streets and to teach-ins to express their views on international trade policies and to exert influence over the future of the global economy, the environment, and their local communities.

It is in the spirit of the protesters' quest for debate, contestation, and collective knowledge-making that we turn a critical eye on the ways in which rural life and literacies have been defined by rhetorics of modernization, preservation, and abandonment, described below. It is also in this spirit that we extend Edmondson's and Giroux's notions of a critical, public pedagogy to our analyses in each chapter, considering in chapter 5 how a critical, public pedagogy that is sensitive to rural literacies can be and has been enacted by compositionists. We realize that enacting a critical, public pedagogy is a complex and challenging undertaking for teachers of writing who already feel pressured by the various mandates they receive from their programs and colleges. Andrzejewski and Alessio cite this as one possible reason why issues of global citizenship are hard to find in curricula, as well as the sense that issues such as global warming are more trends than crises, that global problems seem so insurmountable, and that "educators have not usually been taught about issues of social and global responsibility."

However, part of engaging literacy involves questions of citizenship and social action. To this end, we offer ways of understanding literacy as a resource for democratic citizenship that shapes the potential for rural communities to experience the "economic prosperity, environmental protection, and social equity" desired to make rural communities sustainable places (President's Council).

## Why Rural Literacies Matter

Throughout this analysis, we engage with and challenge representations of rural literacies and argue for a notion of rural literacy based on a concept of sustainability. While we contend that there are no fixed qualities that typify rural literacies, we examine the widespread social, political, and material issues that shape them. We investigate the rhetorics that impact rural communities and rural literacies with an ultimate goal of demonstrating what has been missed in past representations and understandings of rural literacies.

For example, literacy research in our field is skewed toward urban sites and subjects. Many of our theories and research paradigms for literacy presume an urban or semi-urban setting and do not account for the experiences and realities of rural places and peoples. Indeed, our field tends to focus on the "urban" or the "city" as a dominant metaphor for the work of composition studies. In a *College Composition and Communication* article analyzing the politics of space in composition, Nedra Reynolds reports that compositionists have been moving from the metaphor of "community" to "city" because it is more hip, less homogeneous, more cultured, and more postmodern. Examining three imagined geographies in the discipline's discourse and metaphorical approaches to the field, Reynolds unpacks the spaces of the frontier, the city (with a brief stop at the ubiquitous term "community"), and cyberspace. Though Reynolds critiques the conceptions of both "community" and "city," she makes clear that "city" offers two ideologies, "city as embodiment of postmodernism [and] city as a reflection of democratic ideals" (25). The city is espoused as a thriving center for energized exchanges, a notion that harks back to the gathering spaces of ancient cultures that would appeal to rhetorical scholars. In fact, Aristotle's *On Rhetoric* connects the physical space of the town to certain sophisticated rhetorical techniques. As George Kennedy explains in his translator's note to chapter 10 of the *Rhetoric*, "Asteia, or Urbanities": "*Astu* means 'town,' usually in the physical rather than the political sense. . . . In contrast to the country, towns cultivate a certain elegance and grace; thus, *asteia*, 'things of the town,' came to mean elegance of speech, wit, good taste. Latin *urbanitas* . . . and thus English 'urbanity' have similar meanings" (244).

Reynolds is not alone in deploying the metaphor of the city as a productive space for imagining the work of the field. Margaret Himley, in the concluding chapter of *Political Moments in the Classroom*, refers to the city as a useful term for describing the politicized composition classroom. Likewise, Bruce McComiskey and Cynthia Ryan in their collection, *City Comp: Identities, Spaces, Practices*, emphasize the diversity of ways that writing is taught in urban settings. Christy Friend also turns to city metaphors, though her focus is the classroom rather than the discipline. Friend's piece "From the Contact Zone to the City: Iris Marion Young and Composition Theory" addresses the relationship between public discourse and writing done in classrooms. She studies Iris Marion Young's notion of the ideal city as a way to approach this relationship, demonstrating that Young's offering of the city as a location allows a more encompassing alternative than "liberalism's isolated individual and the communitarian idea of small, homogenous communities as the locus of public decision-making" (659). As in Reynolds's description, the appealing aspect of the city is its potential to be the most democratic and to offer the most diverse interactions.

In their arguments for urban metaphors, both Reynolds and Friend are responding to the prevalent metaphor of "community" and its theoretical and pedagogical shortcomings. Specifically, they each address the problem of space and place as one of the downfalls of the community metaphor. As Reynolds explains, "Community too often assumed a transparent space" or a space that was "too limited" in possibilities (25). Friend refers to Joseph Harris's idea that "without a firm grounding in concrete practice . . . the notion of community becomes an empty, sentimentalized abstraction" (663). The term "community" is more slippery and amorphous than "city," where images easily come to mind. Community also has prosaic connotations that do not appeal to a field striving for legitimacy and for a pedagogy of contact zones that works to include dissonance as well as consensus.

We can appreciate the usefulness and appropriateness of the "city" metaphor. However, as George Lakoff and Mark Johnson remind us, a metaphor is a way of seeing and a way of not seeing. How do urban or city metaphors serve to represent rural students and rural teachers and composition programs located at colleges and universities in rural settings? How do such metaphors fail to describe or account for different notions of space, place, and location? While there are valid and complex justifications for assigning the city as a metaphor for the field of composition, in claiming that "naming composition a city marks a moment of maturity in its history," or "to navigate a city requires more experience, skill, or wits than to navigate a small community," scholars reinscribe the notion that urban is more advanced (Reynolds 24, 26). The example of the city as ideal is yet another way in which rural experiences are erased, denied, or deemed unimportant, where those who are rural are seen as having less "experience, skill, or wits" rather than those of a different kind. (Navigating country roads requires another set of skills than does reading a subway schedule.)

Across the chapters that follow, we critically analyze and address commonplace assumptions and stereotypes about rural literacy and rural peoples. Our account is meant, on the one hand, to address the "rhetoric of lack" or deficit model of rural life that is commonly perpetuated in academic scholarship and popular press and media representations. All too often, life in rural America is seen as "lacking": lacking education, lacking economic opportunities, lacking cultural opportunities. Rural Americans are often thought to be illiterate, untechnological, and simplistic—stereotypes that we have encountered frequently as those from rural backgrounds and as educators in American colleges and universities. On the other hand, we also wish to address the often romantic or ahistorical visions of rural life that are as common as the negative stereotypes.

We also upend traditional ways of understanding "rurality" as, essentially, the opposite of urbanity. For those who can't imagine life in a town with a population under 10,000 or a career dependent on the vagaries of the weather, rurality can seem such an odd state of being, outside that of mainstream urban and suburban America, that it can be understood only in terms of not-urban, not-us, not-me. There is a tendency to see rural people and rural places as "other," a trend that was most pronounced during the election years of 2000 and 2004 when the "blue state"/"red state" dichotomy took hold and became a convenient narrative for explaining the presidential election results. The narrative is that the nation was "divided into coastal liberals [blue staters] and heartland conservatives [red staters]" (Wilentz). Lists of characteristics were attributed to each group—red staters were values voters and gun toters, and blue staters were urban liberals and latte swillers. This framing metaphor has become increasingly elaborate and variegated and reinforces an urban-rural split. As the Seattle-based weekly *The Stranger* put it in an editorial following the 2004 election, the red state/blue state dichotomy is a dichotomy of the cities versus rural areas, which are portrayed as the seat of sexism, racism, homophobia, and right-wing Christian fundamentalism:

> It's time to state something that we've felt for a long time but have been too polite to say out loud: Liberals, progressives, and Democrats do not live in a country that stretches from the Atlantic to the Pacific, from Canada to Mexico. We live on a chain of islands. We are citizens of the Urban Archipelago, the United Cities of America. We live on islands of sanity, liberalism, and compassion—New York City, Chicago, Philadelphia, Seattle, St. Louis, Minneapolis, San Francisco, and on and on. And we live on islands in red states too—a fact obscured by that state-by-state map. Denver and Boulder are our islands in Colorado; Austin is our island in Texas; Las Vegas is our island in Nevada; Miami and Fort Lauderdale are our islands in Florida. Citizens of the Urban Archipelago reject heartland "values" like xenophobia, sexism, racism, and homophobia, as well as the more intolerant strains of Christianity that have taken root in this country. And we are the real Americans.

They—rural, red-state voters, the denizens of the exurbs—are not real Americans. They are rubes, fools, and hate-mongers. ("Urban Archipelago")

While the rhetoric in this editorial is deliberately incendiary and provocative, similar versions of the urban-rural divide have been stated in other publications. The problem with the urban-versus-rural framing metaphor is that once again, it reinforces "rural otherness" and oversimplifies politics along geographic lines. The framing metaphor highlights how the Republican Party has effectively utilized the red state/blue state dichotomy to reinforce its hoped-for political divisions and to keep Americans from thinking about common concerns—the war in Iraq, job loss, a failing economy driven further into debt, among other issues. As Sean Wilentz argues, "Reporters and commentators are misleading themselves and their audiences about the actual political state of the Union. Without realizing it, they are also advancing the picture of the nation advanced by the GOP culture warriors, feeding the despair and paranoia of coastal liberals and writing off millions of Americans in every part of the country." To combat the process of othering in framing metaphors like these, we explore the nature of rural life as people who have identified ourselves as and been identified as rural learners as well as rural educators, resisting comparisons with standards of culture and models of literacy that originate from urban settings.

Our project also accounts for how literacy is imbricated in the class structure and economic system of rural areas. The socioeconomic base of American rural life has changed drastically and increasingly due to globalization; however, many Americans and many educators, especially urban and suburban ones, are unaware of those changes and their impact on rural communities, rural peoples, and rural schools. Over the last thirty years, the economic base that once was the heart of rural America—small farms and ranches—has been radically transformed. According to the *Occupational Outlook Quarterly*, Winter 1999/2000, "Of all the occupations in America, farming is facing the greatest decline" (qtd. in "Farm Facts"). Of America's 60 million rural residents, "less than two percent earn their primary living from farming. Agriculture overall—including processing and marketing jobs—accounts for less than twelve percent of rural employment" ("Think Rural" 3). However, many urban and suburban Americans, according to a 2001 W. K. Kellogg Foundation report, still believe that most rural Americans make their living from family farms. Many do not realize that thousands of small farms and ranches have failed financially or been sold off by their owners over the last three decades with devastating consequences to rural areas and communities (see also Davidson).

Not surprisingly, lack of real economic participation among rural Americans has led to many of the same ills experienced in urban areas: chronic unemployment and underemployment; homelessness, hunger, and malnutrition; a rise in cases of battering and child abuse; and also the continued rise of hate groups, a point that was brought home tragically with the bombing of the Oklahoma City Federal Building. As Osha Gray Davidson puts it, rural America has become one of America's many "ghettos," a term he uses to describe the economic segregation and disenfranchisement of many rural areas and peoples (8). In places such as the California Central Valley, where multimillion-dollar subdivisions go up in sight of silos and developers use farmers' fields to break ground not for crops but for strip malls and fast food chain restaurants, the economic imbalance between urban and rural areas is brought into high relief, and the contrast is often an uneasy one. Government policies, educational practices, and modes and ways of living overwhelmingly reflect an urban and increasingly metropolitan focus, what one might even call an "urban bias," and the result of such bias can be inequity, misunderstanding, and impoverishment—realities that active and engaged critical literacy educators must always work against.

As we discuss later in this chapter, this "urban bias" is predominantly a class bias, which stigmatizes poor urban culture as well as rural culture. The "city" metaphor uses the city not so much as a symbol of a particular configuration of space but rather as an exemplar of a rich, diverse, and varied culture. Access to many of the cultural opportunities of cities—museums, theaters, performance spaces, technological resources, universities—has as much to do with class status as it does with one's proximity to them; one can be an urban-dweller and still lack access to what cities have to offer. Moreover, the city metaphor in composition needs to account for the circuitries of global power and capital present in large financial centers like New York, Los Angeles, London, and Tokyo, which, in Saskia Sassen's words,

> accumulate immense concentrations of economic power while cities that were once major manufacturing centres suffer inordinate declines; the down-towns of cities and business centres in metropolitan areas receive massive investments in real estate and telecommunications while low income urban and metropolitan areas are starved for resources; highly educated workers in the corporate sector see their incomes rise to unusually high levels while low or medium skilled workers see theirs sink. Financial services produce superprofits while industrial services barely survive.

Like those decaying industrial cities and low-income urban centers Sassen mentions, small or midsized rural towns and villages have experienced a loss of infrastructure, public services, schools, and living wages. Companies moving into rural areas often capitalize on lower wage rates, and large firms often exploit low-wage immigrant workers in nonunionized agricultural work, processing jobs, and manufacturing jobs. Any use of the metaphor of the "city" in our field should account for how cities are sites for the differential circulation of capital, information, labor, and cultural resources. The same forces must be accounted for in rural communities.

To counteract the metropolitan biases on the part of policy makers and educators, our focus on rural literacies is meant to highlight the need for the continued use of literate action to affect social change for rural peoples and rural communities: to bring real educational and economic opportunities to rural communities. Representing rural America's challenges, needs, and potential is important, and it will take both rhetorical and material action to effect a movement of understanding and action. As the Center for Rural Strategies report states: "If rural communities are going to survive the sweeping economic changes of the 21st century, national policy must better reflect the true economic nature of non-metropolitan America. One place to start this conversation is through public information campaigns that paint an accurate picture of rural communities and their needs" ("Think Rural").

## Resisting Stereotypes of Rural Literacies

To offer a more accurate portrayal of rural literacies, we must actively resist the typical stereotypes that have affected people's perceptions. Consider the following quotations from two different public agencies concerned with rural education:

> The schools are held to be largely responsible for ineffective farming, lack of ideals, and the drift to town. This is not because rural schools, as a whole, are declining, but because they are in a state of arrested development and have not yet put themselves in consonance with all the recently changed conditions of life. (Commission on Country Life 121–22)

> Leaders in rural education are being called upon to help solve problems that are increasingly complex, information-based, and globally connected. What is at stake is the survival and transformation of rural life as well as its traditional and emerging contributions to the national economy and spirit. ("National Issues")

These statements were published almost a century apart. The first is from the Commission on Country Life, convened by Theodore Roosevelt to investigate "the problems of farm life" (9). Its report was published in 1911. The second is from the Appalachia Educational Laboratory's Web site in 2003. Funded by grants from the U.S. Department of Education, the AEL works to improve rural schools in southern Appalachian states.

Both groups want rural education and rural life to be both transformed and preserved. Both see rural education as struggling to meet the "recently changed conditions of life," which, in these days, are "increasingly complex, information-based, and globally connected." Both groups want rural areas to maintain a distinct character from urban life—"its traditional . . . contributions to the national spirit"—while they, at the same time, "catch up" to the modern world and modern times. The Commission on Country Life ultimately leans more toward preserving rural communities as places apart; it advocates rural curricula that are "visual, direct, and applicable" to the agricultural character of rural life and are distinct from urban school curricula (124). The AEL leans toward modernization; many of its programs emphasize using current technology to improve rural schools and supporting ways to get rural schools in line with national standards.

Sustaining the cultural life of a community is not the same thing as preserving it. While preservation can be a useful term, rhetorically, in arguing for resources to address the plight of rural communities, the notion of "preserving" a culture often runs counter to the concept of "sustaining" it. "Preservation," as we describe in this chapter and throughout the book, suggests locking cultural practices into the past, implying passivity rather than active and relevant contributions to culture. Sustainability requires adapting cultural practices to changing economic, ecological, political, and social circumstances to ensure the survival and sustainable development of a community. An important element of models of sustainability is the understanding that economic systems are interlinked, as are ecological systems. As Andrzejewski and Alessio note, while "the [economic, environmental, or social] problems we do see seem to be local or individual," they are in fact connected to much larger systems. The consumer practices of urbanites and suburbanites, for example, affect the ecological and economic practices that shape rural communities. Similarly, cultural practices and attitudes interact across communities and have economic and/or ecological repercussions in ways that are masked by terms such as "preservation."

The modernizing approach also has its problems. In particular, national standards are often referenced to urban or suburban models of literacy and of education and involve assessments that depend on norm-referencing. This creates a situation that is likely to perpetuate the stereotyping of rural regions as subliterate rather than improve rural education. In his fascinating look at the history of "construct-ing normalcy" in *Enforcing Normalcy: Disability, Deafness, and the Body*, disability studies theorist Lennard Davis notes:

> I begin with the rather remarkable fact that the constella-tion of words describing this concept "normal," "normalcy," "normality," "norm," "average," "abnormal"—all entered the European languages rather late in human history. The word "normal" as "constituting, conforming to, not deviating or different from, the common type or standard" only enters the English language around 1840. Likewise, the word "norm," in the modern sense, has only been in use since around 1855. . . . If the lexicographical information is relevant, it is possible to date the coming into consciousness in English of an idea of "the norm" over the period 1840–1860. (24)

Davis attributes the surprisingly recent emergence of the concept of "the norm" to a variety of specific social and historical circumstances. He notes that the idea of "the norm" sprang from concepts of an "ideal,"[4] and he links the emergence of "normalcy" to the appearance of the science of statistics in the second half of the eighteenth century (26). The measurement of literacy through statistics has traditionally been used to name particular populations as "deviant" from the norm. This measure of "deviance" is supposedly objective, unbiased, and free from stereotype—sterile, hard-to-argue-with numbers on a page. Yet a close look at these statistics, especially as they apply to rural areas, shows them to be highly problematic.

In the years after it stopped surveying respondents about literacy and before the institution of the National Adult Literacy Survey/Na-tional Assessment of Adult Literacy in 1985, the U.S. Census instruct-ed those using its data to extrapolate literacy rates from data about poverty and high school graduation rates. Similarly, the summary of the Kentucky Adult Literacy Survey study emphasizes correlations between literacy proficiency, poverty, and school graduation rates and leaves out anyone above the age of sixty-four from its sample ("Kentucky Adult Literacy Survey"). One can imagine how many rural areas would fare under these measures. Many rural areas have high numbers of elderly who may not have graduated from high school at a time when leaving school to work full-time was common—especially in agricultural occupations. Many of these people, though, are quite "literate" by any measure. By many measures currently in use, then, literacy deviance may have little to do with actual reading or writing ability; it is instead an issue of economic and educational class. Here the concept of "literacy" has ceased to have anything to do with itself and is wholly an attribute of something else—code for class status. When literacy level becomes code for class status, a perpetual literacy "crisis" results—society is never all of the same class—and resources are allocated to solve the unsolvable literacy "problem."

Davis also links statistical theories of "the norm" and "the deviant" to hierarchies of class when he writes, "Statements of ideology of this kind saw the bourgeoisie as rationally placed in the mean position in the great order of things" (27). Under this kind of correlation, anyone below middle-class status is below the norm or average; anyone above middle-class status is likely "above average." Furthermore, Davis notes that most early statisticians were also eugenicists who wished to utilize their new "science" in the service of racial purification and "improvement" (30).

Paul Nachtigal notes that "norming" rural communities to the standards of urban, middle-class life has long been the goal of educational policies targeting the rural school "problem." In "Rural School Improvement Efforts: An Interpretive History," he writes:

> As late as 1820 only 13 cities of over 8,000 people existed in the [United States] . . . By 1860, the number of cities had increased to 141, marking the beginning of an urbanization trend that continued unabated. . . . With the modus operandi and standards of [educational] excellence established in the cities, it is little wonder that rural schools were seen as inferior simply because they were rural.
>
> Convinced that within the techniques of industrialization—bigger is better, specialization, proper supervision—lies the secret for efficiency and effectiveness in education, reform-

ers molded rural education into a likeness of urban education. Even before the twentieth century (and paralleling the
industrial development of the country), efforts were made
to systematize rural schools. The best professional thinking
was that even the smallest one-room school could be given a
graded structure with the stuff of learning broken down into
discreet subject-matter courses. . . .
   In the 1890s, the National Education Committee of Twelve
on Rural Schools took steps to prescribe remedies for the rural
school problem, many of which are still being applied today:
"consolidation of schools and transportation of pupils, expert
supervision by county superintendents[,] . . . professionally-
trained teachers." The rural school would teach country children sound values and vocational skills; the result was to be a
standardized, modernized "community" in which leadership
came from professionals. (15–16)

Nachtigal's summary of the goals of these reform efforts is worth
examining in some detail. "Standardization" is code for erasing differences of culture, race, ethnicity, class, and linguistic usage. Perhaps the most shocking example, from a rural context, is the case of
American Indian boarding schools, designed to force assimilation, to
"kill the Indian to save the man."[5] These schools forced English as "the
language of the greatest, most powerful and enterprising nationalities
beneath the sun," strictly punishing the use of native languages.[6] A
more recent example is "English Only" laws, which, as of 2007, have
been passed in more than two dozen states, including states with large
rural populations, such as Nebraska and North Dakota. Such laws can
restrict bilingual education in schools or prohibit multilingual government services, such as courtroom translation, translated driver's
license exams and other government documents, or multilingual
election ballots. In some states, such as Alaska, highly restrictive
English Only laws have been struck down as unconstitutional, but
the movement continues.
   Other rural reformers have pushed a kind of economic standardization, introducing curricula in rural schools that emphasize vocational

and technical training. (American Indian boarding schools were among these, as were Appalachian mission schools.) In fact, surveys such as the Kentucky Adult Literacy Survey are designed primarily to be measures of literacy as a very specific kind of economic resource within a particular economic context. The survey's Web site concludes that overall, "the numbers found in the . . . survey generally should be good news to those whose job it is to promote Kentucky and its work force to employers around the globe" ("Kentucky Adult Literacy Survey").

The economic model to which these school reformers wish to standardize literacy and other types of instruction is most often, as Nachtigal suggests, a "bigger-is-better" model based on a notion of continuous growth. Such models have worked in urban areas, which, as Nachtigal comments, have been growing continuously in the United States since the 1860s. But rural areas require a different type of model for economic stability—one of sustainability instead of continuous expansion. As the nature of farming changed, as is described in detail in chapter 3, rural communities dependent primarily on agriculture lost population. The "modernization" desired by the reformers Nachtigal describes involves the very economic forces that have necessitated rural out-migration, decimating rural communities. Note that Nachtigal depicts the reformers' goal as creating "'communities.'" The double quotes here suggest that Nachtigal does not see the reformers' end-goal as supporting self-sustaining rural communities. These are, instead, semblances of communities, dependent on outside "professionals" to shape their economic and cultural direction.

This situation gives rise to long-standing tensions between rural people and these outside education "professionals"—tensions that have sometimes been used to further the stereotype that rural people are anti-education. In his book *Call School: Rural Education in the Midwest to 1918*, Paul Theobald describes how the common school movement met with resistance in the Midwest and Great Plains:

> Free public schools were the first systematic industrial imposition on agrarian life in the United States. . . . Before 1918 the nation was predominantly rural, and it was abundantly clear that rural residents did not share the problems of the

city. If common schools were at least partially successful in the eastern states as a result of their potential to solve urban problems, this much of the pro-common school agenda was missing in rural areas. (1–2)

Regardless of the eventual outcome of incorporating the common school system, it exemplifies the ways urban models were utilized for the entire country. And in the texts children were reading in schools throughout the country, illustrations of children clearly implied wealth and urbanity. "It wasn't unusual," compositionist Lucille Schultz describes in her history of school-based writing instruction in nineteenth-century American schools, "to see a young girl sitting in a rocker with her feet resting on an upholstered foot stool" (45). Though these urban images did not represent the majority at that time—Schultz reminds us that 90 percent of Americans lived a rural existence—the urban experience was already more valued (45).

As the country has completed its shift from rural to urban, rural students have continued to be unheard, unseen, and under-represented. Since the United States has become industrialized and urbanized, it has scarcely looked back, and the effects of this trend are significant to rural students. Martha Kruse explains that "rural sociologists and education researchers frequently approach the field from a deficit perspective; the investigator describes the rural community in terms of what it lacks in comparison to urban areas" (1).

These long-standing problems continue with national standards movements such as the original No Child Left Behind Act, as signed in 2002.[7] NCLB requires, in effect, everyone to be "normal," and it requires the norm to be continually raised: each class's test scores must surpass that of the previous year's class for a school to be performing well. Predictably, NCLB's penalties will rest most heavily on schools whose constituents fall below the socioeconomic norm, both rural and urban. When norm-referenced tests reflect middle-class values and practices as "the norm" and upper-class values and practices as "above the norm," it is not surprising that inner-city and rural schools fare worst under NCLB's assessments. Punishing literacy deviance becomes a code for punishing class and race.

It is likely that rural schools will not measure well under NCLB policies, reinforcing the long-held idea that rural education is a "problem." NCLB requires rural schools to perform to urban and suburban standards, yet it does little to address inequities in school funding. Its quantitative measures of progress simply do not work when applied to low-population rural schools. How can rural schools use their 1 percent exemption from testing for special education students if the population of the entire school is only eighty? How can schools fairly compare the quantitative test scores of two different third grade classes, one with eight students and the subsequent year's in which only two students are enrolled? In addition, how are rural parents to exercise the "choice" option built into NCLB? This provision allows parents to send their children to a different public school if their local school does not meet adequate yearly progress two years in a row. Is this really an option in places where school consolidation already means a ninety-minute bus ride to the nearest school? Will this lead to greater school consolidation and fewer rural communities with a school at the heart of their social network?

What we see here is the most sweeping set of federal educational mandates in decades that does not take into account the real circumstances of difference in rural education—issues of access, funding, and distance. It ignores and even punishes the inherent strengths of rural schools, such as small class size. And it defines for rural communities the kind of literate practices needed for "success," with an emphasis on particular kinds of economic activities. In essence, national, standardizing movements such as NCLB prevent local schools from acting as local literacy sponsors. NCLB removes from local schools the possibility to define what constitutes literacy and how literacy should be valued in ways that could best integrate literacy practices into the needs and life of the local community.

The tension illustrated by the quotes at the beginning of this section—between preserving the uniqueness of rural life and assimilating rural places to the standards of contemporary city life—is at the heart of a century's discussions of what to do about rural education and rural literacy. Three different types of solutions to the so-called problems of rural literacy have sprung from this tension. The first is to "modernize" the rural population by bringing them into line with the technological, economic, and cultural systems of urban life—a trend that is seen today in the tendency to believe that technology can solve many of the problems of rural school districts. The second is to recognize rural culture as a thing apart from urban life and work to preserve its difference. This manifests itself in modern-day curricula that focus on oral history and other preservationist projects that isolate the historical particularities of the rural experience. The third and most radical solution advocates abandoning rural settlements, consolidating school districts, and making city centers the locus of educational activity.

The origins and consequences of these strategies will be detailed further in chapter 2. Characterizations of rural education and solutions to its perceived problems have been hampered by following certain well-worn rhetorical grooves. These rhetorics—of modernization, preservation, and abandonment—stem from and are sustained by a more pervasive rhetoric of lack, originating from those who are not themselves rural and whose stake in rural communities differs from that of those who actually live there.

### Rural Literacies Imagined and Enacted

We advocate an alternate metaphor of rural literacies based on sustainability because we believe that all compositionists, regardless of where they teach or what they research, can have an impact on the future of rural literacies. One of the key precepts of sustainability is that communities are interconnected and affect one another's futures. The work that compositionists do can change the conditions for literacy in many different types of communities, beyond the local environments of specific universities, in four distinct ways—through research, teaching, literacy sponsorship, and democratic citizenship and public participation. It is in these ways that we can enact public pedagogies for sustainability through our literacy work.

Rural communities have been ill-served in the past by both a lack of research on rural literacy and by research and education initiatives that mischaracterize rural literacy. Considering that, "though sixty-seven percent of all schools in the United States are in rural areas, research into rural literacy beliefs and behaviors is most notable in its absence," even less is known about those rural students who do go on to college (Kruse 4). Of the major studies of community literacy published between 1980 and 2005, less than one-quarter deal wholly or in part with communities that could be defined as "rural." Clearly, there is a tremendous need for research on rural literacy. As initiatives like NCLB try to standardize American education, regardless of local context, and as rural communities struggle to create the economic and cultural infrastructures that will reduce out-migration, understanding rural literacy in context becomes of supreme importance. We cannot depend on the National Assessment of Adult Literacy, the Department of Education, or the National Assessment of Educational Progress to conduct this kind of research. Their methods are quantitative, designed to make the same kind of context-free comparisons between rural and urban schools made by the Committee of Twelve that Nachtigal cites. In addition, decades of research show that literacy development occurs as much in the home and the community as it does in the classroom. If we are ever to usefully change the terms of debate about rural education and rural literacy, we need more extensive qualitative research into the contexts of rural literacy.

As teachers, we have the opportunity to shift our students' thinking about rural areas and about literacy. In the concluding chapter of this book, we provide three models of how writing teachers can enact a critical, public pedagogy that addresses rural literacies. Moreover, we suggest how a critical, public pedagogy for rural issues can be applied in broader contexts: through advocacy efforts on the part of citizen groups, advocacy organizations, nonprofit agencies, and K–12 educators, to name only a few. But there are other ways of understanding how rural literacies, and rural areas, affect our students. Subconsciously, and especially if we accept the metaphor of composition-as-city, we may indicate to students that the kinds of literacy we teach are primarily a resource for the demands of urban life. We may encourage our best rural students to move away from their hometowns, to exercise their literacy skills in what we perceive to be the more sophisticated environment of an urban area. We may suggest to students, intentionally or not, that advanced literacy skills require an urban context for their fullest expression. In fact, though, rural communities provide rich challenges and rewards for a literate life. If we come to understand what those challenges and rewards are, we are less likely to assume that our best and brightest students must be destined for city life.

Beyond our own classrooms and the writing programs we administer, compositionists also serve as literacy sponsors in our local communities. The term "literacy sponsor" comes from Brandt; we use it here to refer to entities that advocate a particular way of understanding, valuing, and practicing literacy. One way that compositionists do this is through their effect on university students who become secondary teachers. As a result of NCLB, which requires all secondary-level teachers to hold a major equivalency in the subject they teach, English departments everywhere are having a greater impact on secondary teachers' ideas about literacy. National Writing Project sites offer opportunities for compositionists to dialogue directly with K–12 teachers about literacy. In addition, compositionists may be active in sponsoring community literacy events such as writers' conferences, youth literacy camps, or community literacy programs.

Literacy sponsorship has the potential to create tensions between groups. When particular literacy practices and values are identified with a certain group of people—the sponsor's group—those who seek to learn from the sponsor may feel they have to alter their relationship with the community from which they come. For example, some of the Appalachian people described in chapter 2 feel or have felt that to adhere to a certain sponsor's values meant devaluing the literate practices of their own families. To become "more literate," according to this sponsor, they had to become less like the "mountain people" with whom they culturally identified. One way to avoid putting people in this position is to gain a richer understanding of the nature and function of local literacies—including rural literacies.

The field of rhetoric and composition studies has not thought enough about the specific challenges and opportunities rural settings provide for educators and citizens; indeed, the presence of many large land-grant institutions in rural areas makes it imperative for faculty in the disciplines to think about the interface between rural communities and the university. Rather than seeing the understanding of rural life and culture only as the province of agricultural or rural sociology programs, we need to work with students to help them see the economic, social, and political issues encountered in rural areas as interconnected with the larger social and political patterns present in urban and suburban contexts and vice versa. In doing so, we help foster literacy work, public pedagogies, and political coalitions that are responsive to the struggles of rural communities and rural people. Such pedagogies and activist agendas need to make literacy in a "public globalized sphere" and citizenship the "centerpiece of a struggle for social empowerment, where citizenship can cross geographic boundaries to engage in a unified movement for social justice" (Edmondson 123).

## An Overview of This Book

Addressing these issues surrounding rural literacies is both a scholarly and personal endeavor for us. The three of us have connections to rural places, and we have experienced firsthand some of the ways rural life and rural experiences are represented in limited or reductive ways. As former college students, we have been on the receiving end of stereotypes about rural people and rural literacies. As educators and as scholars, we have resisted those stereotypes even as we have been successful at navigating the demands of teaching urban and suburban students. At the same time, we have strived to bring the perspectives and realities of rural peoples to the attention of those in our field, and we have actively resisted reductive representations of rural communities and rural literacies.

Our understanding of rural life and rural culture, however, is not homogeneous, and our perspectives, experiences, and scholarly emphases differ in terms of region and experience. For four generations, Eileen's family farmed in eastern Washington State, near Cashmere, population approximately 2,500. The area is known as the apple capital of the world and was once home to hundreds of family farms, mostly apple and pear orchards. In January 2001, facing decreased prices and increased global competition, which led to mounting debt and the threat of foreclosure, her mother and brother quit farming. To pay off debt and to stay afloat, her family began leasing their land to another local farmer and sold off some land tracts for residential development. While Eileen's family is fortunate enough to remain on the land they once farmed, the future of the land is uncertain, and the future of the community and the area is equally so. Like hundreds of thousands of family farmers in the United States and across the globe, Eileen's family has been displaced from their traditional livelihood, told that their farm and their way of life is now obsolete. Corporate farms and global competition have replaced small farms, a shift that she addresses in her scholarly work on the rhetoric of the farm crisis in the wake of globalization.

When Charlotte was eleven, her family moved to Paxton, Nebraska, population around 600, located near the western end of the state. Her father had grown up there, as had her grandmother. While Charlotte was there, it was assumed by everyone that she would leave for college at eighteen and then find a job in a city just a state or two over—Denver, Kansas City, Minneapolis. As a first-year student at the University of Nebraska–Lincoln, her English composition course had ten more students than did her entire senior class in high school. Surrounded by students from Omaha who assumed she grew up on a farm (she didn't—she was a town kid), she was scared to open her mouth, having internalized for years the messages that where she came from was unimportant. In college, she wrote to impress the urban Omaha students, constructing (and trying to exoticize) her hometown through the strong sense of place she witnessed in her grandmother, hoping to show in her writing what she could not say in class.

Over a decade later, she found herself teaching the same composition course at the same university, hearing some of her fellow teaching assistants complain about how small-minded their rural students were before they even stepped into the classroom. She responded to those voices by undertaking research on rural literacies, specifically the literacies of older women in her hometown. Eventually Charlotte became an example of "brain drain," what legislators call the trend of young residents educated in Nebraska who leave the state. She now lives in Fort Worth, a part of the "Metroplex" of north Texas, population over five million, where she finds herself in a state ripe for considering issues of place and where she hears her students from rural areas repeat the same negative lines about their hometowns that she found herself saying in college.

Kim represents the second generation of brain drain. Part of her family comes from a small town in southern Appalachia; lack of economic and cultural opportunities led her mother to move to Asheville, the nearest city, to make her life and raise her family. Kim's interest in rural literacy comes from the impressive literacy trajectory within her own family: from functionally illiterate great-grandparents to Kim's Ph.D. in English in only three generations. The literacy accomplishments of her family contrasted sharply with the representations of Appalachian literacy that Kim encountered in academic texts such as James Moffett's *Storm in the Mountains* and in the popular media. These stark differences have fueled her research into the stigmatizing of rural literacy and the effects of those stigmas on rural people. She has been able to research these issues from two different universities that serve rural regions: Fresno, California, and Grand Forks, North Dakota. At the University of North Dakota, she has seen the many ways that stereotypes and realities of rural literacy affect rural college students, from faculty's assumptions that rural students "have no culture" to students' assumptions that they must leave their home communities for urban areas to best use the literacies the university teaches.

Our separate interests in rural literacies have brought us together to address the subject more comprehensively, though certainly not exhaustively. We collaborated to employ our individual research sites and strengths and also to meet the goals of the book that couldn't be achieved singularly. We co-wrote the first and last chapters, but each of us individually authored the three body chapters because we wanted to be overt in letting our stylistic and methodological differences emerge in order to further disrupt the notion that there is only one way to study rural literacies. As indicated in the chapter overviews that follow, while we work to address many aspects of rural literacies, the scope of this book and our areas of expertise lead us to offer this text as a voice in the discussion rather than as the final word.

In chapter 2, "Rhetorics and Realities: The History and Effects of Stereotypes about Rural Literacies," Kim examines the history of stereotypes about Appalachian literacy as a template for the general history of representations of rural literacy. Drawing upon the work of folklorist David Whisnant and historians Henry Shapiro and Allen Batteau, she argues that the creation of stereotypes about Appalachian literacy established rhetorical patterns that have been similarly followed in stereotyping the literacy of other rural areas. This rhetorical history has negatively influenced the relationships among rural people, outside literacy sponsors, and competing notions of literacy. Ultimately, Kim explores the ways literacy itself may be used as a resource to renegotiate these relationships and work toward a model of sustainability.

To investigate this topic, Kim combines rhetorical analysis of popular and academic discussions of rural literacy with qualitative data collection and analysis techniques. She interviewed ten individuals in an Appalachian town that had been the target of three different waves of outside literacy workers who came to the community to remedy its presumed literacy deficits. By examining the ways these individuals came to use and value literacy in their lives in light of their relationships with these different stigmatizing sponsors, Kim offers an analysis of the role of literacy in shaping the social networks within rural communities and between rural people and outside literacy sponsors.

Building upon Shapiro's imagery of preservation, modernization, and abandonment described in chapter 2, chapter 3 extends the discussion of rural literacies into the economic realm. In "The Rhetorics of the Farm Crisis: Toward Alternative Agrarian Literacies in a Globalized World," Eileen analyzes how popular press rhetorics representing the demise of the family farm shape the American people's expectations and understanding of rural life and make it possible for corporations and politicians to exploit rural peoples and rural areas with little or no public accountability. These popular press accounts of the demise of the family farm follow two predictable lines of argumentation: the pathos-driven rhetoric of tragedy or the logos-driven rhetoric of smart diversification, employing rhetorics of preservation and modernization, respectively. While both rhetorics diverge in their appeals and explanatory narratives, they both promote what Eileen calls "agricultural illiteracy" or the general public's inability and, perhaps, unwillingness to understand how, where, and under what conditions our nation's food is grown, distributed, and marketed. Neither rhetoric enables the reader/viewer to understand how we arrived at the "demise of the family farm" through international trade policies, domestic agricultural policies, and the globalization of capital, nor do these stories tell of the environmental devastation that corporate-run agriculture and factory farming often bring to particular regions.

As a corrective to the rhetorics of tragedy and smart diversification, Eileen advocates an alternative agrarian rhetoric that, as Edmondson argues, "reads rural life with a language that attempts to slow the effects of neoliberalism, to offer more choice, and to develop alternatives aligned with rural sensibilities" (15). She analyzes how the family farm advocacy organization Farm Aid, one of the most visible and popular campaigns to help small farmers in the United States, works to build an alternative agrarian rhetoric that fosters agricultural literacy, sustainability, and community-supported agriculture, thus offering a way out of the impasse created by the impoverished tragedy and smart diversification rhetorics. Farm Aid's alternative agrarian rhetoric accounts, in part, for the impact of globalization, corporatization, and industrialization on agriculture and rural life and provides a lens through which to understand the future of the small farm, the future of agriculture, and the link between what is happening in rural America and other rural parts of the globe.

Chapter 4, "Beyond Agrarianism: Toward a Critical Pedagogy of Place," examines the ways agrarianist thinking has obscured the important social function of literacy work by rural women. Charlotte's chapter begins by analyzing the ways agrarianist scholarship currently shapes narratives of rural life that reinforce rhetorics of preservation and discount gendered issues in rural spaces. To consider a more complicated understanding of what rural literacies can mean and how people can learn from rural literacies, she utilizes David Gruenewald's discussion of a critical pedagogy of place that blends ideologies of critical pedagogies (typically associated with urban settings) with place-based education efforts (identified by rural settings).

Charlotte draws upon ethnographic research on older women in her hometown of Paxton, Nebraska, to demonstrate the ways their literacies are not artifacts but contributions and interruptions to what Giroux names as a kind of public memory, and she argues that the social realities of rural life articulated in such literacies can thus become a more integral part of meaning-making to move toward a critical pedagogy of place. In describing how being sponsored by rural women allowed her to tap into other kinds of literacies not valued by traditional masculinist ways of knowing, Charlotte shares how sustainability of community life can move beyond—even while they may employ—the rhetorics of preservation. Finally, she offers ways women's rural literacy work can offer possibilities for enacting a critical, public pedagogy of place.

While chapters 2, 3, and 4 expose and investigate misperceptions and narrow depictions of rural literacies and begin to offer alternative ways of thinking through and practicing rural literacies, in chapter 5, "Toward a Sustainable Citizenship and Pedagogy," we share concrete strategies for compositionists to participate in pedagogies that are rooted in a richer understanding of rural literacies and that work toward sustainability for all communities. Ultimately, we call for compositionists to play a role as activist intellectuals and literacy sponsors to improve public discourse about rural issues and foster a multiplicity of rural literacies.

There is always the risk in a project titled *Rural Literacies* of seeming to advocate for yet another identity to be added to the string of positional identities in academia. Our goal is to avoid making the argument that "rural" is merely an interesting identity or monolithic position to consider. Rather, our project works to demonstrate how ideas of the "rural" and "rural literacies" encompass questions of space, place, politics, power, economics, community identity, and a myriad of identifications and connections.

At a time when stereotypes of rural people are perpetuated with renewed energy by the popular media through red- and blue-state simplifications, and at a time when the population of rural areas is dwindling due to loss of farms and well-paying, stable jobs, we need a clarifying vision of what rural literacies can mean. Ultimately, we hope that *Rural Literacies* will open up a new line of inquiry into the meaning and function of literacy in rural settings. Americans profess great affection for the "rosy past" of our rural ancestors. If we want to ensure that rural communities remain an integral part of America's future, we must take an honest look at the role rural literacies can play in creating and sustaining that future.

# 2 / Rhetorics and Realities
## The History and Effects of Stereotypes about Rural Literacies

*Kim Donehower*

> Even when pedagogy is related to issues of democracy, citizenship, and the struggle over the shaping of identities and identifications, it is rarely taken up as part of a broader public politics—as part of a larger attempt to explain how learning takes place outside of schools or what it means to assess the political significance of understanding the broader educational force of culture.
>
> —Henry Giroux, "Cultural Studies, Public Pedagogy, and the Responsibility of Intellectuals"

This chapter examines what Henry Giroux calls "the struggle over the shaping of identities and identifications" for rural people in light of the broader public politics of rural literacy. As Giroux argues, culture itself is a powerful educational force in shaping public notions of literacy in rural communities. For more than a century, the most commonly held public perception of rural literacy has been of its inadequacy. From images of illiterate hillbillies to ignorant rednecks, the predominant representations of rural literacy in popular culture have been those of extreme deficiency.

Academic culture has also had a hand in propagating versions of these same negative caricatures, both inside and outside the classroom. A rural student at the University of North Dakota vividly recalled his first experience in the college English classroom in the late 1990s: "The teacher walked in [to the introductory literature class] and said, 'You're from North Dakota. You have no culture. My job is to give you some.'" As teachers who come into contact with rural students in the course of our daily work—and rural students are everywhere, including large urban universities—it is incumbent on us to understand the cultural assumptions that affect our own understanding of rural students' literacies, especially as we work to shape those literacies in the composition classroom. The context of literacy development in rural areas, in general, differs from that of urban and suburban areas in the structure of leisure time, in access to literacy materials, and in economic demands for particular kinds of literacy skills. From different contexts come different ways of valuing and practicing literacy. As they do so often in other situations, these differences inspire stereotyping and stigmatization more often than they do curiosity and understanding. As literacy researchers, it is vital that we break the cycle of stereotyping and work toward more nuanced representations of rural literacies.

To disrupt this cycle, we must acknowledge that rural people in the United States pursue literacy under a stigma of rural illiteracy. The rural illiteracy stereotype, perpetuated by academics, the popular media, and what Deborah Brandt calls "literacy sponsors," holds that rural people lack literate skills and value literacy and education less than their urban and suburban counterparts do. This stigma forces rural people, even if they don't want to identify themselves as generically "rural," to respond to a label they did not seek.

How does the stigmatization of rural literacies affect the development of rural literacies, our understanding of rural literacies, and the relationships between literacy sponsors such as ourselves and rural people? How does the legacy of stigmatization based on literacy affect the identities and identifications of rural people? In this chapter, I first review the history of stereotyping rural literacy in the United States, with a particular focus on the stigmatization of Appalachia as an illiterate region, to document "the broader . . . force of culture" in shaping common notions of rural (il)literacy. By considering the rural literacy research of James Moffett, I investigate how these common notions of rural (il)literacy can affect the relationships between potential literacy sponsors and rural people, creating struggles for identity and identification rooted in different notions of literacy. I then present data from my qualitative research in one Appalachian community to examine the ways that literacy becomes both a site of and a tool for negotiating identities and identifications among rural people and those who would sponsor their literacy.

## Sourcing the Cultural Stereotypes

The American people cut their teeth on stereotyping rural regions through the demonization, and celebration, of Appalachia. The film *Deliverance* and the popularized legend of Davy Crockett demonstrate the paradox at the heart of what America likes to believe about rural people—that they are either barbarians or paragons of the pioneer spirit or, somehow, simultaneously, both. Based on the novel by James Dickey, the film version of *Deliverance* seared into Americans' minds images of Appalachian natives as either harmless-but-creepy retarded banjo-pickers or shotgun-toting rapists looking to prey on any hapless urban males who might have the misfortune to cross their path. Davy Crockett, on the other hand, "king of the wild frontier," was the idol of many late-1950s television-watching boys or girls who begged their parents for coonskin caps. "Born on a mountaintop in Tennessee . . . raised in the woods so's he knew ev'ry tree," Davy was the master settler taming the American landscape, from killing bears "when he was only three" to fighting Indians. "The Ballad of Davy Crockett" was the number two hit song on the Billboard charts for all of 1955.

Henry Shapiro, in his analysis of the history of stereotyping of Appalachia, calls this paradox "a peculiar ambiguity . . . by which the mountaineers became at once like us and not like us" (61). Allen Batteau extends Shapiro's discussion, arguing that both stereotypes spring from "the Puritan separation from civilization and the consequent confrontation with nature" (197). In other words, when civilization becomes defined as distance from nature, the physical setting of rural areas suggests a barbarism, an image Batteau describes as "the embodiment of anti-civilization" (196). At the same time, the ability to tame nature, to work with it and subdue it—to know every tree, to kill bears single-handed—becomes a necessary characteristic for those who would civilize America. In this way, rural people can represent both the "contemporary ancestors" of modern civilization (Shapiro 99) and a threat to it.

This dual stereotype, originally applied to Appalachia, has come to be associated with rural communities in America in general, as I argue later in this chapter. Where do such stereotypes originate? Shapiro, Batteau, David Whisnant, and Peter Mortensen have all documented that the concept of "Appalachia" as a distinct cultural region, with particular problems inherent in that culture, was largely the creation of a battalion of culture workers who descended on the area at the turn of the twentieth century. The region defined as Appalachia did suffer from poverty and a variety of ills that spring from poverty. But the ways in which these problems were characterized, and the solutions that were offered, reveal more about the cultural agendas of the groups who sought to "fix" Appalachia than they do about the region itself. They provide a rhetorical model for problematizing rural literacy and rural education that came to affect analyses of other rural regions and still exert a powerful pull on our current-day understanding.

In *Appalachia on Our Mind: The Southern Mountains and Mountaineers in the American Consciousness, 1870–1920*, Shapiro provides a detailed timeline of the initial cycles of rhetoric about the Appalachian "problem." It is worth summarizing Shapiro's analysis to see connections with the arguments about rural literacy in other regions and to understand the types of solutions that are most commonly proposed to these problems.

First: The region is identified as a distinct region. Shapiro attributes this step of the process to the local color writers of the late nineteenth century and in particular to a single essay published in *Lippincott's Magazine* in 1873, which, he states, is "the first to assert that 'otherness' which made of the mountainous portions of eight southern states a discrete region" (4). Shapiro documents the ways in which magazine articles, short story collections, and novels served to establish Appalachia as both a distinct region and a place apart from, and unlike, the rest of America (3–31). This critical step allowed culture workers, such as missionaries, settlement school founders, ethnographers, and others, to secure funding for and plan their work in the region. As folklorist Dorothy Noyes notes, "Applying for grants, we know we'll do better if we can frame our project around a 'community'—that is, a viable political constituency—instead of a 'practice'" (449). Culture workers thus became invested in cementing Appalachia's status as a distinct cultural group.

Second: The region is identified as a "problem" to be solved. Shapiro documents that by 1890, both popular and professional literature about Appalachia portrayed it as a cultural problem in need of resolution (63). Shapiro describes the problem as one of "otherness"—how to make life in Appalachia more like life in the rest of the United States? Language and literacy issues were central to this sense of otherness, from the supposed "Shakespearean" dialect of the mountain people to limited reading and writing skills and a knowledge base that did not fit mainstream, middle-class notions of "what every American needs to know."[1] In "Representations of Literacy and Region: Narrating 'Another America,'" Mortensen describes the institutionalization of Appalachian illiteracy in both the popular and professional imaginations, beginning with the works of local color writers John Fox Jr. and James Lane Allen at the turn of the twentieth century, through decades of educational intervention in the region by missionaries and other culture workers, to a 1989 episode of the television news magazine *48 Hours* that still portrayed Appalachia as both "other" and illiterate. Mortensen notes along the way that literacy rates in the region at the time that Appalachia's illiteracy was first asserted showed no great difference from those of the rest of the southern United States (106).[2]

Moving from Appalachia in the 1870s through the 1920s to the Great Plains in the late twentieth century, we can see how the process Shapiro details replicates itself in another rural area, despite the differences between the regions in geography, economics, settlement patterns, and the cultural heritages of those who live there. The defining "problem" of the Great Plains, a vast emptiness resulting "naturally" from its topography and climate, is established by contemporary versions of Shapiro's local color writers. In persuasive, poetic terms, Kathleen Norris, Ian Frazier, and Paul Gruchow depict this emptiness, both geographical and, by implication, cultural, that pervades the plains. Similarly, Fox, Allen, Mary Noalles Murfree, and Will Wallace Harney[3] established for Appalachia an "otherness" that sprang "naturally" from its supposedly isolating mountains.

From such descriptions are born particular ways of character-izing the problems of the plains states. The Great Plains, as any other U.S. region, does have its particular difficulties—out-migration, low wages, and the effects of agricultural corporatization. But the ways in which these problems are understood and the proposed solutions to them show that the process Shapiro documents in Appalachia is being applied once again. The source of the problems, in both cases, is an "otherness" that results from a geographically imposed isolation, whether that isolation is the result of vast, open space and a challenging climate or from steep, rocky ridges and hidden "hollers." These geographical boundaries supposedly insulate the populace from the kinds of changes occurring beyond their borders, resulting in a population that is somehow "behind" the rest of the country.[4]

The idea of this isolated "otherness" allows the stereotypes of both *Deliverance* and Davy Crockett to flourish. Separated from the rest of civilization, rural people may be seen to both preserve a former, noble way of life and give in to primal, destructive impulses. How, then, should one solve the "problems" of rural communities as represented by these conflicting rural stereotypes? Shapiro documents three basic types of solutions that were proposed in the case of Appalachia; again, we can see them being offered as solutions for other rural regions.

Solution One: "Modernize" the population by bringing them into line with the technological, economic, and cultural systems of urban life. Shapiro describes a number of different responses to the problem of Appalachian otherness. The first was to "make them more like us" by introducing "modern" conveniences and standards of behavior. Settlement and mission schools in Appalachia, for example, often recruited primarily female students and taught them the latest tech-niques in home economics and "hygiene" while also exposing them to a sort of "great books" curriculum.[5]

Solution Two: Recognize the culture as a thing apart from ur-ban life and work to preserve its unique character. As Shapiro and Whisnant observe, the preservationist impulse by culture workers in Appalachia had much to do with their sense of mountain people as "our contemporary ancestors" (Shapiro 99), "pure" Anglo-Saxons living in the style of their Scottish and Irish forebears (Shapiro 80;

Whisnant 237–46). The version of the culture that workers sought to preserve was altered and edited (Whisnant 55–58) to fit their visions of Appalachian culture's supposed "essential Englishness" (Shapiro 200, quoting folklorist Cecil Sharpe) and its link to a quintessentially American pioneer spirit (84). Language habits and other cultural practices were shaped to demonstrate these romantic images of the culture's meaning for the rest of America.

Solution Three: Relocate the people to urban or suburban areas and abandon the region to nature. This strategy—give up and get them out of there—declared the region uninhabitable and sought to relocate the people to places where they might participate in "modern" American life. In Appalachia, this meant moving the population to Piedmont mill towns to participate in the Industrial Revolution, including child labor (Shapiro 156, 162–80). Poverty combined with a lack of marketable literacy skills created a cheap labor force that could be exploited in the name of benevolence.

Solutions to the problems of the plains states echo those advocated in Appalachia. Contemporary discussions of "modernizing" rural schools center around technology—specifically, computers and distance education. A special issue of the journal of the Education Commission of the States focusing on rural education reports that "distance education overcomes isolation" and that technology is "closing the gap" between rural and urban schools. While distance education does offer isolated areas access to programs they might not otherwise have, little attention is given to the possible pedagogical downside of it—for example, difficulties in having students work collaboratively in groups or the effects of the teacher's lack of a physical presence in the classroom for hands-on activities. Instead, computers and technology are portrayed as the modernizing solution for isolated rural schools.

Preservationist impulses are evident in national organizations' interests in promoting community research and oral history projects in rural schools. The Rural School and Community Trust Web site, under "practices" for rural schools, has a section entitled "Arts and Cultural Heritage." In 2004, its featured stories reported entirely on cultural preservation projects in which rural schools are engaged. Similarly, a significant portion of the National Writing Project's Rural

Voices, Country Schools initiative has been devoted to "connecting students to their communities" through such projects as researching the history of the school building and interviewing community members about what life was like in the community fifty years before. The connections being built are largely connections to a past way of life. Chapter 4 discusses both the positive and negative aspects of this approach.

The preservationist impulse need not have negative consequences. Its rhetoric is an important tool in gaining support for work that sustains rural life. However, as Giroux advocates, "a pedagogy of public memory is about making connections that are often hidden, forgotten, or willfully ignored. Public memory in this sense becomes not an object of reverence but an ongoing subject of debate, dialogue, and critical engagement" (68). We must interrogate the source of our desires to preserve rural places and be ever-conscious of the danger that lies in preservationist models that seek to make of rural places a monolithic symbol of a collective American heritage for those who live in urban and suburban areas, rather than vital and diverse communities that can adapt to economic and demographic shifts. Preservationist projects that seek to turn rural communities into museums essentially ensure that those communities cease to exist, as no one actually lives in a museum.

The third strategy Shapiro documents—that of abandoning rural areas and returning them to nature—has its advocates in the plains and, on a smaller scale, in rural regions elsewhere. Most spectacularly, advocates of the "Buffalo Commons" concept invented and popularized by Frank and Deborah Popper set a goal of returning a million acres of the plains region to nature. People would fence nature out instead of in and would live in even smaller, more isolated settled outposts scattered across the vast natural commons. The Poppers acknowledge that they intended their strategy as a "metaphor"; they note, as well, the power that metaphor has had in seizing the imaginations of those who would like to see rural areas transformed into nature preserves. Interestingly, the Great Plains Restoration Council, the advocate of the million-acre project, is headquartered in Fort Worth and Denver—both cities located on the fringes of the plains.

The abandonment strategy shows up in subtler form in wide-spread debates about rural school consolidation. Often seen as a last resort to deal with the problems of funding rural schools—which receive 22 percent of federal education dollars despite serving over 40 percent of the nation's students, according to the National Education Association—school consolidation abandons the smallest and most isolated schools to concentrate funds toward a centralized school building. While consolidation may be the best use of limited resources, the loss or lack of a school building negatively affects communities in other ways. In a study comparing rural New York villages with and without schools, Thomas Lyson found that towns with populations under 500 that had schools had higher housing values, better municipal infrastructure, more stable employment patterns, and less income inequality. Bruce Miller of the Northwest Regional Educational Laboratory notes that school buildings in small towns serve as cultural and recreational centers as well as sites for civic engagement and community education.

The *Deliverance*/Davy Crockett stereotype can inspire and reinforce all three of the impulses Shapiro describes. Modernizing rural places becomes a necessity to continue the "civilizing" process, where civilization means "progress" away from a land-based economy. Preserving rural places becomes a way to supposedly conserve our own heritage in terms of the nation-building myth we use to define the American character. Abandonment "solves" the whole messy contradiction by attempting to assimilate rural people into urban and suburban life. The stereotyping and othering of rural people, perpetrated and disseminated by the media, leads to policy decisions that can genuinely isolate rural communities. The process of "othering," which, as Shapiro documents, begins with representations of rural people, becomes concretized in the policies that are fueled by the stereotypes.

## The Role of Literacy in the Perpetuation of Rural Stereotypes

The paradoxical dual rural stereotype, of the pioneer and the barbarian, flourishes in both the popular media[6] and the world of professional educators. For the second group, as for the first, the mythos of Appalachia often stands in for ideas about rural communities in general. In late 2002, coordinators of the Rural Sites Network of the National Writing Project—a group with the best of intentions for improving rural literacy and rural education—attended their annual meeting wearing red bandannas as neckerchiefs. Bluegrass music filled the air, and participants were led in an opening cheer of "yee-hah." The symbology here mixes the Old West with Appalachia and the lowland South of *The Dukes of Hazzard*, but it is evident that "rural," in this context, was taken to mean the culture of the rural mountain South. One North Dakota teacher, grimacing at the banjo music, said, "I hate this shit. I grew up listening to disco."

Folklorist and cultural critic Whisnant writes that "to this day there are a thousand people who 'know' that mountaineers weave coverlets and sing ballads for every one who knows that millions of them have been industrial workers for a hundred years . . . or that, today, they shop at the K-Mart and Radio Shack, drive Camaros, and watch as much television as people anywhere" (13). Appalachian people do not all wear bandannas and listen only to bluegrass and yell "yee-hah," and neither do residents of other rural areas. Shapiro calls this "assumptions of coherence and homogeneity" (117), and it plagues our ability to achieve a nuanced understanding of rural regions. Romantic, unified visions of rural America, inspired by the Jeffersonian ideal discussed in chapters 3 and 4 and based largely on literary and media images, offer no basis on which to make sound decisions about, or interpretations of, rural literacy and education. And yet many of us still cling to them.

These stereotypes persist in part because of their widespread dissemination in both mainstream media and academic environments. But there is something more at work—a need on the part of many urban and suburban people for rural places to be this kind of "other." The Appalachian region offers an ideal site in which to examine the motivations for this need. Consider this quote by University of Chicago sociologist George Vincent in 1898 in a work on the Kentucky mountains that he titled "A Retarded Frontier": "We had heard so many stories of the ignorance of the mountaineers that we were somewhat disappointed by their familiarity with a good many things we had expected them not to know" (qtd. in Mortensen 108).[7] As Mortensen notes, the literacy statistics for the South from the 1900 census show that rates in Appalachia were basically consistent with the rates for the rest of the South.[8] This begs the question: Why did others outside southern Appalachia need it to be a locus of illiteracy? Why would academics—professional educators—be disappointed to find that the southern mountaineers were not as ignorant as they had believed?

The reasons are racial, regional, cultural, and political and have to do with these educators' own struggles with identities and identifications. Culturally, the early part of the twentieth century, with its massive rates of immigration, was a time of hierarchicalization on many levels as the United States' social and political elite strove to maintain some kind of nationalist identity amidst the influx of foreigners. Cultural critic Lawrence Levine, in *Highbrow/Lowbrow: The Emergence of Cultural Hierarchy in America*, terms this process the "sacralization of culture," in which particular cultural artifacts (specifically, those of northern European origin) changed from the common property of the masses to sacred objects that had the power to purify the soul and sanctify the mind of the viewer or listener. Levine offers as an example the treatment of Shakespeare's works, which in the mid-nineteenth century might appear on a theater playbill along with "Mr. Stoepel, with his Wood and Straw Instruments" and the "Musically-Educated Seal." By the end of the century, however, this "human Shakespeare who . . . could be parodied with pleasure and impunity" had been replaced by "the sacred Shakespeare," who, one critic argued, was best "off the stage" entirely, read in the privacy of one's own study (69–74).

Levine argues that this reorganization of cultural materials into a rigid vertical hierarchy, with strictly enforced boundaries between "high" and "low" culture, was not a given of American society but was a conscious social construction that occurred in response to political, economic, and social needs for order among the disorder caused by mass immigration, a more diversified population, and other social and economic changes at the turn of the century. In Levine's words, "The drive for political order was paralleled by a drive for cultural order[,] . . . the push to organize the economic sphere was paralleled by a push to organize the cultural sphere[, and] . . . the quest for social authority was paralleled by a quest for cultural authority" (228). Specific types of culture were identified with particular cultural groups. Thus, a set of cultural materials and practices that was devalued within the cultural hierarchy similarly marked the devalued status of the cultural group with which those materials and practices were identified. Groups and individuals could then use certain cultural materials and practices to identify, or dis-identify, themselves with particular high- or low-status groups. Reading Shakespeare in the privacy of one's own study allowed a person to both identify with a high-status cultural group that engaged in that practice and to distinguish oneself as different from groups who had no access to Shakespeare, private studies, or leisure reading time.

This elevation of specific sets of cultural materials and ways of performing those materials created a class of "culture professionals" who resided at the top of the cultural hierarchy and benefited from their close association with "sacred" cultural forms. Culture professionals had to lift themselves out of the popular cultural marketplace, away from the common "mixed audience," to gain authority. They had to continually reinforce certain boundaries, as cultural status came to be defined by the degree of separation from a group clearly marked as cultural and intellectual "others." The concept of literacy became a powerful tool in maintaining this division.

Consider the case of John Fox Jr. as documented by Mortensen. A southerner from the Kentucky Bluegrass region, Fox's fictional accounts of the southern mountains in works such as *The Kentuckians* and *The Trail of the Lonesome Pine* received widespread popular attention. Mortensen sees Fox's goal in these works, and in his representation of mountaineers' (il)literacy, as creating evidence for a literate, cultured South distinct from the illiterate South of the southern Appalachians:

> Each of these works contrasts mountain and Bluegrass culture; each measures progress toward modernity—or distance from it—in terms of literacy. That Fox's work attained such immediate and widespread notice enabled him to advance a theory of southern improvement measured against the low

mark of supposedly primitive, illiterate conditions in the southern mountains. (103)

This is a case of regional scapegoating. The South was seen in the early part of the twentieth century as less literate, less cultured, and more primitive than the rest of America. It was being denied access to the kind of cultural power available as a result of the hierarchicalization that Levine describes. Therefore an explanation had to be developed for the South's lower literacy rates: one part—Appalachia—was dragging the rest of the region down. Southerners such as Fox could use literacy—both their representation of others' literacy and their own literate practices—to define themselves in contradistinction to a low-status group. Literacy functioned as a tool to identify oneself with one cultural group and to dis-identify with another group that was perceived as being of lower status intellectually, culturally, economically, and morally.[9]

The investiture of southern Appalachia as "illiterate" had a racial motivation as well. An important aspect of the mountaineers' characterization as "illiterate" at the early part of the century was the belief that these people could be saved from their illiteracy. The reason for the mountaineers' potential was based on a mythic construction of the southern mountaineer as representative of whiteness, of "pure" Anglo-Saxon culture, protected from racial or ethnic contamination by being shut away in the mountains.[10] This piece of (false) public memory lingers today in the minds of those who still believe that Appalachian dialect is actually some form of "Elizabethan English."

In *All That Is Native and Fine: The Politics of Culture in an American Region*, Whisnant describes how "culture professionals," usually missionary teachers from the northeast, traveled to southern Appalachia to identify and collect Appalachian cultural artifacts (songs, handicrafts, and the like) that were deemed "appropriate" cultural representations of the "hardy mountaineer" and of his or her "pure Anglo" culture. If the cultural artifacts that the mountaineers contributed did not fit in to the missionaries' idea of appropriately "English" works, then the mountaineers were subsequently instructed until their cultural practices met the missionaries' romanticized, and racist, standards.

This excerpt is from a 1938 newsletter from the Hindman settlement school in Kentucky: "A child with a genuine love for music expressing itself in raucous singing of so-called 'hill-billy' songs, learns at our Saturday night gatherings beautiful lasting melodies, and true mountain ballads that are a heritage from English forbears. Her keen ambition to take piano lessons is fulfilled" (qtd. in Whisnant 57–58). In other words, the illiterate, uncultured mountaineers could be saved by getting them in touch with their whiteness. Their "raucous" edges could be smoothed away by exposure to their "true" heritage. Here we see a strict racialist agenda underpinning the entire enterprise of first labeling the people of the southern mountains "illiterate," then rushing in to save them through the systematic revision of their culture. The representation of mountain culture as purely "English" is, of course, another piece of false public memory; the diverse heritage of the southern mountains has been well-documented.[11]

The groups of culture professionals who came to save Appalachian literacy practices were united in their vision of Appalachian literacy as substandard. They differed distinctly, however, in the kinds of literacy they wanted to instill in the region. It is useful to understand these professional literacy workers in terms of Brandt's definition of a literacy sponsor: "Sponsors . . . are any agents, local or distant, concrete or abstract, who enable, support, teach, model, as well as recruit, regulate, suppress or withhold literacy—and gain advantage by it in some way. . . . Sponsors set the terms for access to literacy and wield powerful incentives for compliance and loyalty" ("Sponsors" 166–67). In other words, literacy sponsors offer to groups or individuals a certain set of methods for practicing literacy and particular reasons why literacy should be done. Sponsors don't simply offer these methods and reasons for "free." They demand from their students compliance with the values—linguistic and otherwise—of the sponsor. Here we see an additional motive for the stigmatization of a culture's literacy and subsequent activity to repair that literacy: sponsors seek validation of their own worldviews.

James Moffett's book *Storm in the Mountains: A Case Study of Censorship, Conflict, and Consciousness* offers an excellent example of this motivation and of its potential results. A renowned liberal educator, Moffett traveled to Kanawha County, West Virginia, in the 1970s after the community banned a set of textbook materials for high school English classes that he had edited. He compares his drive to the county to the opening scenes of *Deliverance*, in which Dickey describes the men's trip from Atlanta into the Appalachian wilderness as one into a foreign land (Moffett 8). The bulk of the book is taken up by transcripts of Moffett's conversations with the leaders of the group who wanted to censor his textbook series; in the last section, Moffett provides his analysis of these interviews.

After a detailed and largely respectful investigation into the arguments of the book-banners, Moffett concludes that the Kanawha County people were suffering from "agnosis"—a term he coins to mean, essentially, the desire to be ignorant (184). My own interpretation of the interviews is different, as I describe below. Far from demonstrating some kind of backward mental state, I believe the Kanawha County residents displayed canny rhetorical skills that they used to try to protect themselves, their culture, and their worldview from Moffett, who would label them "ignorant" unless they agreed to critique their sacred texts, relinquish their way of looking at the world, and generally come around to his way of thinking.[12] What resulted was a rhetorical stalemate, with both sides emerging from the discourse more entrenched in their original positions and neither open to the possibility of change—an unproductive scenario for the development of rural literacies.

Eloquent and exciting, *Storm in the Mountains* pits the academic literacy professional against the supposedly "anti-intellectual" non-professional. The second section of the book, "Voices from the Fray," offers largely unglossed transcripts of Moffett's interviews with some of the leaders of the group who banned his textbook. Moffett was ostensibly in Kanawha County to understand how the censorship conflict came about. Yet in "Voices from the Fray," he repeatedly tries to convince his informants of the wrongness of their stance. Using the didactic rhetoric of Socratic education, Moffett asks the kind of leading questions a teacher asks a student (when the teacher already has the "right" answer to the question firmly in mind): "Is there something we should learn from the book controversy about how to get along with people who interpret the Bible differently?" (56). But in these interviews, the students do not go where the teacher is trying to lead them. Time and again, Moffett's informants ignore such leading questions, usually responding to them with a burst of scriptural quotation. Here is one example, taken from Moffett's conversation with the Reverend Ezra Graley:

> Moffett: I think there are a lot of people who would accept that principle of obeying a spiritual law over a human law. The problem comes that equally sincere people have different notions of spiritual law, and then you get into conflict. This is what concerns me.
>
> Graley: Yeah now, I think though it's people more or less don't know what the Bible says. They're good Christian people, seem like, but they said, "Well, we'll do ours a-praying, we'll pray about ours, we'll pray about our problems and let God work them out." Well, I'm sure Joshua prayed about his problem, but he had to march around Jericho seven times, you know. . . .
>
> Moffett: Well, Christians can agree that the Bible is an inspired work of God, but they go to it and they come back with different things. I can see it's partly maybe because people are at different stages of their development.
>
> Graley: I think it's just a lack of understanding really, cause I know a lot of things that I stood for or against back when I first started out for God, I have studied more deeply in the Bible and I've changed my mind on a lot of things, you know, that I would have died for back then.
>
> Moffett: A lot of people have said this, that the reason that they do Bible study year after year is the Bible deepens in meaning as they mature and as they study and they grow, but what it means is that people are going to interpret it differently at different times. It seems to me the practical problem is what do we do about this? Is there something we should

learn from the book controversy about how to get along with people who interpret the Bible differently?

Graley: I really believe that if everybody that's truly been borned again—like Jesus said, "You must be borned again"—I believe if they're borned again, I think they'll see the word of God just about the same, because I don't think that it was written to cause divisions; it was written to—and Jesus prayed in his prayer, "Father, make them one, even as you and I are one." (55–56)

We see here a real struggle over the shaping of identities and identifications on the part of both participants in this exchange. This struggle is rooted in differing notions of how to use and interpret texts. Moffett identifies strongly with the Socratic tradition and tries to "teach" Graley accordingly, attempting to lead him toward an acceptance of the possibility, and the necessity, of differing interpretations. Graley identifies with an evangelical tradition that teaches through acceptance of certain predetermined interpretations. In his identity as an academic, Moffett sponsors a brand of literacy that highly prizes variety in interpretations. The Reverend Graley comes out of a very different literacy tradition that values agreement in interpretation—at least when it comes to the Bible. Moffett thinks that if he can get Graley to admit to differing interpretations of the Bible, the text Graley holds most sacred, Graley will then have to admit to the possibility of differing interpretations of the textbook selections he wants to censor. But for the Reverend Graley, his personal and professional identities are irrevocably tied to his version of biblical literacy. It is unlikely that Moffett will have any success in getting him to alter his position on textbooks through this rhetorical route.

And in fact, the Reverend Graley is able to end up exactly opposite of where Moffett has been trying to lead him: "I really believe that if everybody that's truly been borned again . . . they'll see the word of God just about the same" (56). Graley responds here under the dictates of a very different literacy sponsor from the one who trained Moffett in the practices of interpretation, argument, and the valuing of texts. Graley's literacy sponsor, a fundamentalist Christian organization, has

taught him to value consistency and agreement in interpretation. It
has provided him with training with one particular text, the Bible, so
that he may call up spontaneously a seemingly irrefutable quotation
to suit any rhetorical situation. In this discussion, Graley employs
the literacy system in which he has been trained every bit as well as
Moffett uses the literate tools in which he is expert.

Moffett interprets the informants' responses both to him and to
the books included in his set of classroom materials as their "misunderstanding" his goals and the purposes of the texts, but I would
argue that the mountaineers understood some things very well. They
understood the cultural context in which these exchanges were occurring, a context in which they were labeled, automatically, as "ignorant,"
as having lesser cultural value and less intellectual and linguistic
capital with which to play. Moffett's interviewee Elmer Fike says of
the national media: "They try to make us look like rednecks" (71).
The Reverend Avis Hill says, "I know that as far as the educational
structure and as far as mainstream society is concerned, I was looked
on as nobody" (84), and Hill is right. Within this context, for Moffett's
informants to submit to his teacherly questioning and accept his kind
of logic meant tacitly agreeing with the system that identified them as
inferior, a system of which Moffett was both a symbol and a practitio-
ner. Thus the mountaineers refused to engage Moffett with any of his
rhetorical tools and relied exclusively on their own—heavy scriptural
quotation, parables, and local anecdotes and analogies.

Both Moffett and the censors operated from deeply held com-
mitments to competing versions of textual interpretation, which connected to strongly rooted identities as liberal academic and conservative Christian. For either to budge on issues of textual interpretation
carried the potential of identifying with a group that each perceived
to be his political and spiritual opposite. Perhaps this is why Moffett,
in the conclusion to *Storm in the Mountains*, retrenches as far as he
does into his position on the censors' "agnosis." Similarly, his oppo-
nents retrench even further into their stance on textual interpretation,
which can then be argued as but another example of their desire "not
to know." And so the cycle of stereotyping continues.

## The Case of Haines Gap

The example of *Storm in the Mountains* shows us that the cycle of stereo-typing rural literacies, which both fuels and is fueled by the analytical filters of modernization, preservation, and abandonment, ruptures the possibility for genuine reciprocal relationships between rural residents and outside literacy sponsors such as Moffett. The process of stereotyp-ing rural literacy associates literate practices and values with particular cultural groups, making literacy an explicit factor in struggles for identities and identifications. In this context, one's stance on how to practice and value reading and writing becomes a way to identify or to dis-identify with particular traditions or groups.

As folklorists note, performing particular cultural practices can mark one's identity in at least two ways—by saying, in essence, "This is us," or by asserting, "This is not us."[13] In terms of acquiring new literate practices from potential sponsors, the first option is one of assimilation, an attempt to fully adopt the sponsor's cultural identity through the sponsor's literate practices. The "this is not us" option can be described as rejection of acquiring both the sponsor's literate practices and elements of the sponsor's identity. A third choice exists: appropriation, in which both practices and identities are modified and hybridized. In these ways, struggles over ways to practice and value literacy become struggles over identities and identifications. In this section, I examine the ways these struggles have played out in one Appalachian town, moving from tensions among town resi-dents and outside literacy sponsors who came to "fix" their presumed illiteracy to struggles for identities and identifications among the townspeople themselves.

In the late 1990s, I interviewed ten residents of Haines Gap,[14] a town of 500 people in the mountains of western North Carolina. I chose Haines Gap because it had a long history of "outsiders," to use the locals' term, coming in to "rescue" the mountaineers from their presumed illiteracy. These included Presbyterians who established a mission school, northern teachers who came to work in the local public schools and area colleges, and government literacy programs. I was interested to see how the prevalence of so many different literacy sponsors affected individuals' choices about literacy.[15] I was also curious to discover how the targets of these various literacy efforts responded to the long-standing stereotypes of Appalachian illiteracy—the very stereotypes that motivated these sponsors' presence in the community.

To find potential interviewees, I talked with a longtime resident of the community to identify people who grew up in the town, or nearby, at any point between 1910 and 1965. These years marked the presence of the greatest number of outside literacy sponsors in the community; today, the Presbyterian mission school is long gone, and government literacy initiatives in the area have dwindled. My local contact and I found ten individuals who were willing to participate and who had made a variety of choices in their relationships with various literacy sponsors over the years. This group also represented a range of literacy skills and interests, from a man with little formal education who rarely wrote and whose reading consisted mainly of newspapers and magazines to individuals with post-baccalaureate degrees and one who was the author of a number of books on local history.

I interviewed these people about their personal histories with literacy, having them describe in detail every aspect of their literacy learning and practices that they could remember. The interviews began with informants recalling their earliest memories of reading and writing. As the conversation proceeded chronologically through interviewees' lives, I asked them to describe in detail the kinds of reading and writing they did, whom they did it with, and how they read and wrote. I also asked about their reasons for pursuing certain literacy practices—or not pursuing them—in the ways that they did and about their relationships and experiences with Haines Gap's different literacy sponsors.

Haines Gap intrigued me for its multiplicity of sponsored ways to practice and value literacy, but there is a second reason I chose it as my research site: it is where my family comes from. My own experience of Appalachian literacy stands in stark contrast to what I read about in *Storm in the Mountains* or saw on *The Beverly Hillbillies*. My great-grandfather never learned to read or write. My great-grandmother learned to read in her sixties as part of a government-sponsored program run through the local Civilian Conservation Corps camp. Their youngest child, my grandmother, finished the seventh grade and grew to be a strong reader and writer, a poet and avid letter-writer who read everything she could get her hands on. Two of her children became extremely disciplined readers with a taste for classic literary works as well as for history, philosophy, and political biography. I ended up getting a doctorate in English, and some of my cousins also have advanced degrees. The literacy trajectory in my family was and is startling: from total illiteracy to an English Ph.D. in four generations.

One family's story, of course, does not disprove decades of negative stereotypes. But my family's experience suggested to me that there was not anything inherently "anti-literacy" in Appalachian culture, or at least the part of Appalachian culture with which I was familiar. I went into this study in part to challenge stereotypes; once the interviews began, it was the effect of those stereotypes that became the most compelling factor to address in my study. That the stereotypes themselves were present, and bore little resemblance to the complex literacies in the community, was obvious. The psychological and sociological effects of those stereotypes on individuals' choices about literacy became my primary focus.

Since many negative stereotypes about the rural intellect center on language practices, literacy, in rural areas, serves both as a site of stigmatization and as a set of tools to manage that stigmatization. In Erving Goffman's terms, reading and writing help "manage" the "spoiled identity" that results from being stigmatized for one's linguistic and textual practices. Strikingly, each of the ten informants in the Haines Gap study, when asked, "What's the first thing you remember about learning to read and write?," offered up traumatic memories of being psychologically shamed and/or physically abused. Beatings for writing left-handed and being made to wear a dunce cap for not being able to recite the alphabet backwards were some of the most striking examples. In general, the acquisition of literacy was fraught with the potential for shame and stigma.

These extreme punishments, of course, could simply be part of the punitive pedagogies of the time, but informants also recalled being made to feel inferior because of the ways their Appalachian heritage influenced their literacy practices. Margaret Garvey recalled a college teacher who criticized her pronunciation when reading aloud in class:

> Well, I was taking, I don't remember what course at Berry Hill College, and, she was from, I guess up North some place. Away from here, and . . . she had asked me, how then would I say a Model T, or a T Model. And I don't even remember my answer to her but she asked me a couple of other questions, and she said you know, to be well rounded and educated, you've got to watch what you say, of course. Which I realized that. And I guess maybe she saw the glint in my eye was not too favorable. But anyway, she came back the next week and she said "I have been listening to other mountain people." And she said, "I have come to the conclusion that, you probably are . . . not going to change your way of speaking. And, you probably are not going to move away from here, so, this is the dialect of the mountains."
>
> Q: So she decided—
>
> A: She decided it was okay. Right.
>
> Q: And well, what was your reaction to all of that?
>
> A: . . . I had never, I never had really gave it any thought at all. . . . I just thought, you know, "what in the world is she talking about," you know, "she's out of her league." I guess that's what I thought. (Donehower, "Literary Choices" 354)

Here the outsider teacher sends a clear message that Margaret's language practices are something that must be contained, kept separate from outside cultures. Language practices are represented as a marker both of who you are—in terms of cultural and economic status—and of your potential value. They have the power to contaminate what others might think of Margaret and how she might fare in the outside world. As long as Margaret stays in the mountains, however, these language practices are okay. This teacher seems to operate from both modernization and abandonment perspectives: "modernizing" or standardizing Appalachian language practices is the primary goal, but if residents aren't planning to live outside the community, they may safely be "abandoned" to their substandard practices. The message for Margaret is that the way one uses language, particularly in the context of reading aloud, serves both as a marker of membership in a particular group and as a potential barrier or tool to move successfully among groups.

Sponsors in Haines Gap recruited adherents not only by offering particular ways of valuing and practicing literacy but also by stigmatizing the literacy that was already there. Sponsors such as Margaret's stigmatized directly, bluntly, and without tact. Others, such as the Presbyterian mission school, used a different strategy. Their message, as one informant said, was that "they were there out of their great love for us." Concerned with the fate of the mountaineers' souls, the mission workers offered a kind of literacy that was designed to both discipline the mind and provide firsthand access to biblical scripture. Despite its being cloaked in love and concern, though, the underlying message was the same: your current literacy practices are inadequate to the task of living as one ought.

Acquiring literacy within these scenes of stigmatization creates strong tensions in one's relationship with these potential sponsors. If a person wishes to pursue literacy with a sponsor, she must, to some extent, internalize the negative messages that the sponsor sends about her home community and reevaluate her relationship with that community. This tension is illustrated in these comments from Lucinda Sykes, a local woman who became a public school teacher:

> Q: Well now . . . tell me why you think the grammar is important.
> A: . . . In the way one speaks.
> Q: Okay. Because that's how people—make decisions about you?
> A: Right. . . . Absolutely. . . . And it was drilled into me, and I drilled it into my students. . . . You know your grandparents, and my grandparents, and people who didn't have English grammar stressed at home, their pronunciation and the use of the word, like, "have went," those little helping words,

we call them helping words, down in third grade. . . . And expressions like that, you know, and the pronunciation of "brush," instead of "bresh," and "frush" instead of "fresh," and then—the correct usage of the verb, that—meant so much.

But when they hear it at home, day in and day out, they come to school and they're wearing that there, and it's hard, you have to go over and go over, repetition, repetition, repetition, to get that—out, and then, I had a child tell me once, I had been hammering on something that I was trying to get into them, one of the students came back and said, "Ms. Sykes," said, "They made fun of me at home, because I did so and so." You know? And I said, "Well you just stick to it because you are right." They said that he was trying to put on the dog, using the correct form of the verb or something. But—it was fun, I enjoyed it. (Donehower, "Literary Choices" 345–46)

To Lucinda, adapting local literacy practices to more standardized norms played a vital role in sustaining the local community. Exchanging comfort within one's family circle for "correct" literacy, in terms of the cultural authority obtained, was worth it for her whether her students moved outside Appalachia or stayed, as she did, in Haines Gap. The stress that infusions of new forms of literacy put on community identity, in other words, was worth it for Lucinda to offer her students a sustainable future.

Others struggled more with reconciling the tensions between sponsors' literacy and a desire to retain a certain kind of Appalachian identity. Margaret's husband, Marlon, the principal of the Haines Gap school, made these comments on the training he received in the summers at a state university:

Well, professors in my opinion live up on a silver cloud. They're not down in with it. They need a year in the public school system, a lot of them do. They go by the book. And the book's not always right. Especially psychology and philosophy and whatever, you know. You read it, but—to practice it, it's different. There was one here that was awful. [Gestures

to bookcase.] *How to Read a Book*. That is the awfulest book
that you—
    Q: What's awful about it?
    A: Oh, just read it. How long are you going to be in town—
do you have time to read a book?
    Q: Oh yeah.
    A: Can I give you one to read? [He gives me Jesse Stu-
art's *The Thread That Runs So True*.] (Donehower, "Literary
Choices" 351)

Stuart's book is an account of his days teaching and serving as a
principal in mountain schools in Kentucky in the 1930s and 1940s.
What Marlon rejects here are texts that offer decontextualized knowledge. *How to Read a Book*, as indicated by its title, purports to tell
anyone how to read a book, regardless of their cultural background
or their reasons for wanting to read books in the first place. Marlon
felt his and other mountain teachers' reading time would be better
spent on works that both supplied and explained the local context
in which they worked. It was not that *The Thread That Runs So True*
offered a better pedagogy than *How to Read a Book* did; the book is
a personal memoir and does not advertise itself as a theoretical or
practical treatise on how to teach. Rather, *The Thread That Runs So True*
contextualizes teaching in a particular Appalachian community at a
certain time, describing the local attitudes about education and the
ways that one teacher found to interact with those attitudes. Marlon's
privileging of local context is a common goal for those who wish to
sustain a particular local or regional identity.

What we see here is a clear-cut example of Brandt's concept of a
literacy sponsor and of the struggles over identity inherent in sponsor/
sponsee relationships. The public school system, supported by state
government and the state university, offers to its principals a particular
set of methods for literacy (*How to Read a Book*) and a particular way
of valuing literacy (going "by [certain] books" is more powerful than
considering other kinds of knowledge) and provides incentives for
compliance with these methods and values. (Marlon is required to
attend these summer sessions, and he displays Mortimer Adler and

Charles Van Doren's *How to Read a Book* in his office, despite the fact that he thinks it's an awful book.) Marlon's economic security, his keeping his job, is dependent on his at least being able to appear as though he agrees with this sponsor's brand of literacy. However, in Marlon's view, this sponsor's version of literacy explicitly denies local context, setting up a conflict between his role as an official of the public school system and his identify as a mountain person.

The nature of relationships with sponsors tended to follow one of the three broad paths described above: assimilation, appropriation, and rejection. Lucinda sought assimilation with her sponsor. She became a proponent of that sponsor's literacy values and practices within the community. Marlon rejects many of his sponsor's literacy values and practices while still working as a representative of that sponsor. Others in the study took an appropriative stance. They borrowed some of their sponsor's literacy practices and values but applied them in ways that the sponsor might not approve. For example, Irma, who attended the Presbyterian mission school, kept detailed reading notes in her Bible, as her sponsor had taught her. She took the same kind of marginal notes in her copy of *Love, Medicine, and Miracles*, which, as a cancer patient, she was avidly reading. Irma adapted the literacy practices she learned with her sponsor and applied them in ways that the sponsor might not condone—finding "lessons for living" in a secular text by a Jewish physician who argues that miracles can have human, rather than divine, sources.

The stigmatization of literacy in Haines Gap forced informants to reexamine and negotiate relationships with sponsors, with others in the community, and within their families, as the examples of Margaret, Lucinda, and Marlon demonstrate. It also led some to explore their relationships with themselves, their lives, and the world around them with literacy practices as a tool for this exploration. The infusion into the community of different ways of valuing and practicing literacy initially precipitated struggles and negotiations among local residents and external literacy sponsors. But these struggles and negotiations also rippled out into the community itself, as literacy came to be appreciated as a means of managing one's identities and identifications through opportunities to assimilate, appropriate, or reject different literate practices. In all cases, literacy was both the issue that precipitated these negotiations and a practice through which relationships could be managed.

The situation in Haines Gap, with the stigmatizing power of literacy ever-present in the form of multiple literacy sponsors, taught informants that literacy was a tool to establish hierarchies of class. A common message of all the sponsors was that literacy practices could help a person improve his or her class status. Eradicating telltale "Appalachianisms" from one's speech and writing and a steady diet of the right kind of reading were advertised as holding the key to increasing one's economic status (by the public school, college, and government sponsors) or spiritual/moral status (by the mission school sponsor). It should not be surprising, then, that reading and writing became a means for some informants to manage their class status within Haines Gap, renegotiating their relationships with the various groups that make up the Haines Gap hierarchy.

One should not assume that rural communities, because of their small size, are any less prone to class divisions than urban centers. In Haines Gap, boundary lines are drawn according to family history. My interviews often began, before I turned on the tape recorder, with a sorting-out of the ways in which I might be distantly related to my informant. There are economic distinctions as well, marked primarily between those who own their homes and those who rent. There are class distinctions between those who have been able to leave Haines Gap, especially those who leave to work or pursue schooling, and those who have stayed. Geography also marks status; those who live within the town limits refer to those who live outside those limits as "country people," a term usually used disparagingly. Within the town, those who live "up," on the three primary hills, have higher status than those who live "down," in the areas prone to floods.

Religion marks another hierarchy. While members of each religion might believe their religious group laid claim to the best or most prestigious form of religious belief, each denomination is also associated with a particular group on the socioeconomic ladder. The wealthy Estes family, who owned much of the rich farmland along the river in Haines Gap, was Catholic and established a small Catholic church in the town. Catholicism became associated in some part with their prestige. Presbyterianism arrived with the northern missionaries who founded the mission school; it, too, carried some cultural cachet as being the religion of wealthier and more cultured groups. Methodists, Baptists (Southern and Freewill), and Evangelical/Holiness groups made up the other status rungs on the religious class ladder.

These distinctions marked multiple groups in Haines Gap with which one could claim, or reject, membership. Literacy became a primary tool for many informants in doing exactly this. Consider Ida, the child of sharecroppers who tenant-farmed the land of the Estes family and worked as caretakers for their property. Exposed as a child to the Catholicism of the Estes family, Ida had herself become Catholic and is an avid reader of books with Catholic themes and content. When she checked out a book from the public library by Andrew Greeley, knowing only that he was a Catholic priest, she was shocked by its salacious content. She returned the book immediately, and since the library's check-out records were public, she insisted that the librarian white-out her name on the check-out register. Ida sees public awareness of her reading preferences as a way to signal her religious and moral stature in the community.

As self-appointed town historian, Ida also uses writing to renegotiate her status within Haines Gap. She has published three books on local clubs and on wealthy local families. Through writing, Ida aligns herself with groups—clubwomen (and men) and the local elite—to which her birth as a sharecropper's child might not entitle her. Since the representatives of these groups are long gone, Ida uses writing to inscribe herself into their company. While interviewing the last surviving member of the prestigious Cuthbertson family for one of her books, Ida became such close friends with the woman that she was left some family heirlooms in the woman's will.[16]

Deana also uses literacy to alter her relationships with various groups within the town. She first came to Haines Gap from "the country," putting her at a class disadvantage. Deana pursued literacy vigorously, eventually getting a master's degree. As a local politician and occasional editorialist, Deana turned the critical literacy she had learned in graduate school against the injustices of the town:

There has been a great deal of emphasis in the past fifty years on local women and men going away to school for four years, and coming back. And I feel that this is one thing that's responsible for the low ebb of learning now. . . . We need teachers from outside . . . to challenge. . . . Most people who come in, value honesty. And truth. . . . But . . . it's not the same brand of honesty and truth that we have. This area probably got a good dose of Baptist religion at some time. And that's a little different brand of honesty and truth. . . . What would be oppression to one family, keeping a family poor, because they work for you and not giving them very much advantage, still might be honesty to you, and then a person coming from another area would see that they needed a bathroom, or they needed more clothes, or they needed more books—they needed a greater reward for their labor. And—still, yet the local person would say that he was being fair, if the family did not have a bathroom, if they had no books, [as long as] they were warm and had clothing.

Q: So it's good to have people come in from the outside to sort of—

A: Challenge. . . . I think that we really needed our values—our—livelihoods, our outlook challenged. Because we were pretty narrow. (Donehower, "Literary Choices" 357–58)

Here Deana marks her relationship to various powerful entities in the town—wealthy landowners, religious groups, local educators. She left Haines Gap to affiliate with a sponsor that trained her in a particular brand of critical literacy. She then used this literacy to transform herself from an anonymous "country child" to a central figure in the political life of the town. In her comment about the "Baptist religion," Deana also marks her stance within her family. Deana's mother, Irma, mentioned earlier, is a devout evangelical Christian. Deana's rejection of this type of Christianity, which she articulates with the literacy skills learned from her sponsor, lets her renegotiate her relationship with family members. In addition, by using a new form of literacy to turn a critical eye on her own community, Deana brings the kind of fresh perspective that can help ensure the sustainability of the town. As the economic model of life in Haines Gap changed from a paternalistic system of tenant farming to a marked decrease in agriculture's importance in the local economy, Deana could see that new skills and new literacies—"more books"—would be crucial in sustaining local life on both economic and cultural levels.

Deana is not the only informant who used literacy practices acquired from an outside sponsor to purposely rupture her relationship with various groups within her home community and to advocate for local change. Eliza sought out a sponsor who would offer views different from the ones with which she had been raised. As a child, Eliza bought into the stereotypes of Appalachian illiteracy. When asked how literate the people around her were at that time, she replied simply, "They weren't"—even though her mother is an avid reader and writer. Eliza spent much of her childhood working her way through the books in the mission school library. (Although not admitted to the school, she soon discovered they had a much better library than the public school.) As soon as she was working and could afford it, Eliza put herself through a kind of "great books" reading program, purchasing classic sets of works of American literature and ancient philosophy. She explained that she engaged in all this reading to construct for herself a "philosophy of life," which would then give her a basis for understanding others' philosophies of life. Reading, for Eliza, was preparation to build relationships with others who had different ideas and values from the people of Haines Gap. Ultimately, Eliza brought the new perspectives she had gained from a lifetime of literacy practices outside the community back to advocate for improvements in Haines Gap in her role as a town alderman.

For a few informants in this study, literacy also offered a way to manage one's relationship with oneself, the local context of daily life, and the larger context of the world outside Haines Gap. Pearl, an avid reader, poet, and self-taught artist, typically had no audience for her literate practices. She did not editorialize in the local paper as Deana did. She did not display her reading publicly or write for publication as Ida did. She did not use reading to fuel her conversations with others as Eliza did. Her writing was kept private, without anyone to see and respond to it. She maintained no long-lasting relationships with any sponsor and lived her life entirely within Haines Gap. But Pearl's literacy still let her manage an important set of relationships in her life.

Pearl's literate activities began primarily as a coping mechanism. She raised six children during the Great Depression while her husband was away working on the railroad. She described her intensive reading as a counterweight to the immediate pressures of her everyday life: "Something to—get my mind interested in, y'know. 'Cause that was a hard life then. You know." Acquiring reading materials, at this point in Pearl's life, required a ten-mile walk over a mountain to the home of a neighbor who maintained a small lending library, so the relief offered by reading must have been worth it. Later in her life, painting and poetry provided a way to help Pearl appreciate the subtleties of her daily life. As she explained, writing and painting familiar scenes "brought out some meaning" in her surroundings. These activities offered Pearl a means to deepen and enrich her relationship with the physical setting in which she lived out a very long and sometimes arduous life.

Literacy also gave Pearl a relationship with the world beyond her local setting. She said reading gave her "knowledge. I like to know things, y'know, and understand . . . the whole world." Reading and writing offer Pearl access to ideas beyond those she encounters every day in Haines Gap. Together, reading, writing, and painting help Pearl appreciate her local context more and step outside it when she needs to.

In addition, writing, in particular, helps Pearl nurture her relationship with herself. Pearl explained her poetry and songwriting by saying that she "had a romantic mind." It was her nature, her essence, as far as Pearl was concerned, to do these things. Similarly, Pearl's daughter Eliza describes her own intensive reading by saying that "it's just my nature." One might presume that Eliza's strong pursuit of literacy comes at least in part from following the model offered by her mother. Yet she prefers to see it as something that comes out of her alone. It is a way to value herself, and the practice of certain kinds of literate behavior help Eliza and Pearl reaffirm who they are to an audience consisting only of themselves.

Both Eliza and Pearl, in very different ways, appropriate types of literacy they acquired from sponsors and use them to enrich and develop local life in Haines Gap on both private and public scales. Their acts of appropriation, like Deana's and Irma's, are particularly important in looking at rural literacies through a lens of sustainability. Whatever the goals of their sponsors—to modernize, preserve, or abandon local literacy practices—these appropriative acts put literacy to uses that both fit the local context and serve to reconfigure the local context, helping the society to adapt and grow instead of remaining static or completely losing its sense of local identity. Chapter 4 takes up in more detail the ways in which the literacy work of rural women can have such effects on their communities. Whatever the sponsors' intentions, the multiplicity of ways of doing and valuing literacy that they brought to Haines Gap rippled out through the community in ways that might not have been intended but which were adapted by the local people to best serve individual and communal needs. By explicitly introducing a multiplicity of ways of doing and valuing literacy into Haines Gap, sponsors provided new resources for restructuring the social fabric of the town and the townspeople's relationships to what they describe as the "outside" world.

## Reconfiguring the Relationships of Rural Literacies

I do not wish to suggest that the experiences and choices of these ten residents of Haines Gap offer a model for understanding literacy development in all rural areas. However, I think it is useful to consider how these individuals took up literacy as a resource to help them negotiate the experience of being stigmatized as illiterate and manage their relationships with literacy sponsors and other distinct groups both within and outside their community. Part of the stereotype of rural illiteracy suggests that rural people's literate abilities (or perceived inabilities) are a natural, unavoidable result of their economic and cultural context. It portrays people as either passive illiterates or, in the case of Moffett's analysis, active resisters. But the Haines Gap data show that rural people can and do make conscious, informed choices among different alternatives for practicing and valuing reading and writing, acknowledging literacy's important functions in navigating the complex economic and social realities of rural life.

The alternative rural literacy Jacqueline Edmondson offers in *Prairie Town* both presumes and requires agency on the part of rural people to make choices and adapt practices to ensure the sustenance of their communities. In Haines Gap, we see individuals doing this to ensure their own sustenance—in Edmondson's terms, they are practicing an alternative agrarian literacy. For Margaret, Lucinda, Deana, and Eliza, the kinds of literacy they sought out and learned from sponsors enabled them to pursue careers—as a government employee, elementary teacher, principal and political activist, and secondary teacher and counselor—that would not have been accessible to them had they not chosen to align themselves, for some portion of time, with particular sponsors that were available to them. Their experiences with literacy stigmatization did not shut down their desires to pursue literacy, though it may have led them to reject particular literacy sponsors. Instead, they became very much aware of a variety of practices and purposes for literacy and of the ways literacy might enrich their own lives.

The Haines Gap interviews strongly suggest that literacy work is crucial in shaping, maintaining, and dissolving the relationships that make up the social networks both inside rural communities and with the outside world. The ways of practicing and valuing reading and writing that Marlon, Deana, Irma, Ida, Eliza, and Pearl learned from these sponsors served as tools to renew, strengthen, or weaken their relations with various social groups. The role of reading and writing to construct, maintain, and alter social networks is particularly important in rural communities. Popular media accounts bemoan the failing economic infrastructure of rural places, but social networks are equally important to small towns' survival, as chapter 4 demonstrates.

Literacy has much potential to manage relationships among groups and to continually reconfigure social networks. In the case of rural literacies, these relationships are suffused with a long history of stereotyping and of the problematic purposes of modernizing, preserving, or abandoning rural communities. Is it possible to see rural literacies outside the lenses of modernization, preservation, and abandonment? What would a vision of rural literacies grounded in a model of sustainability look like? How would a literacy sponsor that operated from such a model behave, and what would be the repercussions of such behavior? As we described in chapter 1, Edmondson's call for a "public pedagogy" provides a possible answer. We noted that a public pedagogy would interrogate constructions of rural people and life, investigating, in Edmondson's words, "the extent to which characterizations of the rural match (or not) observations of demographic, social, and economic conditions" (114). In other words, literacy sponsors in rural areas have an obligation to do research, to determine the specifics of local literacies situated in particular contexts, and to assume that past characterizations may be riddled with inaccuracies, given the strong weight of public memories about rural literacies that rely heavily on the *Deliverance*/Davy Crockett stereotypes.

The Haines Gap data suggest that sponsors of rural literacies must also acknowledge the struggles over identities and identifications with which that sponsorship is necessarily fraught and recognize that literacy itself can function as a tool to negotiate these struggles.[17] The presence of multiple literacy sponsors in Haines Gap—each offering a different "brand" of literacy and setting off consequent ripples of new literacies throughout the community—created an active awareness in these informants that a multiplicity of ways of doing and valuing literacy existed. The experience of stigmatization provided a strong impetus for informants to choose among these types of literacy and adapt them to their own needs, altering them in ways their sponsors might not have intended or foreseen.

The classic study of the effects of stigmatization is Goffman's *Stigma: Notes on the Management of Spoiled Identity.* He notes that stereotyping and stigmatizing can be self-fulfilling mechanisms. Goffman explains that "the stigmatized [has] the sense of not knowing what the others present are 'really' thinking about him" (14). As a result, stigmatized people may act toward the nonstigmatized, a group Goffman calls "normals," in such a way as to reinforce the stigma. Goffman gives an example from a study of illiterates: "When illiterates interact among themselves . . . not only do they change from unexpressive and confused individuals, as they frequently appear in larger society, to expressive and understanding persons within their own group, but moreover they express themselves in institutional terms. Among themselves they have a universe of response" (Freeman and Kasenbaum, qtd. in Goffman 20). In other words, internalizing stigmas and stereotypes can lead to responses that reinforce the stereotypes. This can happen unconsciously, as Goffman describes, but it occurs consciously as well as a way to play with the credulity of normals. During a brief stint as hostess at Mom and Pop's Country Store and Restaurant, an Appalachian tourist trap, while on break from college classes, I found myself lapsing into dialect and malapropisms worthy of Jethro Bodine. I loved putting one over on the tourists, exploiting their willingness to see me as a stereotype in exchange for tips to defray my college loans. But such responses only serve to strengthen the stigmatizeds' and the normals' misunderstanding of one another.

How can sponsors and potential sponsees step outside this self-perpetuating cycle of mistrust and misunderstanding? Paul Nachtigal's anthology *Rural Education: In Search of a Better Way* describes the ideal relationship between rural communities and outside education "professionals":

> The close-knit, personal nature of small rural communities results in school and community operating as a single integrated social structure. Useful rural school improvement strategies must, therefore, address needs that are recognized by both the local school and the community and must operate in a style congruent with the local setting. Although outside ideas and resources may contribute greatly to successful plans to improve rural schools, a high level of local involvement is essential in determining the specifics of those plans. (iii)

Examining the data from Haines Gap, we can see the possibilities for a similar ideal relationship between professional, "outsider" literacy sponsors and individual rural communities. The individuals in Haines Gap who are most proficient in their literacy and who have best adapted literacy practices to serve the needs of their lives are those who appropriated various parts of outsiders' literacy practices and values and reworked them through local literacy practices and values. Forcing total assimilation on a sponsee, in this scenario, is an unreasonable and unproductive goal, as we saw in Moffett's exchange with Reverend Graley. It forces an identification that the sponsee is likely to find discomfiting, unless, like Eliza, she is eager to distance herself from her home community. Facilitating appropriative relationships between literacy sponsors and sponsees, then, helps to moderate the tensions of the struggles for identities and identifications inherent in rural literacy work and is another key element in a relationship grounded in a model of sustainability.

Such a model also opens up the possibility of adapting and adopting new practices to enrich and sustain local life—not to alter it completely, or fossilize it into the past, or abandon it, but to help it continue to grow. For people who appropriated sponsors' literacy practices, sponsors' types of literacy were understood as options from which to choose, not as mandates. Ways of practicing and valuing literacy that were offered as models to be adapted to the local context, instead of as rigid prescriptions, were more likely to be well-received. In *Prairie Town*, Edmondson identifies three kinds of "rural literacies" present in the Minnesota town that she studied. One of these, she argues, has as its goal "to offer more choices, and to develop alternatives aligned with rural sensibilities" (15). In Haines Gap, we can see the result of the availability of many different options for ways to practice and value literacy and to adapt or align those with local needs and practices.

Another solution to the problematic relationship between rural communities and literacy sponsors was offered by Pearl, who gave one of the few positive descriptions of "outsider" teachers who had taught her in the early 1900s in the one-room schoolhouse in Sevenmile, a tiny community outside Haines Gap. These teachers, as Pearl perceived it, saw their role as participants in a cultural exchange rather than as outside experts there to "fix" local practices. She explains that "we loved teachers that come from out of state . . . to teach" because "we learned from them and they learned from us":

Q: What do you think they learned from you?
A: Well, they learned our ways, you know. . . . Lots of things. . . . Like, my mother did crafts like, you know, that they were interested in, like spinning wool . . . and all kinds of making yarn and knitting and things like that. . . . Miss ———— . . . was young, and . . . it was real interesting to us to see the things that she could do. . . . She'd give us . . . little parties and things like that . . . which we'd never had anything like that.

The relationship Pearl depicts in this exchange has at its center a notion of mutual identification. Chapter 3 details the importance of a shift from sympathetic identification—such as that exhibited by the Presbyterian missionaries—to mutual identification, as is exemplified by Pearl's teacher here. Mutual identification is a key aspect of a relationship grounded in sustainability. Sustainability, as we described in chapter 1, requires that rural, urban, and suburban residents understand the ways their lives are and might be interlinked. The outsider teacher in this description understood that she and the community might benefit mutually from one another. While she had positive practices to offer the residents of Sevenmile, they, too, could introduce her to practices that could enrich her own life. This teacher did not occupy the "missionary position" of ministering to her Appalachian students because she felt sorry for their deprivations, at least as Pearl describes it. Instead, she sought to offer social rituals that she found enriching—parties, in this case, which could be easily adapted into local existing social frameworks—and to learn whatever new practices she could beneficially incorporate into her own life. A relationship between a literacy sponsor and a rural community that is grounded in sustainability would operate much like this example, as a genuine cultural exchange that recognizes the possibility of mutual beneficence among all parties.

### Implications for Research and Teaching

In this chapter, I have tried to offer an example of rural literacy research that explicitly avoids the preservationist, modernizing, and abandonment lenses in favor of a model of sustainability. I have also worked to foreground the struggles for identities and identifications that are at the heart of relationships between rural communities and academic literacy sponsors such as myself. For literacy researchers seeking to better understand the choices individuals make about literacy and how those choices affect and are affected by social relationships, rural communities offer a microcosm of the many social forces that constrain and encourage literacy choices. Despite their small size, rural towns have their own complex hierarchies of class, ethnicity, and status and are culturally and economically linked to the larger class, ethnic, and social networks of American life.

There are other literacy researchers who study rural areas with an interpretive lens grounded in a metaphor of sustainability.[18] In her book *Literacy in American Lives*, Brandt begins with the premise that "individual literacy exists only as part of larger material systems, systems that on the one hand enable acts of reading or writing and on the other hand confer their value" (1). Brandt's focus on the systemic economic, political, and social forces that shape individuals' literacy development could be applied as well to communities, thereby enacting Edmondson's vision of a public pedagogy that examines how well "characterizations of the rural match (or not) observations of demographic, social, and economic conditions."

Robert Brooke's edited collection, *Rural Voices: Place-Conscious Education and the Teaching of Writing*, demonstrates one way that researchers can practice rural literacies and pedagogies in productive and sustainable ways. The contributors to the book, teachers in the Nebraska Writing Project, write as rural people who are also researchers, writers, and teachers. They write not to prescribe but to model ideas and practices that can be explored in other rural contexts. The collection acknowledges that rural places are not homogeneous and that the techniques that might work in one location could fail in another. It demonstrates ways to think about one's local context in designing literacy curricula, in much the same way that Marlon advocates having Haines Gap educators consider local context through studying a text such as *The Thread That Runs So True*.

For compositionists working with rural students in the college

classroom, the lessons of Haines Gap are these: Perpetuating stigmatization of rural literacies is a poor means of recruitment to new forms
of literacy. Regardless of one's demeanor or relationship with students,
the history of rural literacy stigmatization means that the type of
academic literacy offered in university classrooms may be perceived
by some rural students as requiring rejection of their home communities. This dynamic applies not only to rural students, of course, but
to any student from a background whose relationship with "official"
or academic literacies is fraught with a history of stigmatization. In
this scenario, encouraging appropriation, rather than assimilation, of
academic literacies is a productive way to deal with the struggles of
identities and identifications that the subject of literacy invokes.

To encourage appropriation, we must help rural students value
the knowledge they have to contribute to the university community.
At the University of North Dakota, my students from farming backgrounds have relished the opportunity to apply the critical tools of
academic literacy to analyze the economic situation of family farmers. However, tellingly, I have had to coax many of these students to
believe that their own knowledge of the subject, gained from years
of working on their families' farms, was legitimate material to write
about in the university environment and that this deep knowledge
enhanced their ability to practice the forms of analysis I was trying
to teach them. For some, their knowledge of farming and the food
industry didn't even seem like specialized knowledge. Contrast this
with Eileen's urban and suburban students at Syracuse University
who, in her words, were "almost gleeful in their ignorance of farm
life" but discovered just how much their ignorance could affect their
lives. For both groups, it seems, agricultural knowledge didn't seem
to particularly "count" as knowledge in a school setting at all until
experiences in their courses proved otherwise. As Eileen describes
in chapter 5, we can set up our courses to encourage among students
the kinds of mutual identification and exchange of knowledge so
prized by Pearl in her interactions with her northern teacher. At the
same time, we teachers must find ways to genuinely participate in
such exchanges, considering the ways our students' literacies might
enlarge our own.

Rural students' intellectual insecurities can extend beyond the specialized knowledge they bring to college. Some students in my classes have mistrusted even the official "school knowledge" they gained from rural schools. A not-uncommon response to my question "What most concerns you about taking this class?" has been this: "I am worried that my country teachers didn't teach me right." As rural literacy is suspect, so are rural schools, and some students have internalized and believe in this stereotype, however positive their experiences in rural schools may have been.

There is much that can be done in the first-year composition classroom to address the legacies of stereotypes about rural literacies that negatively affect our relationship with students and their relationships with the university. These are described in detail in chapter 5. The goal is to bring the struggles for identities and identifications among rural and other constituencies out into the open by practicing the basics of argument analysis, identifying the claims, grounds, and warrants inherent in representations of rural literacies. Chapter 3 demonstrates how careful rhetorical analysis can expose the barriers to mutual identification among rural, urban, and suburban people.

The field of composition has traditionally demonstrated deep concern for ways to best serve students from groups who feel a sense of cultural displacement in university environments. Given the long history of stereotyping rural literacies, we must acknowledge that, especially in the literacy classroom, rural students are one of these constituencies. By acknowledging how loaded the topic of literacy may be for these students, by exploring ways to validate students' preexisting knowledge and literate practices, and by encouraging appropriative relationships with the types of literacy we offer, we can best serves as sponsors of these students' literacy.

# 3 / The Rhetorics of the Farm Crisis
## Toward Alternative Agrarian Literacies in a Globalized World

*Eileen E. Schell*

Food is our most basic need, the very stuff of life.

—Vandana Shiva, *Stolen Harvest:*
*The Hijacking of the Global Food Supply*

If you eat, you have a stake in agriculture.

—FarmAid.org

In his often-quoted *Notes on the State of Virginia*, Thomas Jefferson portrayed the yeoman farmer as the embodiment of American character, arguing that the agrarian ideal should serve as the backbone of American society: "Those who labour in the earth are the chosen people of God, if ever he had a chosen people, whose breasts he has made his peculiar deposit for substantial and genuine virtue. It is the focus in which he keeps alive that sacred fire, which otherwise might escape from the face of the earth" (290). As argued here and in chapter 4, Jefferson's yeoman farmer continues to be a powerful image that shapes many Americans' views about farmers and rural people even as the number of small family farms and farmers[1] has declined precipitously in the latter part of the twentieth century—a situation that many have come to call the "farm crisis" (see Davidson).[2] The term "farm crisis" refers to the fact that U.S. small farms, many of which have been in "families for generations[,] are going under, and rural communities are facing economic devastation" ("Fair Prices"). Although the causes are complex, three main factors are responsible for the farm crisis:

- "Chronically low prices that have plagued all crops in all regions around the country"

- "The breathtaking consolidation of agribusiness and the retail food industry," which "has taken away the bargaining power of farmers to get a fair price"
- "International trade policies," which "continue to benefit global agribusiness companies at the expense of family farms, local businesses and rural communities" ("Fair Prices")

In spite of these shifts in agricultural production, a romanticized image of the small family farm still holds iconic sway in American life. Although family farms and farmers continue to decline in large numbers, for instance, many urban and suburban Americans still believe that most rural people make their living from family farms. In actuality, farmers make up only 2 percent of the rural population, addressed in the 2001 W. K. Kellogg Foundation study ("Perceptions"), and nationally, family farms account for only 565,000 of the 2 million farms in existence and 44 percent of all farmland ("Family Farmers").

In general, the situation of agricultural production and agricultural life is often shrouded in mystery or misinformation—one might even say "myth-information." The majority of popular press accounts of the demise of the family farm follows two predictable lines of argumentation: the pathos-driven rhetoric of tragedy and the logos-driven rhetoric of smart diversification. The tragedy rhetoric participates in what Jacqueline Edmondson calls "traditional rural literacy," a literacy that "reads rural life through nostalgia for the past and efforts to return rural communities to the way they once were" (15). In rural communities, traditional rural literacy can lead, on the one hand, to protection and preservation of traditions and, on the other hand, to the "language of despair" as it becomes "more difficult, if not impossible, to retain traditions and conditions of the past" in a globalized world (15). In extreme cases, within rural communities, traditional rural literacy can lead groups to try to keep others out and to maintain homogeneity and isolationism, a rhetoric practiced by hate groups like the Aryan Nation, which has deliberately located its base of operations in rural Idaho and now in rural Pennsylvania (15).[3] Traditional rural literacy is also appealing to those living in metropolitan areas as it allows urban people to see rural areas as repositories of history and "traditional values" and as bucolic landscapes full of quaint small towns and picturesque family farms where people live "simpler lives." When reporters, novelists, and documentarians interpret the farm crisis through the lens of traditional rural literacy, urban readers and viewers often end up feeling "sorry" for family farmers and mourning their loss and obsoleteness rather than considering how the farm crisis is affecting their own lives as consumers of food.

The focus on the quaintness and traditions of rural culture aligns traditional rural literacy with Henry Shapiro's discussion of preservation, as addressed in chapter 2. As Kim notes in her discussion of Shapiro, the culture of Appalachian people—their language practices, crafts, and folkways—were thought to be worthy of preservation efforts as they might shed light on the "uniqueness" of the people and the region and illuminate the pioneer spirit of American character. Thus, the logic of preservation offers a way to maintain an idealized vision of what was essential and vital about a people. In a parallel track, tragedy rhetorics about the farm crisis carry that same preservationist impulse in the form of an idealized and often nostalgic vision of the family farm. Indeed, preservationist rhetoric can be found in the proliferation of "hobby farms" and museums of the agricultural past where old farm equipment, barns, and animal husbandry practices are documented. The danger with preservationist models, as Kim points out, is that they may "seek to make of rural places a monolithic symbol of a collective American heritage for those who live in urban and suburban areas, rather than vital and diverse communities that can adapt to economic and demographic shifts" (see chapter 2). Unless there is a shift in agricultural policy toward giving family farms a fighting chance in the global economy, the family farm will fast become an interesting, albeit dusty, museum display.

In contrast, the rhetoric of smart diversification emphasizes how farmers can survive by "thinking outside the box" through strategies such as niche farming, farm tourism, and technological methods like precision farming—using satellite technologies and global positioning systems to increase crop yields. The rhetoric of smart diversification has two components: one focused on individual adaptability and innovation and the other on a collective embrace of neoliberalism. On the one hand, narratives driven by smart diversification rhetoric often emphasize individualized narratives of progress, grit, and success in spite of the odds. Farmers engaged in organic farming and those who are opening their own distribution sites are examples of a smart diversification rhetoric that emphasizes individual farmers' responsiveness to changing their practices and preserving the legacy of the family farm. This component of the smart diversification narrative carries with it the possibility of transformation as it grants individual farmers the agency to adapt to the larger economic forces—federal farm policies, corporate consolidation, and international trade agreements—that are determining their fates. On the other hand, smart diversification rhetoric emphasizes technological innovation within the structure of industrialized agriculture, using new technologies like precision farming to increase crop yields or trying new inputs, chemicals or fertilizers, or genetically modified seeds to increase crop yields. This second component of smart diversification rhetoric participates in what Edmondson calls a discourse of neoliberalism that "reads rural life through a language that constitutes mass production, efficiency, and more recently, neoliberal principles. This discourse values agribusiness, market-based logic, and fast capitalism" (15); it emphasizes the realization of the principles of the market economy—maximizing profits and efficiency, exploiting resources and labor, and expanding operations, what some farmers have called the "get bigger or get out" principle.[4] This second component of the rhetoric of smart diversification has much in common with chapter 2's discussion of modernization as a solution for the problems of rural areas. Modernization, in a parallel track to smart diversification, is an attempt to bring farmers in line with technological and economic models that emphasize expansion and profit in contrast to the traditional agrarian values of land stewardship and community participation. In fact, the modernization logic of smart diversification often leads to abandonment, the third solution discussed in chapter 2, where whole communities and regions that were once agriculturally rich empty out as few farmers can continue with their farms under the reign of neoliberalism.

While the tragedy and smart diversification rhetorics diverge in their appeals and explanatory narratives, neither rhetoric truly enables the reader or the viewer to understand how we arrived at the demise of the family farm through international trade policies, federal agricultural policies, and the globalization of capital. Nor do these stories tell of the environmental devastation that corporate-run agriculture often brings to particular regions. Many of the narratives of the farm crisis fail to create a rhetorical situation in which the reader or viewer can understand the farm crisis's impact on our lives, on the food we eat, and on the future of agricultural lands and rural communities in the United States and across the globe. In other words, the dominant narratives of the farm crisis foster an "agricultural illiteracy" among the general public whereby the conditions under which our nation's food is grown, harvested, distributed, and marketed are made opaque and inaccessible.[5]

As a corrective to the rhetorics of tragedy and smart diversification, this chapter argues for an alternative agrarian rhetoric and literacy that is grounded in the discourses of rural sustainability. According to Edmondson, an alternative agrarian literacy "reads rural life with a language that attempts to slow the effects of neoliberalism, to offer more choice, and to develop alternatives aligned with rural sensibilities" (15). This alternative agrarian rhetoric and literacy allows rural people to imagine their options and alternatives, whether such options involve the revitalization of family farms or grassroots community organizing "to protect rural people, rural work, and rural lands" (16). The common denominator here is that these alternatives are derived by rural people "attempt[ing] to bridge agency and structure in ways they choose" (16). This alternative agrarian literacy is one not confined to rural areas solely, and, as I argue here, urban and suburban residents can also take part by making critical consumer choices and supporting public policies and organizations that foster sustainable rural development.

Throughout this chapter, I situate my analysis of the rhetorics of the farm crisis in the tradition of critical literacy studies (Edmondson, Freire, Shor) and rhetorical scholarship on social protest and advocacy rhetorics (Morris and Browne). We have already discussed literacy in this book, in Deborah Brandt's words, as a resource—"economic, political, intellectual, spiritual—which like wealth or education, or trade skill or social connections, is pursued for the opportunities and protections that it potentially grants its seekers" (*Literacy* 5). Critical literacy, contends Ira Shor, "challenges the status quo in an effort to discover alternative paths for self and social development" ("What Is Critical Literacy?"). Critical literacy allows us to analyze and rethink' the practices of everyday life and encourages dissenting perspectives on public issues that allow people to connect "the political and the personal, the public and the private, the global and the local, the economic and the pedagogical for rethinking our lives and for promoting justice in place of inequity." Critical literacy, then, "can be thought of as a social practice in itself and as a tool for the study of other social practices." It is a particularly important mode of analysis and action in a world where nations and people are linked globally, on a daily basis, in ways previously unimaginable.

Following the lead of critical literacy scholars, I see critical literacy as a way to help our students and communities move toward creating knowledgeable, literate citizens who are prepared with the "knowledge and skills for social and environmental justice" (Andrzejewski and Alessio). In a consumer-oriented, largely urban society, critical literacy on issues of food production is a particularly important site of intervention, as the way food is produced, marketed, and sold affects everyone on a daily basis and has a daily environmental impact on the planet. Thus, critical literacy approaches and advocacy rhetorics provide rhetorical strategies and tactics that can be used to work against the farm crisis and allow for different ways of conceptualizing and taking literate action to sustain rural areas.

Critical rhetorical studies is also a significant tradition to bring to bear on analyzing the issue of the farm crisis. A critical rhetorical approach allows us to study the rhetorics of emerging activist organizations and advocacy groups that are working to address inequities in agricultural policy and practice and address questions of sustainability and rural development. Groups working under the umbrella of what Vandana Shiva calls "food democracy" are engaged in making farming an accessible and sustainable process, and their advocacy efforts provide alternatives to the tragedy and smart diversification rhetorics that currently guide much of our public discussion of the farm crisis.

Seeing the U.S. farm crisis through the lens of critical literacy studies and critical rhetorical studies helps us avoid the rhetorics of lack and lag that are so commonly utilized to describe rural life. I also highlight and analyze the rhetorical work of one farm advocacy organization—the U.S.-based organization Farm Aid, a 501(c)(3) nonprofit—that offers an alternative agrarian rhetoric and literacy that works in the service of a sustainable future for small family farms.

It is my goal here, in line with Derek Owens's call for addressing sustainability in English and writing curricula, to create awareness of and critically literate action on the "farm crisis" through examining it as a problem of public policy (local, national, and international), public awareness, and consumption practices. It is also my goal to analyze the rhetorical strategies and literate action that organizations, groups, and individuals can take for redressing the "farm crisis" through public policy advocacy work and critical consumer choices. I also argue the case for an alternative agrarian literacy from my own position as an academic who is a member of a third-generation farm family who recently quit farming due to many of the trends and patterns highlighted in this chapter. To better contextualize the economic, political, and social circumstances faced by family farmers and their communities, I provide readers with a brief overview of the farm crisis.

### What Is the Farm Crisis?

Over the past thirty years, the economic base that once was the heart of rural America—family farms and ranches—has been radically transformed. Consider the following statistical information:

- According to the *Occupational Outlook Quarterly,* Winter 1999/2000, "Of all the occupations in America, farming is facing the greatest decline" (qtd. in "Farm Facts").
- Of America's 60 million rural residents, less than 12 percent are employed in facets of agriculture, including farming, processing, and marketing jobs (W. K. Kellogg Foundation, "Perceptions" 2001).

- According to the USDA Economic Research Service, farm profits have dropped from forty-one cents in 1950 to twenty cents on the dollar at the end of the 1990s (qtd. in "Farm Facts"). Meanwhile, production costs—the price for equipment, feed, fertilizer, labor, fuel, and other necessities—have increased; thus, many small farmers are unable to break even or make a slight profit.

- Family farmers who are making ends meet are usually doing so because they or family members have jobs off the farm: "88% of the average farm operator's household income comes from off-the-farm sources" (USDA Economic Research Service, Agricultural Outlook, May 2000, Table 31, qtd. in "Farm Facts").

These statistics are due to changes in the structure of agriculture—namely, corporate consolidation—brought on by post–World War II farm policies in the United States and by international trade agreements that favor multinational agribusiness corporations. Consolidation has had a major impact on U.S. agricultural production as large farms produce a sizable portion of the food we eat. For instance, "2% of farms produce 50% of agricultural product sales" (1997 Census of Agriculture, USDA National Agricultural Statistics Service, qtd. in "Farm Facts"). The reason for this trend is clear. American farm policy, according to the 1998 USDA report "A Time to Act," is structurally biased "toward greater concentration of assets and wealth in fewer and larger farms and fewer and larger agribusiness firms" (2). Federal farm programs favor large farms with tax policies that "give large farms greater incentives for capital purchases to expand their operations" (2). These same farms also "receive exemptions from federal labor laws that allow them the advantage of low-wage labor costs" (2). Like the manufacturing sector, the agriculture sector has seen a turn in public policy that favors corporations instead of small businesses as "programs originally designed to protect the small and medium-sized farmer have instead become little more than mechanisms to funnel taxpayers' money into the pockets of the largest growers" (Davidson 29). For example, "30% of subsidies go to the largest 1% of producers (the so called 'superfarms' with annual sales of over half a million dollars), while 80% of the nation's farms with sales under $100,000 a year receive less than one-third of the government payments" (29).[6] One recent example of the favoring of large farms in U.S. agricultural legislation is the "Freedom to Farm" bill signed in 1996 by President Clinton. Freedom to Farm was touted as a way to take farmers off of government controls or "agriwelfare," as some Republicans called it. Interestingly, Freedom to Farm was passed the same year that the Aid to Families with Dependent Children (AFDC) program was repealed as part of welfare reform, thus challenging two key components of New Deal–era reforms. Freedom to Farm as a piece of legislation "was designed to expose farmers to the so-called free market" and was sold as a bill that would reduce "the level of government interference, which in theory would allow farmers to thrive on the open market, particularly in what was seen as the growing export market" (Lilliston and Ritchie 2). Before Freedom to Farm, which many farmers and farm advocates have angrily deemed the "Freedom to Fail" bill, "price floors" were ensured for commodities such as corn, soybeans, and wheat so that the prices the farmers received would not fall below their production costs. Production controls were also in place that allowed for land to be kept out of production or grain reserves to be maintained until prices were raised. The Freedom to Farm bill was to eliminate this system, in place since the New Deal (1). Farmers were guaranteed "fixed but declining payments to end in 2002" and given the option to plant crops as they saw fit (1).[7] The Freedom to Farm bill, however, benefits large multinational agricultural corporations, not small or mid-sized family farmers, as it encourages overproduction and lowers the price the individual farmer receives from the buyer. Through enabling legislation such as Freedom to Farm and through vertical integration, large multinational agribusiness corporations have an even greater opportunity to dominate the market at the expense of small farmers. As Sheila Ehrich, a Minnesota farmer, says, "Cargill is buying corn damn cheap—we're back to overproducing" (qtd. in Lilliston and Ritchie 3). Ehrich and her husband used to have the option to sell to five different independently owned grain elevators, while "now the five elevators are owned by only two companies" (3).

Low commodity prices and consolidation often make it impossible for farmers to break even, thus driving them further into debt and eventually from their land.

As there is "horizontal" integration on the production side of farming, there is also "vertical" integration of the food processing and retailing industries. Vertical integration involves the corporate control of food from the "farm to the table" (Davidson 29). Examples of vertical integration can be found easily in the meat industry in the form of "factory farms" or Concentrated Animal Feeding Operations (CAFO). These operations, like much of agribusiness, are owned by corporations that "control all aspects of meat production" from the growth, feed, slaughter, and marketing of the animals ("Farm Aid FAQs"). For example, "four meatpacking companies control an estimated 79 percent of cattle slaughter" ("Farm Facts"). Large corporations like Tyson Chicken control virtually all poultry production; "more than two-thirds of all hogs are raised on farms that have more than 1,000 animals. This is double the percentage of ten years ago" ("Farm Aid FAQs"). Many small family farmers have become "contract" farmers who farm for large corporations, assuming the risk and liability of growing food while the corporations are sure to reap the profits. The movement toward consolidation, toward vertical and horizontal integration, and toward farm policies that favor large multinational agribusiness firms makes it clear that the crisis in family farming is no longer a crisis; it is a worldwide shift, a definitive change in how the developed world grows, distributes, and sells its food.

The growth of consolidation and vertical and horizontal integration, what some have come to call the "New Farm Economy" (see Lamb), has had devastating effects on small family farms. While small family farmers continue to leave their land in record numbers, the New Farm Economy has provided a boom economy for agribusiness giants like Cargill/Monsanto, ConAgra, and Archer Daniels Midland. Archer Daniels Midland, the "supermarket of the world," recently saw profit increases from $110 million to $301 million. Cargill, another grain conglomerate, reaped large increases, nearly doubling its net profit in four years ("Global Free Trade"). The fact that these agribusiness corporations make huge profits while small family farmers go deeper into debt or go bust is not well understood by the U.S. public, nor is it widely reported. Says Osha Gray Davidson, "The fact that these giant corporations have been doing well while farmers have not receives little attention. When the phenomenon is mentioned at all, it is usually as an afterthought" (30), a point that underscores the need for critical literacy work and public discussion of this issue.

Some might argue that the loss of small farms, the rise of consolidation, vertical and horizontal integration, and factory farming are small prices to pay if we are going to feed the people in the United States and others across the globe at a fair price and under efficient production conditions. However, the question of efficiency and cost-effectiveness of large versus small scale farms is hotly debated. Some small farm advocates claim that larger farms are not necessarily more efficient farms; "the cost per unit for agricultural production is no better in larger commercial operations than in family farms" ("Farm Aid FAQs"), while agricultural experts and economists claim that "consolidation has occurred because larger production units have lower per-unit production costs" (Lamb 10). Efficiency, however, has to be put into perspective. How are costs measured beyond the tangible ones of feed, seed, and equipment? What about costs to the environment, consumer health, and food security? For instance, residents living near CAFOs often report physical health problems such as "nausea, vomiting, coughing, and headaches," likely due to higher levels of "nitrogen, phosphorous and other nutrients in the soil, air and water" ("Farm Aid FAQs"). Antibiotics used in close confinement meat production and antibiotic-resistant bacteria can be passed through the meat supply. Toxins that seep into the soil and groundwater from CAFO manure lagoons can pollute and contaminate area waterways and fields. For instance, in 1995 in North Carolina, "35 million gallons of animal waste" from corporate hog farms "spilled into . . . riverways, killing 10 million fish."[8] The costs of such environmental spills are mind-boggling and will have an impact on the land and waterways for years. The price for the "cheap food" and goods that many Americans purchase at Wal-Mart Supercenters and other grocery outlets is quite high, carrying an environmental and societal price tag that costs taxpayers millions every year.

Edna Bonacich, professor of sociology at University of California–Riverside, calculates the cost-benefit ratio of big-box stores like Wal-Mart, noting that the cost-savings passed on to consumers is offset by reductions in wages:

> There's a kind of cyclical process of poorer workers needing cheaper goods, needing poorer workers to produce those goods, in a kind of ratcheting down of standards. What happens is that inequality is increasing in the United States. The middle class is kind of being hollowed out, and there are more and more workers who find that it's hard to earn a living wage. They don't make enough in order to live. The distinction between the earnings of workers and the earnings of management, that division has grown huge. It used to be something like 60–1, [what] the highest executives made versus their workers. Now it's something like 600–1. ("Interview")

With small farms and ranches on the decline, many rural Americans struggle to make ends meet and to sustain their communities. State and local government officials tend to see rural economic development as job-creation at any cost, not as a sustainable enterprise. Davidson characterizes "rural development" as a process of devastating compromise with huge consequences to rural people: "In a desperate attempt to bring jobs to their devastated regions—and then to keep them there—state and local governments attempt to outdo each other in making concessions to manufacturers, offering businesses a variety of inducements such as tax breaks, job training programs, and development bond financing" (134). These economic development programs are often quite good at providing low-paying, non-union service jobs, which constitute more than half of all rural jobs (W. K. Kellogg Foundation, "Perceptions" 2001, 5), but such jobs fail to provide a real future for rural communities. Low-paying service jobs often lead to further out-migration of local residents and in-migration of a pool of exploitable immigrant labor. Many of the service jobs in food-processing industries are staffed by migrant workers from Mexico and Central America; the conditions under which they work rival those of the meatpackers portrayed in Upton Sinclair's classic novel *The Jungle* (see also Schlosser). Therefore, rural economic development often becomes a synonym for "low wages, antilabor laws, [and] inadequate environmental protections" (Davidson 134). Indeed, a chronic challenge for rural communities is balancing environmental concerns with economic development.

The policies and economic decisions that have fueled the farm crisis and worsened rural poverty, however, are not limited to the United States. Farmers in other parts of the world also have been affected by national and international policies that favor large farms and multinational corporations. For instance, George W. Bush's Farm Security and Rural Investment Act of 2002, a "ten-year, $190 billion bill," has increased "government support [of farms] by $83 billion more than the cost of existing programs" (Edmondson 117), providing subsidies that will mostly go to the wealthiest who own large farms or tracts of farm land (10 percent of all farmers). This legislation reversed the notion perpetuated in Clinton's Freedom to Farm bill of 1996 that "agriwelfare" for larger farms would end and encouraged more "corporate welfare" for agribusiness. In addition, this policy has reverberated throughout the agricultural community across the globe, affecting countries that heavily depend on agricultural exports such as Chile, Guatemala, and Canada. Criticism of the policy has been voiced by "the European Union, Canada, Australia, Brazil, and others" who see American farm policy as protection for the wealthy farmers even as the U.S. government extols the virtues of free trade while "manipulating so-called 'free trade'" (117-18). Moreover, the Farm Security and Rural Investment Act stands in contrast to the policy proposed by the "Doha Ministerial Declaration" ratified at the World Trade Organization (WTO) symposium, which called for correcting the uneven playing field of "free trade" whereby farmers from "first world" countries receive subsidies. The Bush administration's backtracking on its support of "free" agricultural trade was a particularly devastating move for developing countries that "must not only struggle against the double standards expressed in the conditions for 'free trade' (i.e., U.S. markets won't purchase bruised fruit or vegetables and therefore will not buy fruit from Third World countries), they must also compromise their economic growth capacity to support a handful of rich American agribusinesses farmers" (118).

The result of the 2002 Farm Security and Rural Investment Act has mostly been more profit for U.S. agribusiness and the furtherance of what Shiva deems "food totalitarianism." Shiva, an internationally renowned environmental activist, defines food totalitarianism as a system "in which a handful of corporations control the entire food chain and destroy alternatives so that people do not have access to diverse, safe foods produced ecologically" (17). Hiding beneath maxims about efficiency and productivity and slick advertising campaigns about feeding the world's growing population, global corporations like Cargill/Monsanto have used trade agreements, property laws, and new technologies to gain dominion over local agriculture. Older, more sustainable and diverse forms of agriculture have been replaced by monocultural agriculture, a system of food production focused on producing one type of food through industrialized agriculture. Monocultural agriculture coupled with "free" trade agreements—or what many have come to call "forced trade" agreements—is increasingly wiping out sustainable agriculture and decimating small farms and agriculturally rich communities in places like Shiva's home country of India, a country that hosts one out of every four farmers across the globe.

The brave new world of global agribusiness is reshaping centuries of agricultural practice through trade-related policies and intellectual property rights. For instance, the practice of family farmers sharing and saving their seeds, a time-honored practice of conservation that ensures biodiversity and food safety, has been challenged by the recent trend toward seed patenting, the seizing and patenting of indigenous seeds by corporations. Aided by the WTO's Trade Related Intellectual Property Rights, which makes it illegal for farmers across the globe to share and save their seeds (Shiva 8–9), large agribusiness corporations are racing to file patents on seeds developed over centuries by multiple generations of small farmers. Rice-Tec has claimed a patent for basmati rice; Calgene, a division of the Monsanto Corporation, carries a patent for soybeans (9). Shiva puts it succinctly: "Centuries of collective innovation by farmers and peasants are being hijacked as corporations claim intellectual-property rights on these and other seeds and plants" (9). The development, marketing, and dumping of genetically engineered foods on developing countries also has been a new and hotly controversial trend under the WTO's Trade Agreement on Agriculture.

What these trends and patterns portend is that we are losing our right to determine where our food comes from and how it is produced: "Decisions about how our food is grown and by whom are made behind closed doors. Trade and agricultural ministers have allowed multinational corporations to gain unprecedented power and control over our food system. As a result, America's reliance on imported foods has increased" ("Global Free Trade"). Meanwhile, consumers are "largely left in the dark about the negative impacts of cheap imports within the domestic food system." Furthermore, the move toward so-called free trade means that the United States and many other industrialized nations have become dependent on a global food economy where export crops are featured prominently. The environmental consequences of global food are worth noting, especially in a time of diminishing fossil fuel resources. Helena Norberg-Hodge and Steven Gorelick argue that global food systems are usually monocultures, which "require massive inputs of pesticides, herbicides, and chemical fertilizers." Furthermore, a global food economy requires that millions of dollars be spent on fuel for food transport, thus "making food transport a major contributor to fossil fuel use, pollution and greenhouse gas emissions." In the United States, "transporting food within the nation's borders accounts for over 20 percent of all commodity transport" and "120 million tonnes of $CO_2$ emissions every year." In an age of depleted fossil fuel resources and global warming, the logic of "global food" has reached a critical juncture and has caused many rural advocacy organizations and environmental groups to argue for a return to local and regional systems of food production. Local or regional food costs less to transport, requires less preservation or modification, and is not as dependent on pesticides and nonorganic fertilizers that are common in monocultural production. Community-supported agriculture, farmers' markets, food co-ops, and "buy local" campaigns are among the practices typical of "local food" initiatives. Another strategy is the idea of land trust, which preserves lands for agricultural purposes rather than allowing it to be sold off to developers at bargain basement prices.

While this brief sketch does not do justice to all of the economic and agricultural trade-related trends and patterns currently in play, it outlines the challenges that national and global trade policy poses to small family farmers and those concerned with the food system. The current trend toward consolidation and the attendant movement toward global food trade underscore the need for citizens to engage in movements for the protection and sustenance of local food systems, what Shiva refers to as "food democracy." Food democracy, Shiva argues, is a social justice movement that favors the majority of the world's population instead of the industrialized North and the corporations that originate there. It involves the support of local food systems. Mobilizations toward the realization of an ideal of food democracy can be found in global, national, and local advocacy organizations and citizen-based movements such as Food First, Farm Aid, and the Community Food Security Coalition and in loosely structured coalitions of farmers, environmental activists, consumer activists, public-interest scientists, farm-to-cafeteria activists, college students, and others who have raised a public outcry about global agribusiness and international trade agreements at meetings of the WTO. Together, these groups are working toward the realization of a food democracy—a system that will have a positive effect on sustaining the economic well-being of rural communities in the United States and across the globe.[9]

The economic patterns, social inequities, and environmental consequences surrounding food production are important issues for critical literacy educators to take up. Not only is the future of small family farms at stake but also the health of our citizens, the welfare of farm lands and small farms, and the future of the environment. One significant way to begin addressing such issues is to seek alternative discourses and advocacy rhetorics that offer food consumers and farmers sustainable alternatives.

## The Rhetorics of the Farm Crisis

As the economic realities of the farm crisis continue to unfold in rural areas across the globe, popular press representations of it—the main venue by which most of our largely urban and suburban society encounters farmers and agricultural production—largely fail to account for the complexities discussed earlier. As mentioned previously, stories of the farm crisis are usually driven by two major plotlines: the pathos-driven narrative of tragedy and the progress-driven narrative of smart diversification. The first underscores the human-interest dimensions of the farm crisis; the typical domestic U.S. news story is usually that of a farm family's slippage into debt, foreclosure, bankruptcy, and public auction. As William Greider contends: "The media's usual take on this new farm crisis is a tearjerk feature story that begins with a worried farm couple poring over bills at the kitchen table, children crying in the background; and it closes with a romantic elegy for Jefferson's doomed yeomanry. Too bad, but that's the price for progress, end of story" (12). Such a narrative is driven by appeals to pathos; the viewers are witness to the suffering of the farm family, their interrelational dramas, and their likely dispossession, which is portrayed as the "cost" for modern efficiency. At times, the family farmer in the story triumphs against the odds, but all too often the story of the farm ends with the public auction, an image photographer Dona Schwartz refers to as "an easily digestible synecdoche" of the farm crisis presented for media consumption:

> Over and over, images of farm auctions appeared on the television screen or the printed page. Sound bites featuring the inexplicable cadence of the auctioneer as he offered equipment and machinery for sale served as a backdrop for the dramatic tension built up in these stories. People were shown bidding competitively for the spoils of the sale, while friends and family nervously paced at the edges of the crowd and the defeated farmer tried to appear proud and resolute, unbroken by the loss of his livelihood. Sometimes women were shown weeping.

Images such as the public auction of farm implements or the worried farm couple poring over bills portray the visible socioeconomic realities of contemporary farming, but they do not emphasize the structural realities and federal and international policies that have brought us to this moment. Media reports tend to portray family farmers as "heroic, beleaguered individualists struggling against adversity, quintessentially American," but such reports skip or gloss over "farmers' dependence on a complicated network of economic and political forces beyond their reach" (Schwartz). Farm crisis narratives often represent the farm situation as a result of a "brief economic downturn, coupled with bad luck or poor management skills." Seldom is the farm crisis represented as what it is, "a more complex web of changes that have been transforming rural life," the result of specific agricultural policies and trade policies pursued in the interest of multinational corporations.

In the case of the "tragedy" narrative of the farm crisis, some urban and suburban readers and viewers sympathetically identify with the suffering and loss of the American farm in popular press tragedy narratives. By identification, I am referring to Kenneth Burke's often-discussed definition of identification in *A Rhetoric of Motives* as seeing one's interests as joined or identified with another through the act of persuasion (20). Persuasion through identification involves one being identified with the other, becoming what Burke called "'substantially one' with a person other than himself. Yet at the same time, he [the individual] remains unique, an individual locus of motives. Thus he is both joined and separate, at once a distinct substance and consubstantial with another" (21). In my use of Burke's term "identification," however, I wish to distinguish between the idea of sympathetic identification, which involves feeling sad or sorry for others going through hardship and suffering, and mutual identification, which involves feeling a sense of connection and solidarity with the struggles of others.

Through sympathetic identification with the farm crisis tragedy narrative, readers may be persuaded that the loss of farms is a problem and may even mourn that loss briefly. They may be compelled to identify with the theme of human suffering and grief over displacement from one's occupation and the land. Also, they may feel nostalgia for family farms and may identify with the Jeffersonian view that small farmers are somehow more noble and more representative of American character and therefore worth "saving" or at least publicly mourning. Such a view participates in the traditional rural literacy of nostalgia that Edmondson analyzes and results in farmers being viewed as objects of pity or as an endangered species that needs to be saved. The 1980s farm advocacy "motto" "Save our Farms," reminiscent of the 1980s motto "Save the Whales" ("Rethinking"), makes the majority of small farmers seem as if they are passive victims rather than active agents.

The question of agency—the agency accorded to farmers and to readers/viewers—becomes extremely pertinent here. Through the tragedy narrative, the reader may be persuaded that the loss of family farms is a terrible thing achieved by forces much greater than a single person and, therefore, an issue that cannot be fought even as the reader/viewer's voting patterns and consumption choices have helped facilitate that crisis. Since the tragedy narrative usually emphasizes ruin and downfall, hardship and suffering, the material realities—policies and practices—by which the food production system came to this point are underplayed and mostly invisible; therefore, critical literacy on the farm crisis is the furthest result of the tragedy narrative.

My frustration with the tragedy narrative is both personal and political. The story of the farm crisis is my family's story. For four generations, a total of eighty-three years, my family, the Schells, were owners and operators of a small family apple and pear orchard in eastern Washington State. My mother, Neva Schell, spent her married life on the farm; my late father, Robert E. Schell, spent his whole life on the farm except for eight years of college, graduate study, and military service; and my brother likewise has spent his whole life there except for the four years he attended college. My sister and I also worked on the farm until we went to college and left home to pursue nonfarm occupations. Although my sister and I left the farm, we remained stockholders in the incorporated family farm, and I occasionally assisted with work on the farm during the summers.

In January 2001, my mother and brother decided to leave farming as they were unable to make a profit. Their debt ratio was driven up by soaring production costs coupled with poor prices in spite of bumper crops. The warehouses my family sold to were consistently taking a good cut and giving them pennies, driving them deeper into debt every year. Apples from China and other countries flooded the

U.S. market and drove the price down. Local and regional overproduction of apples and pears—a direct result of "get bigger or get out" policies—also was factored into the mix. My mother and brother were given an ultimatum by the bank that for years had carried their crop loan: pay up in ninety days through liquidating assets or selling out, or they would face potential foreclosure. My mother and brother liquidated all they could, selling off orchard land to be converted to housing tracts. Some of the original farm remains in business, leased and operated by a neighbor who has expanded successfully. My family's story is hardly unique, as many farms in the area underwent a similar fate.[10]

It would be easy to see my family's story as a tragedy narrative; I prefer, however, to see it as a case of neoliberal rural literacy in action where industrialized farming in a globalized age is taken to its logical end, which for small family farmers usually means financial ruin, loss of land, and loss of a way of life that has been declared "obsolete" and "inefficient." In my home region, it is not an unusual sight to see huge bonfire-sized piles of fallen apple and pear trees in large open fields, funeral pyres of the small orchard industry. The end result is often abandonment, as discussed in chapter 2. The land is abandoned as farmland and sold off to developers who sow subdivisions instead of crops or who build Wal-Marts that eventually empty out the downtown businesses

In contrast to the tragedy narrative, the narrative of smart diversification emphasizes how individual farmers or collective groups can pull themselves out of poverty and ruin through practices such as niche farming, direct marketing, and precision farming. Smart diversification narratives emphasize the Yankee ingenuity and adaptability of farmers, and such narratives are often heartening as they portray small farmers succeeding against the odds, another quintessential American narrative of the underdog or the bootstrapper. Later in the chapter, I provide examples of how smart diversification rhetoric can be utilized successfully if it is coupled with a discussion of sustainable agriculture.

At the same time, both the tragedy and smart diversification rhetorics tend to emphasize "individualism": on the one hand, farmers' individual hardships and losses, and on the other hand, farmers' Yankee ingenuity. Neither narrative tends to question the systemic forces that have driven our national agricultural system of small farmers and farms into what the USDA National Commission on Small Farms report "A Time to Act" has deemed "some of the worst years since the Great Depression of the 1930s" (2). Neither rhetoric enables readers/viewers to see "the big picture" of how international trade policies, domestic agricultural policies, corporate concentration, and neoliberalist rhetorics of rural development have created and sustained a collective loss of small family farms.

While both narratives rely on forms of rhetorical identification that ultimately allow the readers and viewers to see the "farm crisis" as a public issue that warrants attention, they fail to communicate how the "farm crisis" affects the lives of their families and communities—after all, food is being grown somewhere; supermarket shelves are packed with food and Americans are increasingly facing a public health crisis of obesity. Thus, the questions not raised by the typical rhetorical strategies for addressing the farm crisis are these: How did we get to the point where small farms have virtually collapsed in America and are fast waning in other parts of the world? Is it simply nimble market forces and the inevitable march of technology overwhelming an old-fashioned way of making a living, as many news stories would have us believe? The point that is absent in most of the popular press literature on the farm crisis is that American agricultural policies and the rise of agribusiness have exacerbated our current situation.

To transmit the message of the "farm crisis" effectively, farm advocacy organizations and media outlets have to work to find ways to get the story out to emphasize how it matters to all of us. The organizers of a consulting firm called ActionMedia, a group that helps progressive organizations reframe their organizing rhetorics, argue that we need a more inclusive way to frame the "farm crisis," a way that will emphasize issues of sustainability and participation for all Americans, especially urban Americans, who make up the majority of the population. Farm advocacy and rural advocacy organizations need to shift from the rhetoric of "Save the Farm and Farmers," a rhetoric of sympathetic identification, to a rhetoric that addresses how the agricultural crisis affects all populations, the rhetoric of mutual identification. The rhetoric of mutual identification emphasizes the common interests of farmers and consumers, that is, "what corporations have done to farmers and small towns, they could do (are doing) to my city/neighborhood too" ("Rethinking"). Instead of identifying farmers as victims and objects of pity, as they are often portrayed in the tragedy narrative, readers/viewers can begin to see the situation of farmers as interconnected with their own concerns for healthy communities and healthy food. Rhetorics of the "farm crisis" that practice mutual identification demonstrate how farmers and consumers can be united around common issues of concern such as food safety, E. coli outbreaks, use of hormones and pesticides, environmental policies, rural migration and out-migration, immigration policy, corporate control, and overdependence on a few large corporations to provide all of our food ("Rethinking"). Arguments about the "farm crisis" that are based on mutual identification emphasize sustainability—sustainability not only of rural communities but of urban and suburban communities as well.

An alternative to the rhetorics of tragedy and smart diversification can be found in advocacy organizations that are currently working to change from global food systems to local and regional food systems. To illustrate the promising trends and patterns currently underway in food democracy movements, I analyze the rhetorical strategies of Farm Aid. Although there are a plethora of farm advocacy and local food organizations at work in the United States, such as the Center for Rural Affairs, the Institute for Food Development and Social Policy, and the Community Food Security Organization, as well as international organizations such as the International Society for Ecology and Culture, to name a few, I have chosen to analyze Farm Aid because it has been and continues to be one of the most visible and popular campaigns to help small farmers. Farm Aid's star-studded rock concerts and its public education campaigns have brought widespread attention to the farm crisis and have begun to promote an alternative agrarian rhetoric and literacy that largely contrasts with the tragedy and smart diversification rhetorics described earlier.

## Farm Aid's Creation of an Alternative
## Agrarian Rhetoric and Literacy

According to its official Web site, Farm Aid was an outgrowth of Live Aid, the July 13, 1985, rock concert to provide relief to famine-stricken residents of Ethiopia. At the Live Aid concert, Bob Dylan made the comment on stage: "Wouldn't it be great if we did something for our own farmers right here in America?" ("Beginning"). Spurred by that statement, musicians Willie Nelson, Neil Young, and John Mellencamp, all of whom grew up in rural areas, formed a core group that began to organize a concert to benefit farmers struggling in the United States. The first concert, put together in just six weeks, took place in Champaign, Illinois, on September 22, 1985, attracted 80,000 people, and raised over $7 million in aid for farmers. Since this initial concert, Farm Aid has sponsored a yearly concert and has also taken consistent action to advocate for small family farms ("Beginning"). Farm Aid brings together high-visibility, popular musicians with farm advocates and small farmers to accomplish four points of action:

- Raise awareness and funds with an annual signature music concert
- Award grants to farmer and rural service organizations that directly support family farmers
- Develop and fund programs that promote outreach, education, and the development of long-term solutions that support family farm–centered agriculture
- Build partnerships and educate the public to raise funds and to promote activism in support of family farmers ("Farm Aid Mission Statement")

While fulfilling its stated mission, Farm Aid has shifted its rhetoric from the typical tragedy rhetoric of "Save the Farm," with its focus on sympathetic identification, to a rhetoric of sustainability based on mutual identification. Farm Aid's initial campaign was organized around a "relief effort" similar to that of Live Aid, and the goal was to create awareness among Americans that family farms and farmers were in trouble and needed to be "saved." In 1986, Farm Aid sponsored a national farm conference that resulted in the establishment of the United Farmer and Rancher Congress. Follow-up local and regional events were organized to address what the national forum had revealed about the farm crisis. In 1987, Willie Nelson and John Mellencamp, along with a group of family farmers, testified before the U.S. Congress, spurring senators and representatives to pass "the Agricultural Credit Act which said that the Farmer's Home Administration (FMHA) could not foreclose on any family farmer unless the FMHA would make more money through foreclosure that [sic] they would by investing in making the farm profitable" ("Beginning"). In 1989, Willie Nelson took Farm Aid on tour; he held press conferences at sixteen concerts, detailed the farm crisis, and urged the media to talk to local farmers about the economic realities they faced. At Farm Aid's 1990 concert in Indianapolis, the organization brought together musical artists, environmental and consumer advocates, and farmers and began to transform its message, moving away from the rhetoric of saving the family farm to a message centered on the idea that farmers are stewards of the land. As the historical overview on the Farm Aid Web site notes: "A new message emerged from that effort: the well being of our land, food and water supply depends on a network of family farmers who care about how our food is grown" ("Beginning"). The shift from sympathetic identification—"Save the Family Farm and Farmers"—to mutual identification, that the stewardship of rural lands and a healthy food supply is an issue for us all, signals a turn in the rhetoric of the organization toward a rhetoric of sustainability and, as I argue below, an alternative agrarian literacy based on the same ethic of sustainability.

## Farm Aid as Critical Literacy Sponsor of an Alternative Agrarian Literacy

Farm Aid's mutual identification message was further developed by a national campaign launched in 1994 entitled the Campaign for Family Farms and the Environment, "a national effort to stop factory farms and those commodity groups that work against the interests of family farmers" ("Factory Farms"). In 1995 in Louisville, Kentucky, Farm Aid held a national town meeting where farmers urged President Clinton "to veto any farm bill that would force family farmers from their land." Unfortunately, the Freedom to Farm bill of 1996 discussed earlier did pass with huge consequences for small farmers. In response, a Farm Aid concert in Bristow, Virginia, in 1999 drew many farmers to the Washington, D.C., area to lobby their legislators about the Freedom to Farm bill. The message for this campaign was "Act now to stop the destruction of family farms," a message that emphasized that family farmers had been sold out by federal farm policies that favor large farms and multinational corporations. Most recently, the campaign for stewardship has been broadened to address the globalization of the food industry and the free-trade agreements that support it ("Beginning"). This thumbnail sketch of Farm Aid's history does not fully address its myriad campaigns, but it does give a sense of the overall priorities of the organization.

To address how Farm Aid's advocacy rhetorics were developed and modified to fit the shifting terrain of agricultural life in the twenty-first century, I analyze how the organization, as a "literacy sponsor" (Brandt, "Sponsors" 166), uses its Web site to deploy the available means of persuasion to craft a rhetorical message about the future of family farms and the importance of critical consumer action and choice. The main thrust of Farm Aid's work as a literacy sponsor is threefold. First, it works through its advocacy rhetoric to educate food consumers from urban and suburban backgrounds about the shift from family farming to factory farming while encouraging them to take literate and material action to support family farmers. Second, it helps small family farmers continue farming and urges farmers, farm advocates, and citizens to create public policies that allow small family farms to continue. Third, it tells the story of the "farm crisis" in a way that ensures mutual—rather than sympathetic—identification between farmers and food consumers. Rather than falling back on the tragedy rhetoric, Farm Aid deploys a rhetoric of mutual identification that allows urban, suburban, and rural people alike to see their mutual interests and to use literate action to reach the possibility of a sustainable family farm system of food production.

My analysis of Farm Aid's work as a literacy sponsor addresses the Web site's advocacy resources since it is the primary vehicle, along with its e-mail newsletters and signature concerts, that the organization uses to communicate with consumers and fellow advocates. While some items are omnipresent on the Web site, such as the organization's mission statement and historical narrative, the Web site, unlike a print pamphlet or flier, is constantly in revision and flux and is responsive to changing political and economic circumstances. As the material of the Web site has changed, my analysis will be limited to a specific temporal period—the summer of 2004.[11]

The visual rhetoric of Farm Aid's Web site says a great deal about the rhetorical message being advocated. At the top of each Web page, including the home page of the Farm Aid Web site, which I will examine in detail in this chapter, Farm Aid features its logo: the silhouette of a farm tractor being driven by a farmer with an American flag. Alongside that image is Farm Aid's banner image, a photo of what most modern farmers might consider to be an old-fashioned farmscape and what many urban viewers might consider to be a traditional small family farm: a looming red barn and split rail fence with horses peacefully grazing out front (see figure 1). A white farmhouse stands in the background flanked by trees and fields stretching to the horizon ("Farm Aid Home Page"). This image can be read in a variety of ways, depending on one's relationship to and knowledge of small family farms. Urban and suburban viewers may read the image through the lens of "traditional rural literacy" or through the lens of nostalgia for the past (Edmondson 15). Rural advocates and small farmers may read the image through the lens of what Edmondson calls a new agrarian literacy that resists neoliberal values that have led to the rural landscape being dotted by huge factory farm facilities instead of small farms (15). The image of the small farm, then, is not merely nostalgic but an image of resistance to neoliberalism and factory farming: a place that is rooted in family and community where the principles of the market do not take precedence over producing safe, healthy food at a fair price that will allow farm families to stay on their land. The image of the family farmscape, then, is both nostalgic and resistant, depending upon the audience accessing the site.

Figure 1. Farm Aid home page, July 5, 2004. Used by permission of Paul Natkin and Farm Aid, a nonprofit organization working to keep family farmers on their land.

In the foreground and off to the left of the farmscape depicted in the banner image, the viewer glimpses four noted musicians—Dave Matthews, Willie Nelson, Neil Young, and John Mellencamp. Although they stand at the left periphery of the photograph, their images are enlarged so that they seem to loom over the farmscape. All four stand together with their arms around each other, almost as if they were the proud owners of the farm in the background. Matthews, Nelson, and Young are dressed casually in jeans and T-shirts and Mellencamp in coveralls; Nelson and Young wear cowboy hats. A few touches distinguish them as musicians beyond their famous visages: Young and Nelson sport the trademark long hair of many performers, and Mellencamp and Young wear sunglasses. The only visual feature that distinguishes them as activists is that they appear on the Farm Aid Web page, and Young wears a "Stop Factory Farms" T-shirt. By making these well-known singers part of the bucolic farmscape in its banner image, Farm Aid foregrounds the ethos of the artists as the ethos of the organization. The four musicians are taking a "stand" for rural America and for small family farms. The symbolic message offered by this image is that they are standing for rural America because it is what stands behind them: their "country roots" of small family farms, rural communities, and rural people. As a section on the Web site later explains, three of the four men (Nelson, Mellencamp, and Young) are cofounding members of Farm Aid and serve on the board of directors, while Matthews joined the board in 2001.

An all-male cadre of musicians serving on the governing board is perhaps not surprising given the dominant masculinist narratives of rock stardom in our culture and the patriarchal narratives of agriculture discussed in chapter 4. Although female staff are a large part of Farm Aid, female artists are frequently featured in the concert lineups, and the four male stars are depicted later in the Web site with Farm Aid's female executive director, Carolyn Mugar, the Web site does convey indirectly the commonplace cultural impression that family farms are patriarchal structures, which, of course, many of them are, although numbers of female farmers are increasing, "jumping nearly 13 percent from 1997 to 2002, according to preliminary findings from the U.S. Department of Agriculture's latest census" (Green). As will be evident later, the spokespeople for some of the positive examples of small family farms drawn from the 2004 Web site are male farmers, although the depiction of these farms also shows how imbricated they are in the family structure and how various members contribute to the running of the operation, even as the patriarch is the spokesperson.

Underneath the banner image, the main links and visual images on Farm Aid's Web site largely construct and authorize the audience of the Web site as consumers of food rather than as producers. Farmers—the producers—can click on a link in the left-hand column of the page if they are in need of assistance. The remainder of the page hails the reader as a consumer of food whom the organization would like to educate about the state of farming in the United States and about critical consumer choices. Below the banner image stands a large box entitled "10 Ways to Ensure Healthy Food for You and Your Family," flanked by a fade-out image of a stand of wheat at sunset and a photograph of a well-to-do white woman choosing fruits and vegetables in a modern supermarket. Viewers are urged to click above the image to learn more. Below this image is the official greeting ("Welcome to Farm Aid") and a brief overview of the organization with a link to click to learn more. A newsletter registration follows that along with a box with a special advertising offer to "read Farm Aid's review of Rodale's recent book *Fresh Choices: Easy Recipes for Pure Food When You Can't Buy 100% Organic.*" The items at the middle to the bottom of the page are educationally oriented with two major items focused on critical questions that consumers have or should have about the food they are buying. The first is "What's in a Label?," a brief overview of how food labels should be critically read and a link to more detailed information about the vocabulary of food labeling. The second is an information item entitled "What Is Mad Cow Disease?" To the right of those items is a column entitled "Action Center," which entreats readers/viewers to "Take our online survey," "Buy *The Meatrix* T-shirt," "Tell a friend about Farm Aid," "Write to elected officials about Mad Cow Disease," and "Say no to irradiated meat!"

The effect of the opening page of the Web site is to anticipate questions viewers might have about the food they buy and eat and to remake those readers into agriculturally literate and critically aware consumers of food. Information is provided at key junctures to explain the challenges faced by small family farms and to explain the factory food system and the national policies that buttress it. Under the auspices of the "Farm Aid Information Center," the organization provides a plethora of information—fact sheets, FAQs, and policy statements—regarding the farm crisis and urges viewers not only to donate to their organization but also to take action by changing their buying habits and supporting local farmers. Those who follow major links on the Web site learn about trends and patterns that are taking hold in agriculture, about policy decisions that have driven these trends and patterns, and about the economic realities in rural areas brought on by these policies and practices. The literacy sponsored by the organization is clearly critical literacy aimed at helping consumers make better individual choices and work to collectively change the system so our food choices include family farmed and organic food.

In addition, the materials provide human-interest stories that largely make appeals to pathos and logos—to the tragedy and smart diversification rhetorics mentioned earlier in this chapter but with a movement toward a rhetoric of sustainability. For instance, making appeals to logos and pathos, a fact sheet housed on the Farm Aid Web site offers a brief definition of factory farming as "megafarms or Confined Animal Feeding Operations," briefly narrates their supposed benefits ("higher production levels, lower retail costs, and greater efficiency"), and then offers an opening question that allows for a critical interrogation of factory farms' supposed benefits: "But cheap food at what cost?" The emphasis throughout this fact sheet is on constructing factory farms as operations that are "ruining the legacy of family farms" and "costing" consumers: "Every new factory farm forces 10 family farmers out of business. With every small family farmer that has to leave the farm, communities lose access to fresh, healthy food and a thriving local economy" ("Factory Farms"). The claims that follow illustrate how factory farms are "abusing animals," "polluting the environment," and "threatening our health." A final section narrates how Farm Aid, along with the Campaign for Family Farms and the Environment, is resisting factory farming.

The visual rhetoric of the page is notable as well, as appeals to pathos are dominant here. Below the banner image described earlier, the viewer encounters three photographs that stairstep down to the bottom of the page. The first is a close-up of a pig packed into a factory farm stall. The pig's eyes and mud- or excrement-covered snout are apparent within the crowded stall, while next to it another stall obscures the image of another pig, revealing only part of its body. The photograph is suggestive of a vast expanse of stalls, exactly alike, that contain other pigs, crammed together in inhumane conditions before being slaughtered. The photographic credit underneath reads "Animal Welfare Institute." Below that photograph and to the left is a photograph of an egg factory farm. Hens are packed together inside cages and stretch their necks out and above the cages, suggesting that they are so densely housed that they are straining to be released. At the bottom of the page and in the far left-hand corner, the viewer sees a group of protestors at a rally holding Farm Aid–emblazoned signs with pro–family farm slogans. The photo caption reads, "Farm Aid friends at a rally against industrial agriculture" ("Factory Farms"). The visual images of factory farms, crowded animals, and protesting citizens make visible the changed landscape of farming through appeals to pathos and make it difficult for the reader/viewer to profess ignorance about how the majority of commercially available food is produced. In short, the effect is to produce a critical literacy moment where readers/viewers come face-to-face with the images of industrial agriculture and where they have to confront their own consumption practices and choices and think about alternatives.

The images are also meant to urge consumers to take material action: to seek alternative food sources by patronizing markets and outlets that sell family farmed food, by donating money to Farm Aid's advocacy efforts, and by getting involved in various campaigns for policies that support family farms. A link at the bottom of the factory farm page takes viewers to a letter authored by Farm Aid president Willie Nelson, who appeals to consumers to make the right food purchases. "Right now, we still have a choice—a choice between food that is grown and raised locally by family farmers or food that is produced on factory farms. But this choice is disappearing each day as local family farms—the producers of fresh, healthy food—are displaced by giant food factories" ("Dear Friend"). The key theme in the letter is "choice," a rhetorical appeal that is familiar to urban and suburban readers/viewers who have been culturally constructed as "consumers" who have the right to the "best choice" and "value" for their money. Rather than simply emphasizing the tragedy narrative of the farm crisis and the loss of the small family farm, Farm Aid seeks to construct a critically literate consumer of food who has the agency—and the income—to make the right choice. The right choice, contends Nelson, is buying "organic and family farm–identified food that ensures that family farmers will continue to offer us a choice of the food we want."

One of the challenges of the consumer choice message offered by Farm Aid is to assume that the reader/viewer has the economic resources to access family farmed food. As a literacy sponsor, Farm Aid has constructed food consumers in visual images and in their implied rhetoric as well-educated, mostly white, middle-class people with access to cars or public transportation that can take them to markets or outlets where they can purchase family farmed food. The July 2004 version of the Web site presented visual images of white farmers, white staffers, and white food consumers. People of color as farmers, consumers, or staffers, until more recent versions of the Web site, have not been well represented, which presents a question about how Farm Aid imagines and portrays its audience, the U.S. food consumer, and the U.S. farmer. These representations also raise questions about access to family farmed food for those who do not fit the Web site's implied demographic profile. Although an increasing number of urban areas offer centrally located farm stands, urban gardens, farmers' markets, or food cooperatives, low-income residents who receive public assistance or who are without reliable transportation may not be able to access those outlets. Also, while a number of farmers' markets are authorized to receive food stamps and coupons through the federally authorized Farmers' Market Nutrition Program (FMNP), approval must be gained through state agencies, and farmers or farmers' market authorities must apply ("WIC"). Therefore, the FMNP benefit might not be available at all farmers' markets. The rhetoric of critical consumer choice, therefore, has its limitations even as it offers a compelling case for white middle-class consumers from urban and suburban areas. Other nonprofit agencies, community gardening associations, food banking organizations, and food pantries focus on connecting low-income, working-class people, black, white, Latino/a, and Asian, to sources of local food. In some cases, food banking and food pantry programs include local fresh fruits and vegetables in the weekly or bimonthly food pantry bags that are given out to community residents in need. In other cases, urban and rural community gardening groups have helped low-income residents set up and maintain their own community gardens and community kitchens, providing an opportunity not only for the assurance of a local food supply but also for residents to learn—and, in some cases, re-learn—how to grow, cultivate, and preserve their own food. In some cases, working-class communities, urban and rural alike, have for decades, without any outside sponsorship, cultivated garden plots and conducted local informal networks of food swapping, bartering, and preserving.

On the public school front, local farm–to–public school cafeteria programs have brought locally farmed foods to schools that cater to low-income students in urban and rural areas. School garden and urban garden projects across the country have encouraged local city youth to get involved in growing and eating their own food and often involve young people in setting up urban farm stands. Groups like the Community Food Security Coalition (CFSC) are leaders in such projects to encourage local food initiatives for all community members, including low-income residents. Indeed, organizations like Farm Aid have lately joined with the CFSC to sponsor national conferences that highlight such efforts.[12] Chapter 5 discusses CFSC's programs in more detail.

### Farm Aid and Globalization

While Farm Aid's Web site educates readers/viewers about the domestic crisis in U.S. agriculture and offers strategies consumers can use to access family farmed food, it also poses free trade agreements as a critical issue to consider. In a fact sheet entitled "The Global Free Trade of Food: Trading Away Family Farms and Consumer Choice," "free trade" is clearly framed as uneven or unfair trade:

> Agricultural "free trade" movements, like NAFTA, promote the trade of agricultural products with little regard to the negative impacts on local communities and producers. Countries, including the U.S., have been flooded with cheap food imports. The low-cost appeal of these imports to consumers has caused farmers to lose their local markets. Free trade agreements pose a threat to domestic food security—a problem that affects people worldwide. ("Global Free Trade")

What follows this statement are a series of grim facts about the impact of NAFTA—the North American Free Trade Agreement—signed in 1994, which removed trade barriers between Canada, the United States, and Mexico. As a prominent feature of this page, the phrase "free trade" is repeated three times, accompanied by a critical claim about it:

> Free Trade: Forcing farmers from the land, spreading rural
> poverty and hunger. . . .
> Free Trade: Unfair profits for multinational agribusiness
> corporations. . . .
> Free Trade: Taking away consumer access and choice for
> local, fresh food. ("Global Free Trade")

Following each claim is a series of economic statistics that show how "free trade" has undermined family farm agriculture and the general well-being of American, Canadian, and Mexican peoples. For instance, in response to the first claim that "Free Trade" has "forc[ed] farmers from the land, spreading rural poverty and hunger," Farm Aid cites statistics to demonstrate this: "100,000 family farmers were forced out of farming between 1996 and 2001" in the United States; in Canada, 11 percent of family farms were lost; "between 1992 and 2002 the percentage of the rural Mexicans living in extreme poverty grew from 36 percent to 52.4 percent" ("Global Free Trade"). The fact sheet also notes that "cheap food imports have pushed [Mexican] farmers off their land and into crowded cities." Clearly, the message here is that NAFTA has not delivered the economic prosperity promised by neoliberal rhetoric. What NAFTA has delivered are large profits for multinational agribusiness corporations largely based in the United States.

By examining the impact of NAFTA, Farm Aid begins to examine how free trade policies have affected farmers across the globe. The organization's resource materials on "global food" make a populist appeal to local food and consumer choice. Also contained in the rhetoric is a nationalist appeal against becoming too dependent on "imported foods" at the cost to domestic small farmers. Farm Aid argues that "each country must retain the right to determine how to meet its domestic food needs while protecting its family farmers. . . . Free trade policy is typically unfair trade policy" ("Global Free Trade"). Embedded in this claim is not only a concern about food exports undermining our own system of family farmers but a more subtle rhetoric about food safety and availability that has increasingly emerged in the wake of the September 11, 2001, terrorist attacks on the World Trade Center and the Pentagon. Stated directly and implied as well is the idea that food grown at home by family farmers is safer and also supports our system of national small farmers. Thus food sovereignty and food security are emphasized.

While this nationalistic rhetoric clearly supports family farmers, it also cuts another way as it does not fully address how small farmers across the globe, especially in areas of the developing world, are faring much worse than American farmers and often in response to agricultural policies proposed by the United States. While Farm Aid effectively urges U.S. consumers to sustain and support local family farmers and organic distributors, the organization has only begun to address the interconnectedness of American consumers with farmers in other parts of the globe and the need for global fair trade initiatives. In 2003, on the eve of the WTO meeting in Cancun, Mexico, Farm Aid signed, with thirty other U.S. organizations, a letter to U.S. elected officials, U.S. trade representative Robert Zoellick, and other global fair trade advocates. The letter, entitled "A Declaration for a New

Direction for American Agriculture and Agricultural Trade," highlights food security, food sovereignty, and just working conditions for farm workers and calls for "a comprehensive re-examination of the impact of global trade policy on food security, farmers' livelihoods, and local, sustainable food production" ("Call"). Along with other groups, Farm Aid pledged to "educate all Americans about the need to redesign international trade agreements to support and promote rural development, poverty reduction, sustainable agricultural development and food security for all, not only in the United States but across the globe" ("Call"). In doing so, the organization moved toward embracing an alternative agrarian rhetoric and literacy that urges U.S. consumers to become agriculturally literate and active in promoting critical literacy in their communities.

The alternative agrarian rhetoric and literacy practiced by Farm Aid bears resemblance to the rhetorics of alternative globalization movements that have gained increasing attention since the November 1999 WTO protests in Seattle, Washington. On November 30, 1999, more than 700 organizations and an estimated 40,000–60,000 people gathered in Seattle to protest the WTO's Third Ministerial Meeting. The Seattle protests sparked unexpected coalitions between groups that normally do not identify with one another: human rights activists, labor activists, indigenous people, farmers, environmentalists, teachers, artists, and others. United by a sense that "free trade" is not fair trade and by the disparity of wealth between nations and peoples, these activists proclaimed that "open borders, reduced tariffs, and forced trade" do not " benefit the poorest 3 billion people in the world" (Hawken). As Naomi Klein asserts in *Fences and Windows: Dispatches from the Frontlines of the Anti-globalization Debates*, these movements have put globalization "on trial" because global trade policies have put up fences that shut people "out of schools, hospitals, workplaces, their own farms, homes, and communities" (xxi). Rather than being anti-globalization, this movement is, as Klein argues, against global corporations ruling the day, "opposing the logic that what's good for business—less regulation, more mobility, more access—will trickle down into good news for everybody else" (4). Like Farm Aid, the alternative globalization movement argues for trade policies that are responsive to "labor rights, environmental protection, and democracy" (5). What both share is a commitment to critical literacies that make working people stakeholders in discussions of the future of their communities, their workplaces, and the kind of world they imagine for future generations.[13]

## Reframing the Family Farm as a Sustainable Enterprise

The other main thrust of Farm Aid's work as a literacy sponsor is to help readers adopt a rhetoric of mutual identification that allows urban, suburban, and rural alike to see their mutual interests and to use literate action to reach the goal of a sustainable family farm system. The information pages of the Web site emphasize stories about family farms that are struggling to survive and that are receiving aid from the organization and, conversely, stories about family farms that have found a way to survive and thrive. The tragedy rhetoric and the smart diversification rhetoric are present here, but they are mostly tempered by rhetoric of mutual identification and sustainability. For instance, if the reader/viewer clicks on a graphic of a farmer's letter to Farm Aid from the opening page, he or she will find two letters sent by farmers to the organization in the spring of 2004. One is an appeal by a sixteen-year-old boy for Farm Aid to help him save his father's dairy farm, which was plagued by a drop in milk prices and mounting debt. Another letter is displayed from a Montana wheat and durum rancher affected by drought, debt, and impending foreclosure ("Support"). These stories are presented as typical of the e-mails and letters the organization receives weekly from struggling farmers. Presented here, with the identifying information removed, the letters give the reader/viewer a sense of the hardship and crisis faced by farmers—low prices, debt, drought, and uncertain weather conditions. The letters also convey the urgency of supporting Farm Aid through donations and supporting family farmers through buying their products.

In contrast to those stories of hardship, Farm Aid offers "success stories," such as one foregrounded under the link "Farm Aid and YOU Saved a Family Farm," which emphasizes how the organization, through member support, was able to save a family farm from foreclosure in North Carolina. After hearing from the farmer's college-age son that the farm was in trouble, Farm Aid referred the family to a local farm advocate who helped counsel the family about financial options and paperwork that enabled them to save their house and land from foreclosure. In this case and others like it, Farm Aid acted as a critical literacy broker. Through the Farm Aid hotline, farmers can get access to trained farm advocates who can help them decipher and navigate the financial quagmire of loan paperwork and legal options. In contrast to the tragedy rhetoric that is so common in popular press representations, the story of the North Carolina farm emphasizes how disaster was averted through the networking efforts of Farm Aid–supported advocacy organizations and advocates working in concert with farm families ("Farm Aid and YOU").

While Farm Aid serves as a critical literacy broker for struggling farmers and educates consumers about their "choices," the organization also skillfully reframes an image of the family farm as a profitable and sustainable enterprise instead of as a failed and obsolete institution, thus avoiding the typical tragedy rhetoric. Through deploying "success stories" of small family farms—stories of family farms that adopted organic farming practices and direct distribution and marketing—Farm Aid reframes the story of farm crisis from one of tragedy and ruin to one of possibility, survival, and sustainability. The monthly success stories contained in the 2004 Web site, and in successive versions of the Web site, make use of an alternative agrarian rhetoric and literacy that emphasizes how farmers are adapting to changing times; the stories also educate food consumers about how they can access family farmed products by providing links to distribution sites for organic milk or meat in their area ("Not Your Average Pigs"). In particular, the 2004 Web site features the stories of two families who are practicing sustainable farming and making use of direct marketing strategies: the Seeleys, who run an organic dairy and storefront in northeastern Pennsylvania, and the Snavelys, swine farmers from Fredericktown, Ohio, who run Curly Tail Organic Farm.

These farming success stories draw on two rhetorical strategies: the component of smart diversification rhetoric focusing on individual adaptability and innovation, and an alternative agrarian rhetoric and literacy that, as Edmondson argues, shows rural people resisting the effects of corporate consolidation and vertical integration by developing "alternatives aligned with rural sensibilities (15) and "attempt[ing] to bridge agency and structure in ways they choose" (16). Although each story differs in the type of farming practices described, several plot outlines are emphasized: community involvement and stewardship of the land through organic practices; the importance of direct, local distribution as opposed to relying upon national and international commodity markets; and the preservation of the institution of the family farm through embracing organic practices and local distribution. Through interview narratives with farmers Ed Snavely and Kim Seeley, readers/viewers can learn about the transitions these farmers made from industrialized farming to organic farming, the forces and concerns that led them there, and their philosophies of farming, community participation, and stewardship. The Seeleys and Snavelys are depicted as farmers who made the choice to "go organic" and, in doing so, protected the future of their land and family farming legacy, discovered a niche market for their milk and pork products, and found local distribution sites, thus ensuring their profitability.

The Seeley and Snavely farm families are portrayed as stewards of the land and as vital participants in the communities surrounding their farms. Kim Seeley, a third-generation dairy farmer with a 180-head sustainable dairy farm, views farming as a form of community engagement: "Community concern and commitment to growing safe, healthy food are high on Kim Seeley's list of priorities" ("Out of This World Milk"). Likewise, the Snavelys see themselves as "committed to being responsible stewards of the earth" who "produc[e] healthful, chemical-free food" ("Not Your Average Pigs"). Community concern is manifested through the way the Snavelys and Seeleys grow and market their food. On the Snavely farm, the pigs are raised according to organic methods. They are fed a "high-fiber diet" made from "grains grown on" the farm; the pigs are also "finished" or grown in seven months as "opposed to a factory farm finishing time of about four and a half to five months" ("Not Your Average Pigs"). This longer "finishing" time allows for pigs to be raised under healthier, more natural conditions. The visual rhetoric of the Snavelys' story is notable as well. The photograph of pigs at Ed Snavely's family farm contrasts sharply with the factory farm pigs depicted in the Web site's portrayal of factory farming. A young pig is shown nestled against two other pigs: clean and pink and content-looking without bars or metal crates obstructing the animals from one another, thus supporting Farm Aid's argument that family farmed food is safer and healthier.

On both farms, direct distribution is key to the success of the operation; the Seeleys sell milk to local people through their store on the farm and through distributing it directly to "local supermarkets, a local county jail, and the Pennsylvania College of Technology," a culinary school ("Out of This World Milk"). Likewise, Ed Snavely and his family market their pork products "directly to local restaurants, to local people through on-farm sales, and at two local farmers markets" ("Not Your Average Pigs"). Moreover, the Snavelys are engaged in raising rare breeds of hogs, Large Blacks and Tamworths, which are considered "critical" and "rare" breeds since they are not usually raised on most swine farms. Through this practice of raising rare breeds, the Snavelys are engaged in preserving "the biodiversity that is threatened by factory farm practices, which favor plant and animal species that fit the rigid production specifications for a highly uniform, industrial system of agriculture."

Furthermore, the two "success" stories promote critical literacy about agricultural consolidation and emphasize ways that family farmers and consumers can combat it by making different choices. Both Ed Snavely and Kim Seeley comment that in an age of corporate consolidation, it is necessary for small farmers to utilize new methods of farming and distribution. Snavely argues that due to consolidation, small family farmers cannot make it without changing their practices:

> I truly believe that the family farmer can't make it anymore as a commodity farmer. You have to try a whole new approach. It used to be you could go to your local grain elevator and your local stockyard and get a fair price. You can't do that anymore; the same companies that own the huge corporate farms own the grain elevator and stockyard. Sometimes you can't even cover your cost of production. ("Not Your Average Pigs")

Kim Seeley also comments directly on the problems with corporate concentration— the fact that dairy farmers have fewer choices of which cooperatives to sell their milk to, thus driving prices down:

> We have been told for years that we will have more power if
> we consolidate the dairy industry into fewer cooperatives, yet
> in the last 10 years we have done that more than ever, and
> the price of milk is still the lowest it's ever been. This is glar-
> ing proof that controlling more power among fewer people
> doesn't solve farmers' problems. It only makes them worse.
> ("Out of This World Milk")

Seeley feels that consumers are the "key to unleashing . . . a simmer-ing agricultural revolution. As soon as we empower the consumers, they can put pressure on politicians and food companies to make changes. They hold the power" ("Out of This World Milk"). A message of mutual identification is offered here. If farmers and consumers see their mutual interests, both will ultimately profit. The consumer who patronizes family farmers such as the Seeleys and the Snavelys will be putting money in the pockets of those farmers, not large agribusiness corporations, and buying a safer and healthier product.[14]

The success of the Snavely and Seeley operations has made it possible for their farms to continue and to be passed on to the next generation of family members. Both "success stories" end with a dis-cussion of the family farm as a legacy that will be handed down to the sons in each family: Shon Seeley and Brandon Snavely. The family metaphor is a particularly important feature of Farm Aid's "success stories" as it provides food consumers with a framing vision of what kinds of farms they should rely upon for their food; in essence, the food consumer is brought into the "family farm" operation and in-vited to become a member of the extended family of the farm—the consumer family. They are urged to develop a relationship with their local farmers and to put a "face" on farming. In doing so, they can take part in an alternative agrarian rhetoric and literacy by making critical consumer choices and supporting public policies that foster sustainable rural development.

By emphasizing these sustainable farming success stories, by educating consumers about their options for safe and healthy food that supports family farmers, and by offering critical readings of domestic and international farm policies, Farm Aid creates a narrative of farm life that differs from the tragedy and smart diversification rhetorics so pervasive in popular cultural representations of the farm crisis. Instead, Farm Aid offers a vision of farm life based on social, economic, and environmental sustainability—an alternative agrarian rhetoric and literacy that provides hope for the continuation of the family farm into the twenty-first century.

## Teaching Food Politics

As consumers of food and as concerned citizens, we cannot afford to ignore the farm crisis; our human need for food means we all have a stake in agriculture. We also have a stake in engaging in critical literacies that will lead to food democracy, whether it is through modifying our daily food consumption practices, working locally to raise awareness and change public policies, or teaching about these issues in our college writing courses.

As we argue in the concluding chapter, literacy educators at the college level can play a vital role in perpetuating critical literacies about rural life and rural issues such as the farm crisis. While advocacy rhetorics like those perpetuated by organizations like Farm Aid can serve as a useful resource in guiding this critical literacy work, a number of critical pedagogical resources in our field also can help us begin this task: for example, Shor's well-known example of students analyzing the politics of the fast food hamburger in *Critical Teaching and Everyday Life* and Owens's interrogation of place, work, and sustainability in *Composition and Sustainability: Teaching for a Threatened Generation*. In chapter 5, we provide models of writing curricula that engage rural literacies issues, including a food politics course that I have designed that takes Eric Schlosser's *Fast Food Nation: The Dark Side of the All-American Meal* as a central text for perpetuating critical literacy about the food industrial complex. Through critical literacy work on the food industrial complex, our students can begin to understand the extensive network of community and global linkages that currently shape our lives as food consumers and can begin to consider practices that will make those linkages more sustainable and equitable. Chapter 4 considers how sustainable linkages are built in rural communities through the everyday literacy work of women—work that is often hidden and unacknowledged, although vital to the sustenance of rural communities and economies.

# 4 / Beyond Agrarianism
## Toward a Critical Pedagogy of Place

*Charlotte Hogg*

Chapter 2 of this book traces the history of stereotyping that stigmatizes rural literacies and analyzes the ways literacies within the context of stigmatization are negotiated between rural people and those who sponsor their literacy. Chapter 3 analyzes the ways in which agricultural literacies are misunderstood, or even absent, in the dominant narratives of our culture and argues for an alternative agrarian literacy rooted in discourses of rural sustainability. In this chapter, I examine how particular discourses of agrarian life may undermine sustainable rural literacies by overshadowing other gendered, "ordinary," and social literacies of rural life that are often unseen or dismissed. Chapters 2 and 3 demonstrate the ways broader discourses of stereotyping, stigmatization, and traditional rural literacies that overlook the agricultural realities in the United States—discourses laden with preservation, abandonment, and modernization metaphors—affect the ways rural people negotiate their literate lives. With such analyses in mind, I shift the lens here to consider not how rural women have been affected by such systemic forces but to ask how their literacies might influence others in their own communities and beyond. In short: what opportunities for understanding and complicating rural literacies already exist in rural places?

There is much to learn from rural women about the ways literacy is produced and shared in a rural community. In my hometown of Paxton, Nebraska, for example, older women have used writing to create and sustain clubs ranging from the Garden Club to Friends of the Library, to historicize the town, to decide what books will be in the town library, and more. In performing these literate acts, they both provide important local resources and information for the town and model ways to sustain a rural place through creating and affirming social spaces. Within this local space, literacies are transgenerational, in which older women teach younger residents and vice versa, so social activities such as giving a lesson at the Garden Club become a space for meaning-making activities that can potentially give rise to sustaining the community. And yet the literate acts and documents from these women—conceived as "only" women's work—have not been valued as they could be (by the women themselves and by others) and thus not considered tools for a critical, public pedagogy toward sustainability.

Instead, dominant discourses on rural identity and education rely heavily on ideologies akin to male agrarianist scholarship originally inspired by Thomas Jefferson. The texture of rural women's lives and contributions to the social good of their communities are often less visible to outsiders because community work operates on microlevels and because it is unpaid labor—it is "women's work," the work of supporting the lives and actions of others. Yet it is the crucial work of cultural production and should be seen as an integral part of a critical, public pedagogy fostering literacies that connect the local, national, and global for a more synergistic relationship.

In the first section of this chapter, I examine the ways agrarianist scholarship and literature often reinforce masculinist narratives of rural life and overlook social realities in a community (even while the term "community" is ubiquitous in the scholarship), leading to depictions of rural life that are celebratory and preservationist in nature. To complicate such representations, I offer educational theorist David Gruenewald's "critical pedagogy of place" as an alternative to agrarianist discourses that dominate rural education. His term blends place-based education and critical pedagogy (usually focused on urban contexts, despite its Freirean influence) in order to address critically and comprehensively ecological, social, economic, and cultural issues that face rural areas. Using Gruenewald's critical pedagogy of place as a framework, I describe the rich, everyday literacy practices that demonstrate how Paxton women contribute to the sustenance of rural spaces. I posit that one way to achieve a critical pedagogy of place is to put their literacies in the context of public memory, described by Henry Giroux as "critically examining one's own historical location amid relations of power, privilege, or subordination ("Cultural Studies"

68). Through performing literacy work that both contributes to and disrupts public memory—compiling histories, writing memoirs, and working to preserve records and places—the Paxton women enact a multifaceted notion of rural literacy that has preservationist qualities but also gives an alternative understanding of rural community largely absent in much scholarship on rural life, providing tools to forward a critical pedagogy of place. In the final section, I explore how Paxton women's literacies, as well as two other sites of women's rural literacies, constitute a critical, public pedagogy.

### *Agrarianism and Rural Literacies*
### Understanding Agrarianism

Agrarianism, as I use it in this analysis, is defined by anthropologist Deborah Fink as "the belief in the moral and economic primacy of farming over other industry, rest[ing] firmly at the base of the collective U.S. ideological framework," which places the masculinist Jeffersonian agrarianist model at the center and does not make a space for the lives of women in agrarian settings (*Agrarian Women* 11). Unlike the alternative agrarian literacy laid out in chapter 3 that embraces complexities of agricultural realities and rural experiences, I refer here to agrarianism and the shortsighted ways that it can uncritically invoke the Jeffersonian legacy.[1] Literature and scholarship that employ agrarianist ideologies fit what Jacqueline Edmondson calls "traditional rural literacy" (15), which, as discussed in chapter 3, falls short of the increasingly complex realities of rural life.

Fink argues that the notion of agrarianism promoted by Jefferson relies on the assumption that agrarian culture is more noble or moral than urban culture but reminds the reader that "farmers are not closer to nature or more moral than any other people" (*Agrarian Women* 194). The legacy of agrarianism values working with the earth above other pursuits, particularly in the face of industry and technology. Much about the agrarianist model depends on a regional definition that provides a patriarchal history and description of farming and ranching in which women are seen merely as helpers to this lifestyle. Further, Fink argues, "[Jefferson's] agrarian vision hinged on the subordination of women," which she supports by citing numerous examples of his belief that women were to comfort and support men (19). With this ideology of superior morality of the male farmer, Jefferson believed that "women should keep house, soothe men when they came into the house, and not interfere in important male affairs" (195). As long as Jeffersonian ideologies are the foundation of well-known literature on rural areas and place, women's contributions will not be a significant part of the conversation. Further, descriptions of rural areas become focused solely on physical spaces and abstract, idyllic notions of community as the social realities are glossed over.

In the anthology *Rooted in the Land: Essays on Community and Place*, editors Wes Jackson and William Vitek include voices often anthologized in writing on place (Vitek, Jackson, Berry, Orr, Sanders); the pieces are by twenty-seven men and seven women, a signal to the ways in which this field is gendered. An excerpt from the introduction to *Rooted in the Land* illustrates how agrarianist ideals prevail: "Many of the contributors . . . share Jefferson's assumptions about agriculture, civic virtue, and the need for decentralized, interdependent community landscapes. In addition, much of the contemporary resurgence in community thinking has originated in the practice of agriculture, by those who have a working relationship with the land" (3). The word "community" is everywhere on the pages of essays arguing for a deep investment in one's place; yet these pieces offer little of the daily social lives in a small town and focus more on ecological issues connected to conservation of place. We aren't offered, for example, specifics of the goings-on in rural towns that actually show what makes and sustains a community. Social networks in rural areas are where a town's identity and culture thrive, not just within school walls but at the bank, grocery store, post office, and the like, and without any sense of these specifics, it is too easy to slip into representations of rural that are less realistic, both culturally and economically. Community is usually constructed in abstract ways that promote a rootedness in land and local ecological issues without describing specific details of social lives in communities apart from connections among those who work with the land. In the section on "Community Criteria," only one of the four male authors referred to an actual town event with characters. In these hazy or absent descriptions of community, the agrarianist ideology persists, implicitly reinforcing the assumption that living off the land is still as pervasive and viable in rural areas as it has always been and that community is sustained through individuals' relationships with the land instead of with each other.

It's no surprise that this version of rural land and community runs through these texts; after all, many contributors to *Rooted in the Land* revere authors like Aldo Leopold and Wendell Berry, who are viewed as forefathers on issues of place. When education theorist Paul Theobald defends in Jeffersonian style "the moral tie to the farming life" in his rural education work, he suggests Leopold and Berry—along with twelve other male writers—as part of the curriculum "for every rural child" (*Teaching the Commons* 87). No female agrarian writers are mentioned. Theobald entitled an ERIC Digest article "Rural Philosophy for Education: Wendell Berry's Tradition" and noted that the *New York Times* dubbed Berry the "prophet of rural America" (5). He argues that to "consider [Berry's] views of rural life and rural education" would greatly benefit rural spaces and schools who exacerbate rather than curb out-migration in rural towns (5). Berry has undoubtedly made significant contributions to agrarian thinking, but scholars fond of him often invoke his ideas with a less critical eye. While again there is much use of the word "community" in Berry's piece in *Rooted in the Land*, any identification with community seems tied to the land or agrarianist ideologies. When Berry outlines tasks for local community members to work toward if they want their community to cohere, he notes that the rules he uses are "derived from Western political and religious traditions, from the promptings of ecologists and certain agriculturists, and from common sense" (82). The actual kinds of community work being done by women are not part of Berry's consideration and in his rules would likely fall under common sense, seen as something obvious and requiring no skill. Masculinist philosophical and historical traditions inform not only his notions of community but also the notions of those who contribute to *Rooted in the Land*.

In her book *Agrarian Women*, Fink raises concerns with Berry's reliance on Jeffersonian agrarianism and the way sexism is reinforced through his agrarianist ideologies in his book *The Unsettling of America*:

> Berry's agrarianism was gendered, the major actors being male, and he tied his vision directly to the institution of marriage and to women's fertility. Berry considered marriage the primary connection among humans and agriculture the primary connection between humans and the earth. Sexuality, he argued, should not be separated from fertility; modern birth control technology destroyed the natural order and fostered sexual amorality. (193)

Fink further describes how a review of a 1980s novel of Berry's brought only slight admonishment for objectifying women, but "once again, the treatment of women was overlooked for the good of the farm" (194). Thus, not only are women rarely a part of meaning-making, at worst they are footnoted or reduced to biological definitions. Although these particular examples do not speak for Berry's views of women in his entire body of work, they do show that he places women's work and contributions to rural life in a gendered frame that limits an understanding of their full range of activities and contributions. While there is no doubt that many see Berry as a spokesman—if not *the* spokesman—for rural America, his work raises questions about how women's contributions to rural life can be understood and valued. His work exemplifies agrarianist literature.

## Place-Based Education and Agrarianism

Readers from a variety of contexts—citizens and educators interested in agrarian literature and environmental texts and rural educators whose mission it is to help others see the value of rural places—draw upon agrarianist literature. This is particularly so for rural revitalization efforts such as place-based education, a movement that puts one's local place at the core of learning in a range of disciplines. Place-based education is defined as "specific to the geography, ecology, sociology, politics, and other dynamics of [local] place[,] . . . inherently multi-disciplinary . . . [and] experiential[,] . . . reflective of an educational policy that is broader than 'learn to earn[,]' . . . and connects place with self and community" (Woodhouse and Knapp 4). Despite these extensive descriptors, the term is often interpreted literally and sometimes privileges ecological aspects of place and celebratory notions of community. Yet place-based education was largely borne out of the same motivation that led us to write this book: rural places and education are misunderstood or ignored altogether.

Primarily found in K–12 schools, place-based initiatives, programs, and scholarship are often at the forefront of movements focusing on rural education and revitalization. I describe this movement because it is where some of the most generative work on rural literacies is being done but also where agrarianist ideologies endure and where critical, public pedagogy efforts have yet to be fully actualized. The need for programs attentive to rural education issues has been highlighted by Paul Nachtigal, former director of the Annenberg Rural Challenge (a branch of a more comprehensive fund for education in the United States specifically dedicated to rural school reform), who explained in 1982 in *Rural Education: In Search of a Better Way*, "The commonly held view of professional leadership through the years depicts rural education as the poor country cousin of the public school system" (15). This country cousin status was amply illustrated in the pervasive assumptions between the 1860s through the 1970s that guided the thinking of rural education, which led to problematic notions and isolated outcomes, trends that accentuated a rhetoric of lack. All of these assumptions devalued the contexts and needs specific to each type of school, rural and urban, and reflected the ways that rural education was often read in response to urban education.

Those committed to rural education—to all education—began to search for ideas to revitalize rural towns, and several programs and initiatives across the United States were launched. In the state of Nebraska, for example, Paul Olson, native of the state and scholar from the University of Nebraska–Lincoln, convened a task force that "hoped to counter the attitude that a small-town existence is inferior to life in the big city," and with help from UNL, schools, agencies, and businesses, Nebraska's School at the Center began in 1992 (McGuire 1). The program "involves the entire state system in a comprehensive, long-term effort to support community-based education. Schools and communities from all over the state are working together to develop plans that include economic development (especially entrepreneurship), housing, community-based science, distance learning, and local heritage" (Annenberg Challenge).

As a former rural student, I've long been a proponent of these programs in my home state of Nebraska. Theorists and practitioners of place-based education promote worthwhile rural revitalization projects. However, within these efforts, some who employ agrarianist ideologies uncritically do not allow place-based education and the rural people it seeks to sustain the broadest and richest possibilities for a public pedagogy as a "critical practice designed to understand the social context of everyday life as lived relations of power" (Giroux, "Public Pedagogy as Cultural Politics" 355). If the intent of place-based education is largely focused on "celebrat[ing] community," the work of moving beyond preservationist tendencies of traditional rural literacy becomes even more difficult (Theobald, *Teaching the Commons* 123).

I am guilty of rendering my rural experience in only celebratory ways and sometimes recognize the tendency from other scholars who describe themselves as rural-identified. When I moved to Oregon for graduate school and faced more overtly the misperceptions and stereotypes of rural people and places, I developed a renewed interest in the landscape and people of Nebraska. After re-viewing and researching my home place, however, correcting others' false assumptions meant resisting what was negative about Nebraska and only honoring it instead. In reading literature on rural education, I found I fit a common narrative of people who have returned to their home place, whether literally, through their ideologies, or even through nostalgia. As I read through Robert Brooke's collection, *Rural Voices: Place-Conscious Education and the Teaching of Writing*, I found that some contributors' narratives have a similar trajectory to my own re-engagement with place. Those who teach in rural areas often left and returned, many times by circumstances rather than by choice, only to feel a renewed interest in their home place and to wonder why it seemed there was nothing there before. As contributor Carol MacDaniels writes, "The refrain is common: 'I never knew'" (157). Her words articulate my reaction when I re-engaged with my home place. People with rural identities who return to home communities literally or in their work feel that first and foremost they have to defend this place against the kind of stereotyping discussed in chapter 2. And in doing so, the preservation model can be useful, perhaps in part because nostalgia is a force in re-seeing one's rural place, in making the shift from abandonment to a defense of place.

While celebration, nostalgia, and preservation should certainly be valued and utilized aspects of rural literacies, their pervasiveness has limitations. In my case, they led to binary thinking—to go against negative stereotypes, I chose to be celebratory. Assisted by agrarianist literature that usually defines community in abstract ways, celebrating local place in uncritical ways risks becoming the end point in one's thinking rather than the beginning. The act of both celebrating and critiquing local place should be an integral component of a critical, public pedagogy that moves toward sustainability.

## Toward a Critical Pedagogy of Place

Gruenewald, in "The Best of Both Worlds: A Critical Pedagogy of Place," examines the ways place-based education and critical pedagogies could be well-served by more explicitly sharing theories and ideas, arguing that "if place-based education emphasizes ecological and rural contexts, critical pedagogy—in a near mirror image—emphasizes social and urban contexts and often neglects the ecological and rural scene entirely" (3). It's ironic, Gruenewald notes, that Freirean tenets of critical literacy have become so associated with urban contexts. Yet, "in its focus on local, ecological experience, place-based approaches are sometimes hesitant to link ecological themes with critical themes such as urbanization and the homogenization of culture under global capitalism" (4). There are signals that this is changing, exemplified by critical literacy scholars like Edmondson, but more work remains to be done by place-based educators and critical pedagogues alike to acknowledge the specific social and economic contexts of rural communities. While many place-based educators talk about local space in terms of community, "place" is most readily associated with the ecology, landscape, and (an often patriarchal) history of a rural area. Rarely is place conceived as a construct that allows for the critique of local-regional-national-global interconnections. Gruenewald offers what he calls a "critical pedagogy of place" that seeks to make more overt the ways place and critical, public pedagogies could be more conjoined:

> Place . . . foregrounds a narrative of local and regional politics that is attuned to the particularities of where people actually live, and that is connected to global development trends that impact local places. Articulating a critical pedagogy of place is thus a response against educational reform policies and practices that disregard places and that leave assumptions about the relationship between education and the politics of economic development unexamined. (3)

Gruenewald's call for a critical pedagogy of place is not dissimilar from Edmondson's alternative agrarian literacy; he argues "people must be challenged to reflect on their own concrete situationality in a way that explores the complex interrelationships between cultural and ecological environments" (6). Yet as agrarianist ideologies persist, specific social and cultural contexts are hard to come by in the scholarship on place that many rural educators are reading, even as community is a widespread term amid its pages.

Further, Gruenewald makes the distinction that "like critical pedagogues, place-based educators advocate for a pedagogy that relates directly to student experience of the world, and that improves the quality of life for people and communities. However, unlike critical pedagogues, not all place-based educators foreground the study of place as political praxis for social transformation" (7). In other words, critical tools are often not an integral part of some rural education programs, and thus the issues we've discussed throughout this book may continue, as "traditional rural literacy" is the dominant discourse in rural areas. But as Giroux explains: "Refusing to decouple politics from pedagogy means, in part, that teaching in classrooms or in any other public sphere should not only simply honor the experiences students bring to such sites, but should also connect their experiences to specific problems that emanate from the material contexts of their everyday lives" ("Public Pedagogy and the Politics of Neo-liberalism" 500).

Gruenewald puts forth two objectives for achieving a critical pedagogy of place—decolonization and reinhabitation—"for the purpose of linking school and place-based experience to the larger landscape of cultural and ecological politics" (9). Reinhabitation, from the ecological place-based perspective, is defined as "'learning to live-in-place in an area that has been disrupted and injured through past exploitation'" (Berg and Dasmann, qtd. in Gruenewald 9). Decolonization, "unlearning much of what dominant culture and schooling teaches," is a necessary part of reinhabitation when blending critical and place-based pedagogies: "If reinhabitation involves learning to live well socially and ecologically in places that have been disrupted and injured, decolonization involves learning to recognize disruption and injury and to address their causes" (9). Significantly, Gruenewald argues that the two concepts together recognize, rather than dismiss, various kinds of local knowledge: "As [C. A.] Bowers points out, decolonization as an act of resistance must not be limited to rejecting and transforming dominant ideas; it also depends on recovering and renewing traditional, noncommodified cultural patterns such as mentoring and intergenerational relationships" (9). Understanding literacies that illustrate how meaning-making occurs socially within a local culture, then, is a crucial part of a critical pedagogy of place that relies on the interdependence of decolonization and reinhabitation. Local literacies can be utilized not merely to celebrate and preserve a vision of the past that is out of step with current economic realities—though celebrating and preservation are a part of the work to be done, to be sure—but also for sustaining local place as well as for dissonance and critique that allow decolonization and reinhabitation to emerge.

One way to move toward this productive tension is to recast everyday literacies, such as local written histories (and those who produce them), not as relics but as a part of public memory. Giroux argues that a cultural studies lens analyzes public memory "not as a totalizing narrative but as a series of ruptures and displacements" ("Cultural Studies"

68). History, then, becomes "not an artifact to be merely transmitted, but an ongoing dialogue and struggle over the relationship between representation and agency" (68). Giroux's pedagogy of public memory, as described in chapter 2, is about "making connections that are often hidden, forgotten, or willfully ignored" and "in this sense becomes not an object of reverence but an ongoing subject of debate, dialogue and critical engagement" (68). In this way, local narratives are not static artifacts for preservation but openings for delving into questions of power and representation, beginning with whose voices are prevalent and whose are absent. The literacy work of women in one rural community—from their artifacts to the reciprocity of sponsorship they promote—becomes a site of inquiry rather than something ignored or exhibited. In the next section, I investigate the ways women in one rural community seek to describe and historicize the culture of their place through their literacy practices, illuminating the kinds of daily activities that should be conjoined with, rather than dismissed by, rural revitalization and advocacy efforts working toward a critical pedagogy of place. Following that, I show how their activities and work can be compared within and against public memory to help foster a critical, public pedagogy of place.

### Literacies of Rural Nebraska Women

In my western Nebraska hometown of Paxton, population around 600, literate acts abound. Literacies of older women in my hometown are largely informed by place—their identities as rural Nebraska women shape what they read and write in their lives and for the community.[2] The data I employ here come from a small sample—in this case, older white women in the Great Plains—in order to allow for a deep understanding of the context of rural life there and thus is limited. To put this sample within the demographics of the state, Nebraska is 89.6 percent white, followed by 5.5 percent Latino/a, 4 percent African American, 1.3 percent Asian, and .9 percent American Indian. In terms of age, Nebraska's population over age sixty-five is 13.4 percent, compared with the national average of 12.4 percent ("Nebraska Quick Facts"). The work of these women in a village in Nebraska is one example (though their work is not unlike that produced in Haines Gap) of the kinds of literacies that abound in a small town—literacies ignored because women's work is seen as quaint, ordinary, or apart from the masculinist, agrarianist mindset that influences rural ideologies. As with chapters 2 and 3, however, what is likely more generalizable are the ways we see the larger social and economic context influencing local spaces.

Between 1997 and 2000, I interviewed women between the ages of seventy-eight and one hundred, adult children of these women, and women in the community who worked closely with the older women in clubs. I learned that there is much literate work being done by older women in town that shapes the community in subtle and more obvious ways. This kind of work should be conjoined with rural revitalization efforts more overtly so that the women are more involved in meaning-making and acknowledged for their work in sustaining rural communities. In many ways, the goals of place-based educators and these women are not dissimilar: they both support revitalization of rural spaces. At worst, these older rural women are often narrowly viewed by both outsiders and insiders of their community as relics, largely as subjects to be interviewed about the "good ol' days." As I knew from living there and later uncovered through my qualitative research, the literate worlds of these women are far richer: for example, the women serve as a different kind of sponsor than do outsiders, working to benefit the community but also benefiting themselves in some way, gaining a kind of power in providing historical and community information to the town. I demonstrate in the following descriptions how Paxton women employ a strong sense of place and loyalty to place through socially based literacies that reconsider public memory and complicate (even as they often adhere to) masculinist thinking, as well as the ways this work can contribute to decolonization and reinhabitation necessary for a critical pedagogy of place.

Paxton is found along Interstate 80 at the edges of the Sandhills—20,000 square miles of dune-shaped hills covered with stubby grass that is a lush green only in the spring and considered some of the best cattle-grazing land in the world. Nearly any stranger who passes by the town approaches from the interstate; from either the east or west, there is no other exit for twelve miles. A traveler sees that farm or ranch land surrounds the town, and it might give the impression that the landscape is all anyone can think about in this village with just two downtown blocks. Paxton fits the rural cliché, having just gotten a blinking red stoplight in the mid-1990s. Trains frequently pass through along the railroad on the southern edge of town, which, in fact, began as a depot station in 1867. Paxton's claim to fame is its watering hole, Ole's Big Game Bar and Grill, mentioned in *Sports Illustrated* in the last decade as a place to see (which I still can't help but mention, as this national nod felt significant). Ole, now deceased, opened the bar on the midnight that Prohibition ended in 1933. Having shot big game on five of seven continents, his trophies decorate the bar—from an elephant to a giraffe to a giant polar bear encased in glass right inside the front door. Once a dim and smoky local favorite attracting travelers who'd heard of it by word of mouth, the bar was sold to a local entrepreneur who now owns the other bar in town and a Days Inn and convenience store by the interstate exit. The air in the bar is cleaner than it used to be, and tour buses often stop on their way to or from a destination for Nebraska beef or Rocky Mountain oysters.

That's what the traveler sees, and the owner of Ole's has capitalized well on travelers' assumptions when they stop. But moving to this small town with a family whose income did not come from farming or ranching instantly disrupted what I imagined as rural when I arrived at age eleven. Naturally in the early 1980s, agriculture was at the heart of the town's identity, but because I lived within two blocks of the grocery store, bank, Methodist church, two bars, and one of the town's larger employers, a manufacturer of slotted pipe, rural was hardly synonymous with isolation. (In fact, the 2000 census indicates that the population of Paxton rose since 1990, an accomplishment for a rural town on the plains.) And while the stereotypical farmers in seed caps were found drinking coffee at Swede's Café every morning, it was the activities of women in town that were omnipresent. Women in my hometown were bank tellers, bartenders, librarians, teachers, lawyers, secretaries, stay-at-home moms, hairdressers, and postal workers, and the largest contingent was retired, like my grandma and much of the congregations at the three churches in town.

The various literacy practices and artifacts created by these women could be found all over town as well. They composed articles for local newspapers and wrote histories of the library, cemetery, churches, and local clubs as well as created family histories and genealogies. They beautified the town through the Garden Club and administered the Yard of the Week. The library board and Friends of the Library did much of the work to complete the new library from money left by a former resident. They led Sunday school, taught in the consolidated school, and ran clubs such as the Just-for-Fun Club. For these women, the local was the center: making sure children and grandchildren valued their home place was important, as was presenting Paxton in positive ways for the many tourists dining at Ole's. Because the women enacting these literacies were older and took on the patriarchal agrarianist ideologies more obviously than they subverted them, it was often assumed they were simply replicating a way of life that reinscribes narrow roles for women and relying on preservationist narratives. To some extent, that plays out, though growing up I observed many women who were not naive about the rural economy and who believed that moving forward with education, technological resources, and the like was good for the town, and as I demonstrate, the work they did and still do is meant to move the community forward, not leave it fixed in the past.

Fae Christensen was likely the most prolific of the older women I interviewed, but her endeavors typify the kinds of literacy work undertaken by older women in Paxton that are an example of reinhabitation, or social activities that lead toward sustainability. Born in 1916, Fae has lived in or around Paxton since she was six months old. She went to a country school that went through the tenth grade and graduated in 1933. At the peak of the Depression, she stayed home and worked for a year before attending college in Lincoln, where she studied for a nursing degree. During some time off, she met her husband, Orvel, at a dance in North Platte, half an hour from Paxton. She then worked on the farm while raising three kids, leading the 4-H Club, and staying active in the North River Extension Club. Later, she returned to school for her teaching degree, telling me that she became interested after teaching Sunday school and realizing that they needed the money with two kids in college. During those years between schooling, she said,

"I think in the back of my mind was always the dream of finishing college; literally, I dreamt I was in my cap and gown being up there." With her three years of college credit she had earned before she was married, she finished within one year (though she had to live away from home in Kearney, two hours east) and began teaching third grade in Paxton in her late forties, retiring twenty years later in 1985. By this time, she and her husband lived in town just down the street from the swimming pool and park, and her community participation increased even more after retirement.

In the name of faith, family, and community, Fae is an incredible literacy contributor to the town and her family. Her work includes, but is not limited to, putting the cemetery in order, writing town histories for the local library, and doing extensive volunteer work for the church (writing newsletters and sending cards to shut-ins) and various clubs and services of the community, such as the Just-for-Fun Club and Meals on Wheels, and annually since 1953 she's typed a Christmas letter detailing events of the year. Her work at the cemetery near the Interstate 80 interchange has been her most visible contribution to the town. Fae informed her husband that when she quit teaching third grade, she would organize the cemetery records, motivated by the following episode, best told in her own words transcribed from our 1997 interview at her kitchen table:

> It was when Orvel was mayor of the town. I was still teaching at that time but getting along towards retirement, and there was a gal from Minnesota had dropped down some flowers. Her mother had given them to her and said, "When you get to Paxton, I want you to stop and put these on my sister's grave." And she couldn't find the gravesite. So she came to the mayor of the town, and he goes out and the two of them couldn't find the gravesite. And it got dark and they ended up with a flashlight and still couldn't find the gravesite, and that was when I saw the deplorable condition of our cemetery records.

Fae went on to describe the amount of work it took to single-handedly research over one hundred unmarked graves in the cemetery:

I went out there and worked it all summer long, and I'd find markers made with pieces of broken glass, old railroad spikes five inches long, barbed wire. I guess it hadn't been done because once in a while there's lots where they put little cement—they called them aprons. They were perfectly located. I learned that I could start from there and measure and identify and label all the others. But there was over 100 people buried out there that were not on our records.

After our conversation, Fae took me downstairs to show me the extensive records she had put together, all stored in her basement. For each member of the cemetery (which, she noted in the town history, was about the same number as those who have graduated from the school in town), Fae used a form she created in order to document information about the deceased, including a mini-biography of the person's life ("How Old" 10). The form, entitled "Cemetery Record of Paxton Resident from Here to Eternity," states, "It is the writer's fondest dream that these records will be an on-going event and 100 years hence when we are all just a memory, folk will still be keeping this book updated," making clear the historical purpose Fae finds in keeping not only records but, when possible, brief narratives that provide insight into the lived experiences—insight that non-locals or younger residents would not otherwise be privy to—of those buried at the Paxton Cemetery (2).

She catalogued not only the Paxton Cemetery but also other cemeteries in that district, such as the Glen Echo and Pickard cemeteries, as well as a private plot, supplemented with these forms. She told me of the work involved in surveying the Pickard cemetery: "But here again that map has been lost, totally lost, we can't find it anywhere. So I went out there and started measuring and creating a map just from the existing stones. And one stone was close to the trunk of an old, old tree and the only way I could get writing off of that was to get on my belly." In addition to the artifacts themselves—map directories, forms, and more—the rendering of that research and work allows her to incorporate religious messages, recasting that work as more of a mission or service than a job, allowing her to negotiate her role in an agrarianist setting. Her authority as messenger enables her to better navigate, for example, a cemetery board comprised of all males. Her endeavors do more than honor the deceased—and in fact I believe it is those in the present and future Fae is so mindful of when doing her cemetery work—and thus can be recognized as reinhabitation. Genealogists from states as far away as California have contacted or been referred to Fae to find their relatives, and some make the trek to visit their dead. Fae also has a desire to ensure that this information is documented so that the cemetery space does not become a relic but a resource for residents and outsiders (genealogy being a motivation for people to travel to rural communities such as Paxton).

During our conversation, Fae told me that her writings include "church writings," especially for "people in the region who have been traumatized in the past week. Birth, death, wedding, hospitalization—I probably average four or five of those a week." Each week she also sends out a letter to around thirteen people, such as family and pen pals from over the years. After our interview, she sent me a personal letter and enclosed a sampling of correspondence to other Paxtonites who were hospitalized or in nursing homes and a copy of her weekly letter, labeled with the date, time, and the amount of rain and titled, "A Crisis Day!" The single-spaced page was a detailed scene of Orvel's low blood pressure and a trip to the nearest town with a hospital (twenty miles west) for a blood test, a listing of the deaths of the week (acknowledging their move to the "Silent City" south of town), and a request for advice from her kids. In addition, Fae composes the *Paxton Senior Citizen News*, noting accidents, illnesses, deaths, and celebrations and reminding seniors about lunches offered downtown every weekday. Of the death of a beloved town member, she writes, "Pneumonia proved her nemesis. In one brief week it did what 53 years of polio could never accomplish and she traded in her [wheelchair] for a pair of wings." In marking and sharing the events of the town, Fae's writings document the daily, lived experiences within Paxton, particularly for seniors, and show how she refuses to view the work of older generations as unimportant to the town's livelihood. It seems that her goal is to buoy the older residents by allowing them to be in the know about town events. Through allowing for this sense of connection among residents who are likely housebound, she seeks to sustain a part of the community.

For the Lutheran church and the town library, she submitted local histories largely culled from area newspapers. It was from Fae's library histories that I learned about the founder of the town (Edward Searle, an eighteen-year-old telegraph operator for the Union Pacific railroad; his namesake was the first white child born in the county), and it is from Fae's perspective that the history of settlement of the West, at least pertaining to the southwest part of Nebraska, is rendered. She editorializes, noting for November 27, 1897: "First burial in Paxton Cemetery . . . was the infant daughter of Simon Stowell (the story of her death is in the cemetery genealogies—very tragic!). Simon was also instrumental in moving burials from outlying areas into the official cemetery, an astronomical task" ("How Old" 7). A historical document such as this invites exploration: What do her editorial choices suggest about the kind of history she hopes to pass on? What is the significance of reading a history that includes such details that couldn't be known by outsiders? Is it a way of keeping outsiders out or of inviting them in? In what way does her editorializing help others see local details that have not been a part of public memory? In what way does it mark her authority as a historian?

This work by Fae is just one example of literacies produced in town. Older women's contributions involved history, genealogy, botany, and more, all pervaded with a sense of place. For years now, Mona has invited school-aged children to come out to her ranch where she shares with them her extensive collection of native grasses.[3] When I spoke with Mona in her living room with the large picture window overlooking the Sandhills as our backdrop, I was fortunate enough to see the entire collection of native Sandhills specimens—dozens and dozens of them—carefully attached to construction paper as Mona explained where she gathered each particular stem. In sharing with future generations her intimate and lifelong ecological knowledge, she is participating in reinhabitation.

Mona has also produced a thick book for relatives, in which she has culled various published histories of the Sandhills and local counties with genealogical histories and photographs, and when we spoke in 1999, she was taking notes for follow-up texts called *Sandhills Saga* and *Beyond Tomorrow* that are also set in the area in which she has spent her life. My cousin Liza, also a Paxton resident, has traveled across the country to conduct genealogical research and in the last decade has made efforts to stay on top of this work through becoming more technologically skilled, purchasing a computer to contact relatives via e-mail and search records on the Internet. Another woman, Cathy, a retired nurse and president of the Garden Club in town, has gone on trips to photograph wildflowers and then prepared slides and talks to share with her club and other clubs. Each of these women in her own way has produced and disseminated her knowledge of local place in an effort to teach others about the people and environment of her home place.

Housed in the new library downtown (built from fund-raising and a large donation from a former female resident) is one of the richest literacy artifacts: an anthology entitled *Early Paxton*, a collection of memories of Paxton by those born before 1925. The editor, Joyce Lierley, who later published a book of family letters from the Civil War, contacted women (and a few men) in town and asked them to contribute to the book of memoirs. Twenty-nine women and four men submitted manuscripts: some wrote brief biographies that read more like a genealogy listing, and others shared stories and memories. In this leather-bound three-ring notebook (done purposely by Joyce so others could add their stories if they desired), readers can learn about daily life in Paxton. My grandma, Dorlis Osborn Hogg—whose piece is the lengthiest at forty-four pages—describes school days:

> It was at this time that we had a man teacher, my first and only one while in grade school. The poor fellow was small, crippled, and looking back I believe he had suffered a stroke, as one side of his mouth sagged and saliva trickled from that side. . . . This was also my first experience with male chauvinism. . . . One of the boys forced some improper advance toward my sister and she proceeded to rough him up a bit. The teacher punished my sister and the boy came off scot-free. (73)

Not only does she describe the sexism she witnessed, my grandma acknowledges the incident as such, complicating the assumptions some might make of the one-room school experience as quaint and idyllic. She disrupts public memory, marking what is "willfully ignored" in romanticizing the rural past (Giroux, "Cultural Studies" 68).

Other observations describe how national events like the Depression and World War II were experienced through the daily lives of these rural women. My grandma describes making bread without shortening while rationing during the war. Not seeing any shortening on the shelves, "I started to search the shelves thinking I might find some fish packed in oil," only to later learn that the clerk was hiding it from another customer in the store who hoarded lard (101). In these descriptions and stories, the authors call attention to the everyday social realities—particularly gendered realities, such as domestic life—that have been unseen or dismissed in agrarianist literature and in public memory. In creating these narratives at all, the women assert the authority of their lived experiences; they deem themselves responsible for sharing histories of their local place and for shaping a local public memory. Despite the messages they had received all of their lives—my grandma told me in her late eighties that she thought the histories she read when she was younger seemed to be only about the kind of people who wrote them (read: white males)—these women made the assumption that what they had to say was interesting or useful and enacted the assumption through their writing.

*Early Paxton*, as is obvious from its title, focuses on the history of the families and the town and in that respect does not challenge the stereotype that rural spaces and people long for the past, and certainly many of the pieces are rife with nostalgia with the writers explaining that they weren't bored in their youth, like kids are today, since back then they had plenty of box suppers, spelling bees, and traveling shows. Many of the texts do not surprise, but some memoirs resist sentimentalizing, as the school example above illustrates, and as does one woman's description of how much she dreaded coming to live in Paxton, challenging the idealism of heading West. Elsie Holmstedt Windels, my grandparents' neighbor for years, does not call up a rosy past: "Sounds like the family was a perfect one. Indeed not. There were arguments when it seemed someone would be murdered. There were fights. fist fights, cob fights, and even rotten egg fights when available" (229). Many women describe the grief of and adjustment to their husbands' deaths. Rosa Reitz, a fixture from the Lutheran church, writes about the death of her husband and the life-changing events that followed: "The herd of Herefords was sold, then all the farm equipment. I had to learn to cope with financial problems. I was fortunate to find a helpful attorney and C.P.A." (175). The nuances of individual narratives can challenge easy conclusions about rural womanhood and rural life through descriptions resisting stereotypes of women as quiet agrarianist helpmates or unassuming little old ladies. In complicating and revising public memory through this specificity, the narratives on a small scale participate in decolonization by providing realities different from dominant messages of this time and place.

In addition to their extensive writing, the women in my study are a strong social presence in the community, from school to church to library to grocery store to clubs that directly affect the community, such as the Garden Club. In the process, they nourish a kind of reciprocal sponsorship in which town members seem to take on literacies that benefit individuals mutually. This move is not unlike mutual identification, described in chapter 3, though it happens on microlevels, in which individuals support each other's common interests through their literacy endeavors. Thus, they participate in an act of decolonization that Bowers describes as reclaiming "noncommodified cultural patterns" that focus on relationships across generations (Gruenewald 9). My dad, for instance, has placed Fae's cemetery records on a Web site so that others in search of genealogical materials can find them. My mom, who knew our friend Gerta was missing her native German language in the nursing home, visited and asked her to help translate the carols from a Christmas German service. Fae wrote to my grandma in the nursing home, putting notes in the margins for me, as she knew that I was one of the persons who read mail to her. She explained that she wanted to help me with my research. She also contacted me to let me know that Mona would be a great person to talk to for my research (she was right). I came to understand, as I interviewed women in my hometown, that there was a literacy synergy among us. I knew most of these women, and all of them knew my grandma, and it became clear that they felt a kind of claim upon my literacy skills. One woman from my study, Janice, in her mid-fifties and deeply involved in volunteer work at the school, the Catholic church, the library, and nursing homes, told me:

> Today [when you visited the book club] they were all so glad to see you, because you're one of ours. I think of Hillary's little village raising a child. You are what you are because you came from Paxton. . . . I don't think that's bad. [We] take pride in what our kids are doing . . . because if you went out and murdered somebody we'd feel terrible. We'd take part of the blame for that too. We may not admit it, but deep down we would feel bad.

It mattered to these women if I wrote, and not merely because I wrote about Paxton but because I was from there. Below I detail the reciprocity among us:

> I was invited to speak at the Paxton Book Club in the summer of 2000. In 1999 I sat in on one of their meetings; they were reading the Mitford series by Jan Karon. The book club has been going only for a few years; most of the members are parents of my high school classmates, former teachers, women I knew from church, as well as the librarian and the Methodist minister's wife. In the past they've gone to nursing homes to read to women like my grandma and Gerta—women they were in clubs with and who, I suspect, would be in the book club were they able. I was invited to their book club the second time as a guest speaker and author [rather than as researcher]. We met in the Paxton Library, a circle of chairs filling all the floor space in the adult fiction section. There was a table in our circle with brownies, lemon bars, and iced tea. Some women brought extra folding chairs; they'd invited friends who were not in the book club to attend, and thirteen women—some of whom I've interviewed—were there.

They wanted to know about my research, my writing life, my writing. I read to them from short stories and essays, passed around journals with my published essays, shared with them my rejection letters from various literary journals, and told them some of the ideas from my research in Paxton. Joyce asked what I wanted to do with my degree. They listened as I told them my plans. (Hogg 128)

In this activity, we shared meaning-making and talked about ourselves as readers, writers, and Paxtonites. They corrected some information I read to them. Growing up rural and being sponsored by these women—learning to see my home place differently than the messages from outsiders communicated—complicated public memory and life in that space.

Together, these women for years have been researching, creating, and sharing literacies at the local level, not unlike what is being called for by scholars of rural education. What's different is that the focus is more on the social realities; the daily or "ordinary" is foregrounded.[4] Much of what motivated (and still motivates) their work was a hope to teach others a local history of the town. Engaging with such texts, rather than assuming that they can only be read as quaint or sentimental because of the authors' positionality as rural, older women, allows readers to see how rural ideologies are inscribed and shared locally. While this alone would not be an obvious enactment of a critical pedagogy of place—we don't see within these histories a dismantling of dominant ideologies—their texts and literacy activities demonstrate a more nuanced understanding of rural women and literacies that offer a different way of knowing from what the dominant culture offers, hence exemplifying the kind of decolonization Bowers articulates. Reinhabitation occurs in their efforts toward sustaining the town through social endeavors that seek to keep the town moving forward.

Employing alternative rural literacies instead of the Jeffersonian agrarianist model can create productive tension for celebrating and critiquing rural places and complicating public memory, allowing the decolonization and reinhabitation components necessary to a critical pedagogy of place to emerge. In 1973, my grandma wrote a brief biography as a nominee for Keith County Centennial Queen that was distributed in a booklet about all contestants. Her conclusion explains: "Her hard-working law abiding ancestors who came to Keith County in their covered wagons with visions of the good life in Nebraska have left her a heritage of which she is proud. By her life she prays that she may pass that same heritage on to her children and grandchildren" ("Dorlis Osborn Hogg"). While the comment by my grandma is emotionally very meaningful to me, that doesn't mean I subscribe to the same ideologies of my home place that she did. While pride best articulates her feeling for Paxton, I am both proud of and uncomfortable with aspects of my hometown. Regarding the latter, for example: the images of covered wagons that she values so highly bring to my mind the relocation and genocide of American Indians from the area that is now Nebraska, and so my reaction to the images is not the same as hers. These women are largely uncritical of the dominant ideologies and histories surrounding their home place, and that point alone invites inquiry. On the one hand, then, it can be said that the women in Paxton contribute to the preservationist model we've described earlier: through rendering the past in their writing, through being motivated by wanting to share their lived history with the community and then rendering that past in their writing projects, and even through being viewed as historical resources to others.

Yet, as we argue elsewhere in this text, these historically based activities are not meant to preserve the past in a passive and fixed manner but as a source for current community work that embodies reinhabitation. The town is not static for them, and they are not wishing for a return to 1940s Paxton; in fact, witnessing change is something they do with pride, and helping the town move forward is a job they have taken up, which comes out also in suggestive ways: the fact that my grandma would often fight for newer books in the library, for example, or their eagerness to build a new library and tear the old one down.

It is perhaps more in how they treated their home place and the people in it than the actual literacy documents themselves that counteracted the many messages about my hometown I received from outsiders. While these women celebrate and romanticize the past, for many of them, their literacy work that came later in life is deeply fulfilling; thus, it is the act of historicizing that highlights the kind of work not recognized by agrarianist literature. The act of historicizing, a form of reinhabitation, also allows these women to affirm and build social relationships in the present as they share their work in clubs and other town activities. What's more, historicizing is only one part of their literacy achievements: they produce extension club and Garden Club lessons, create family memoirs, plan funerals, write newsletters for the church, send letters to those who are homebound or in nursing homes, and select the books and materials the library obtains, giving a texture to the town and making space for learning and socializing in ways that enliven, not fossilize, the town.

However, in a rural setting dominated by the views of outsiders like the media, the social, literate work of women—particularly older women—is deemed negligible by those who subscribe to the view of rural women as helpmates, as unpaid labor in a world where men's paid labor is paramount in the construction of the agrarianist identities prominent in place-based literature. Again, Fink puts these gendered economic issues into context. In her first book on rural women in 1986, her premise is that "the material reality of women in a small, rural community is significant. These [rural Iowa] women struggled to make a living and to create links with each other in order to have some control over their world" (*Open Country* 3). Surveying women pre– and post–World War II, she charts the ways women moved from working for the family business to working outside the home, often commuting to factories in nearby larger towns. More broadly, Fink crystallizes how gender affects material conditions, particularly in rural areas: "Researchers who have examined rural development in diverse settings have asserted that women have shouldered extra burdens with development and that women have not realized the primary benefits of development" (4).

What exacerbates this issue is that rural development in the United States "has been used in many ways as a model for development programs around the word, [thus] this assessment of the benefits and losses experienced by women contributes to an evolving understanding of the human factors in technological and economic change" (Fink, *Open Country* 4). Fink goes on to describe the ways the patriarchal structure of rural spaces allowed men to own the land and control the jobs that paid living wages. Nowhere is this clearer than in her most recent book, *Cutting into the Meatpacking Line*, which highlights the material realities of rural life and challenges stereotypes of rural women as only white women who "help" on the family farm, stereotypes that, as described in chapter 3, pervade the media. Fink worked for four months at an IBP pork-packing plant and writes about the rural working class in the 1990s, describing the sexual harassment, sexism, racism, and workers struggling to make a living wage.

Traditional rural literacies usually don't represent the working class, at least by rural standards (meaning, what was middle class in my hometown sometimes resembled, demographically, working class in other places).[5] The women in my study often put together a patchwork of income when necessary (such as employment at the grocery store or telephone company) during their working years, but if they could work at home on the farm and with the children, they chose (perhaps with societal pressure) to do so. Much of the literate work I describe in regard to them took place in post-retirement years, but the women were still conducting these activities in this same patriarchal and agrarianist environment. Further, retired women, women who were or had been stay-at-home moms, or teachers who had the summer off made up a majority of groups like the Paxton Book Club and Friends of the Library (and, for that matter, membership often overlapped between these two groups), and thus the voices of working rural women, a demographic steadily rising, is not accurately represented. What power they felt in the community was provided to them by these literate activities, though that power was limited in that they didn't work to significantly alter their agrarianist environment. The information they gave to the town through their work for the newspaper, library, clubs, and churches was used and appreciated by the town, but the women did not receive a wage for this work.

Insiders often are complicit in the behavior of devaluing literacy work, particularly since "agrarianism was a filter through which [rural] white women interpreted their lives" (Fink, *Agrarian Women* 12). What's more, Fink reminds us that rural women usually concur in the agrarianist thinking in assuming the men's lives have greater importance, all the more reason to work toward a critical pedagogy of place (*Open Country* 8). Complicating agrarianist thinking begins with seeing and valuing the literacy contributions of rural women; that work must be a more active part of a broader conversation leading to a critical pedagogy of place. And this work need not be done at the cost of important work by agrarian scholars but rather under the assumption that both the ecological and the social are important to sustaining rural life and should be put into dialogue. In the final section of this chapter, I consider gendered possibilities for a critical pedagogy of place; specifically, I offer Paxton women's literacy work as an opportunity for investigating how local knowledge is shaped, disseminated, and utilized as well as describe two sites of rural women's literacy—one in North Dakota, one an on-line community—striving to enact a critical, public pedagogy.

### Toward a Critical Pedagogy of Place

Imagine if the work of the Paxton women could be seen to forward decolonization and reinhabitation instead of as static historical documents used, if at all, merely to see how people lived in the past on the plains. Fae's local history, not even twenty pages long, mentioned earlier, is also a site of inquiry about who tells history, how it is shaped, and what choices are made in rendering such a document. What if students, college or K–12, instead of asking Fae about the good old days, asked how she learned the history, what kind of research she conducted, and how she made the editorial choices she did in terms of selection? What if Fae's history was regarded as a product of complex and deliberate decisions influenced by her place-based positionality?

Putting Fae's history within the contexts of other histories could also invite scrutiny, for instance, if her history was read against a history book published when she was a student and one published currently: where would there be connections and where would there be dissonances? A similar example of this kind of reading demonstrates the opportunities for such scrutiny. I recall researching water issues around Paxton, searching on-line to find the history of various dam projects, and coming across the Central Nebraska Public Power and Irrigation District (CNPPID) Web site that provided a thumbnail history of the south-central part of the state. Just a few days before, I'd read *The Plains Indians* by Paul H. Carlson, and I noted the stark contrast between the ways Native conflicts were framed by Carlson and by the CNPPID, for instance, the 1854 skirmish termed "the Grattan affair" by Carlson and the "Grattan Massacre" by the CNPPID site (Carlson 143; "Brief History"). The latter describes a cow stolen from a Mormon camp that was "killed and butchered," whereas the former says a young Miniconjou Lakota "shot a lame cow" ("Brief History"; Carlson 143). The history text says that Lieutenant Grattan became "impatient" and "ordered his men to fire" (Carlson 143). Grattan opened fire, according to the Web site, "in what might be termed an ill-advised over-reaction" ("Brief History"). These disparate renderings of the same event are ripe for the kind of rhetorical analysis Giroux says can raise issues of power and privilege when treating a historical text as public memory. What was at stake for the authors of each project, and how does their positionality mold their texts? How might an examination of these two texts speak to and against local texts produced by women like Fae who live near the CNPPID? What is significant about the absences in any and all of the texts? This kind of local analysis gives students opportunities to see how public memory is constructed.

The *Early Paxton* narratives could also serve as exploratory sites to complicate the agrarianist mindset, perhaps coupled with and against published texts by writers like Berry and Theobald as well as women writers of the plains and West. Writers who offer an alternative to the traditional masculinist lifestyle include women writers such as Mary Clearman Blew, Elizabeth Cook-Lynn, and Linda Hasselstrom, to name only a few. As Krista Comer clarifies regarding Blew's memoir, *All but the Waltz,* "She implicitly forwards an alternative narrative of the nation, secured far less by western landscape than is that of cow-

boy mythology and culture. In Blew's family, this alternative program
is associated with 'women's values,' which means both community
but also education" (230). Blew grapples with contradiction without
sentimentality, acknowledging deep commitment and love of place
while exploring its realities and problems, displaying a tension that
endorses a critical pedagogy of place. How might her texts speak to
Berry's and *Early Paxton* memoirs? Where do they fill in each other's
gaps, and where do they deviate?

In short: how does putting "ordinary," local women's writing in
conversation with and against more established authors allow them
each to be read against the grain? Instead of assuming that "ordinary"
women's literacies must be less than that of other writers, consider
whether a literary lens is the only way to see these texts, which is often
how ordinary writing is relegated in comparison to published texts. As
Jennifer Sinor explains, reading women's diaries with a literary lens
is to view them one way that "has been shaped historically by certain
assumptions and expectations about what is waiting to be seen at the
other end of the lens" (33). It's just as important to see what is missing
in the local narratives as well. In what ways do they inscribe dominant
ideologies generally and particularly about western Nebraska and
the plains? How do we know this from the context surrounding the
various published and local texts?

Of course, a challenge with critical pedagogies is in contesting
dominant ideologies and the ways they pervade mainstream culture.
I once sat in on a Rural Institute in Nebraska, a writing project class
comprised of women teachers and community members ranging in age
from their forties to their sixties. At times, agrarianist ideologies persisted
in our discussions. On the day I did my teaching lesson, I described
a lesson plan involving reading aloud brief passages from *Leaning into
the Wind*, an anthology of Western women writers, and then having
first-year college students discuss and write about their perceptions of
rural women within and against the reading. In the one-page summary
handout, I posed questions to my peers at the institute, such as

• How do you think others perceive rural women? What are
  the positive and negative connotations with this role?

- What are the ways that your activities affect the community (through children, grandchildren, other community members)?
- How were you shaped/influenced by a rural woman?

After I finished, one teacher commented that she was very impressed with the way I had talked about rural women and their contributions without sounding feminist. She said she was more open to receiving what I had to say about rural women because I didn't seem to have a certain political agenda. Of course, I did have an agenda, as does everyone who makes a claim, but it was not the one she was prepared to resist—I was both celebrating and critiquing my home place and its traditions in the discussion. I offer this anecdote as an example of an attempt I've made to reframe women's writings as a point of departure for critical inquiry; the response I received suggests to me that my audience appeared receptive to my framing of rural women's literacies in an unexpected way, one that, had I approached the conversation differently, could have seemed threatening to certain beliefs.

In working to help residents, teachers, and students in rural areas see the value of their places, interrogating rural life can at first feel counterintuitive. Even with assistance from scholarship and activities that challenge decades of negative stereotyping, recognizing aspects of rural life to celebrate is sometimes no small feat. But in my research, I noticed a contradiction: at the same time people knew the seriousness of economic issues—they were living it—there wasn't much conversation on how to engage in these issues. Acknowledging and incorporating women's literacy contributions to interrogate public memory reframes these literacies as tools for decolonization.

In other rural contexts, there are women probing social and economic realities in ways that more overtly suggest the traits of decolonization and reinhabitation integral to a critical pedagogy of place. Lisa Swanson Faleide's work embodies these goals as she seeks to amplify opportunities for rural women; in thinking about public dimensions of literacy in her rural space, she imagines possibilities for a critical, public pedagogy fostering change. Faleide, raised in a North Dakota town of 500 people, actively strives to create support networks throughout the state for individuals with similar hopes for change. For example, she has formed an on-line "compañera circle," consisting of a handful of women who research women's studies, rural issues, and writing and operate throughout the state as educators and activists. From e-mails and a phone conversation, I learned Faleide plans to open a Prairie Commons Center for women in her hometown and potentially beyond. While her plans for the center have yet to be realized and at this point are somewhat nebulous, her narrative describing the kind of center she envisions keenly emphasizes the neglected importance of the social in rural sustenance:

> The Social Enterprise is an additional category of development—largely on the fringes of our awareness—that is currently pressing for recognition as a viable and necessary complement to existing development endeavors.
>
> Prairie Commons Center for Women seeks to be just such a social enterprise, one that will make the needs and capacities of rural women part of the cultural consciousness in a way that supports rural women's desire for access to opportunities. (1)

Her rationale for Prairie Commons includes education, quality of life—where women have a space not connected to commerce and other demands—and strengthening relationships with women that become the "force for positive change" in the community, forwarding leadership, empowerment, and advocacy networks

- that support economic empowerment and help establish local alternative economic systems through time dollar networks, bartering, informal economic support groups and establishment of a micro-enterprise/micro-lending group;
- that bring together small groups of women with like interests but who may not be connected through usual peer networks;
- that connect women to each other who would like to advocate for a particular issue or needed service but don't belong

to a group with the critical mass (or desire) to unite behind
an advocacy effort; and,

- that help women to become more fully themselves through
the sharing of information and mutual support. (2)

Faleide imagines modeling Prairie Commons as a cooperative as
that term was formerly conceived, in which farmers' union organizations used to be local (and have since become countywide and involve
more bureaucracy and larger corporations). Her ideas for programming
and curriculum include but are not limited to "developing websites,"
"research[ing] and develop[ing] alternative economic systems," and
creating a "rural women's micro-lending group" (3, 4).

Faleide, in short, seeks to create a space where both interrogation
and celebration of rural life with a particular focus on women's issues
can occur. She is similar to the Paxton women in that she seeks to
sustain her community mainly through educational means but differs in that her perspectives and resources for doing this work are
influenced largely from studying rurality and gender, and thus she is
engaging in the process of decolonization in challenging dominant
ideologies. And Prairie Commons embodies reinhabitation, creating an active space for social, economic, and ecological education
for sustainability. Faleide's enactment of a critical pedagogy of place
goes beyond the classroom to "link teaching and learning to social
empowerment," exemplifying a critical, public pedagogy we've argued
for in this book (Edmondson 33).

More realized and extensive than Faleide's Prairie Commons Center, the Rural Womyn Zone (RWZ) is a technological network that
seeks to critically educate rural women. The RWZ describes itself as
a "a grassroots international network of rural women which started
using the Internet in 1997 to provide information, outreach, support
and a networking base for rural women and their nonprofit organizations and grass roots activities" ("First Chance Project"). The RWZ
also seeks to "publish news and information for rural women and by
rural women" and help rural women utilize technology, make connections with other rural women, and access news and other resources.
Through providing access to resources that would take rural women

hours to amass on their own, the RWZ demonstrates one way technology can endorse and support literacy and education and be a critical, public pedagogy of place. Despite the expense and unavailability of Internet technology, particularly high-speed access, for some rural citizens, the site explains its intention as an on-line space to gather:

> One challenge faced by scholars involves how to avoid colonizing the voices of rural women, and how instead to seriously face and understand the different contexts of rural women's lives. . . . Feminist theorists . . . remain caught in a bind. We call for marginalized groups of women to add their perspectives to feminist discourse and practice in order to enable subjects to speak for themselves, but we realize that the academic and literary worlds are closed or alien to many of these women. (Carolyn Sachs, qtd. in "Why RWZ Is Online")

The RWZ stands out from other examples in that it begins from the assumption that dominant ideologies in mainstream rural culture and the United States more broadly are to be questioned and examined: it begins from a position of decolonization. This is suggestive, for example, from the spelling of "womyn" in the title, signaling the strong feminist orientation of the group. While this might make it more difficult to locate in an on-line search, the RWZ remains inclusive to those who may not hold the same ideologies: "You do not have to identify with the women's movement or with feminism in order to belong to this group. But the list assumes the validity of the women's movement and explores the gap between feminism and rural women's experiences" ("About Ruralwomyn").

Its decolonization goals are also clear on the home page in its emphasis on political action, featuring news articles in 2005 such as "How Are We Going to Bring Our Troops Home?" and "It's a Long, Long Way to Towanda, Kansas: The Price of Neglecting Rural America" (*The Rural Womyn Zone*). Reinhabitation goals lie alongside these articles that question mainstream beliefs. Links to the left include "Sustaining Rural Living," a page notifying participants about conferences and books related to sustainable agriculture; Native Shop, "a project of the Native American Women's Health Education Resource Center market[ing] products as an economic development project to raise funds for the resource center's programs"; product development and marketing ventures by rural women; the Landless Workers Movement, "the largest social movement in Latin America and one of the most successful grassroots movements in the world"; and more ("Sustaining Rural Living").

The RWZ is a rich and vibrant resource for rural women that facilitates discussion and analysis of a host of issues ranging from domestic violence to World Rural Women's Day perspectives from Chittagong, Bangladesh, and Sturgis, South Dakota. In and of itself, it serves as a kind of critical, public pedagogy that scrutinizes various rural issues to highlight issues of power and privilege. The site can also be a literacy tool as I describe with the writings of Paxton women, debating and engaging public memory. What might it look like to read essays by RWZ contributors alongside memoirs from the Paxton women and also Wendell Berry, for example? How much richer could conversations about place become for students and researchers when the issues these women attend to conjoin those traditionally associated with agrarianist writing?

Placing women's literacies and agrarianist literacies in dialogue is just one of many ways to engage in inquiry that complicates rural literacies. While this is important work for rural students, teachers, and citizens to invest in, our goal throughout has been to dismantle the idea that rural literacies are just for rural people to pay attention to. In our concluding chapter, we describe how to enact a critical, public pedagogy both in the composition classroom and as activist intellectuals, employing the metaphor of sustainability that centers on the relationships among rural, urban, and suburban people and literacies.

# 5 / Toward a Sustainable Citizenship and Pedagogy

*Kim Donehower, Charlotte Hogg, and Eileen E. Schell*

Throughout this book, we have argued that literacy educators need to examine rural literacies in context and work against the urban biases that inform much of the literacy research in our field. Literacy has traditionally been used as a wedge to separate rural from urban and suburban, symbolizing rural people's perceived otherness from the rest of America. Until we recalibrate our understanding of rural literacies, it will be difficult to see beyond the public rhetorics of red state versus blue state, rural versus urban that separate us. As part of revising what rural literacies can mean, we advocate a critical, public pedagogy that questions and renegotiates the relationships among rural, urban, and suburban people. Student and citizen involvement in a critical, public pedagogy makes way for an alternative metaphor for rural literacies—that of sustainability—to emerge.

As George Lakoff and Mark Johnson note in *Metaphors We Live By*, metaphor is not simply a characteristic of language; it shapes both thought and action (3–6). As we have argued, for too long the operating metaphors for understanding rural literacies have primarily been those of preservation, modernization, and abandonment. Under a sustainability metaphor, there is no comparison of rural literacies against urban and suburban default models; rather, the sustainability metaphor allows us to see rural literacies as adaptive practices that change over time to respond to the short- and long-term needs of the communities those literacies serve. And, instead of setting rural, suburban, and urban communities in opposition, the sustainability metaphor allows us to see the ways literate practices can connect those communities to ensure a stable future for all.

How, then, can rural literacies be incorporated into the curricular and pedagogical practices that reach students at American colleges and universities? The composition classroom is the primary site in which undergraduate students negotiate their relationships with disparate forms of literacy, from those they bring with them to college, to those of their classmates, to the teacher's, to the institution's. Many first-year students need to look no further than the books they carry to class to see the traditional images of rural literacies perpetuated. These textbook readings are worth considering in some detail; they model rhetorical strategies and ways of thinking that our students are likely to emulate, particularly if they are unsure of their own thoughts on the issue at hand.

Three common types of composition readers that can shape impressions of rural literacies are those whose readings focus on identity and diversity, those that deal directly with literacy as a topic for inquiry, and those that interrogate particular issues, such as the environment. In the first category, the majority of textbooks omit place-based identity—one of the few exceptions is *Writing Places* (Mathieu, Grattan, Lindgren, and Schultz), which directly encourages students to explore identity in terms of "where I'm from"—or they include it in indirect ways, as in Gary Columbo, Robert Cullen, and Bonnie Lisle's *Rereading America: Cultural Contexts for Critical Thinking and Writing*, which includes readings on "the myth of frontier freedom" (v). Still, in a text whose goal is to "encourage students to grapple with the real differences in perspective that arise in a pluralistic society like ours," *Rereading America* does not explicitly deal with differences in urban, suburban, and rural viewpoints. Many first-year composition readers that take the "diverse perspectives" approach still work within the trinity of race, class, and gender or deal only with race and ethnicity. While these anthologies do valuable work, identities tied to region, place, and geography are often left out, aside from some environmentalist writing that celebrates or interrogates our relationship with nature.

Literacy-focused readers are hampered by the availability of depictions of rural literacy that push beyond the standard rhetorical frames. Susan Belasco's *Constructing Literacies* represents rural literacies with essays by Andrea Fishman on the Amish and by James Moffett referencing the censorship battles of *Storm in the Mountains*. Both depict rural literacy as deeply religious with a fundamentalist bent and therefore resistant to engaging in critical interpretation. Linda Adler-Kassner's *Considering Literacy* also uses the Fishman essay. Granted, the stated goal of Belasco's and Adler-Kassner's textbooks is not to represent a diversity of perspectives, as in *Rereading America*. Instead, they have gathered thought-provoking pieces on the nature of literacy and the purposes of higher education. Yet in this mix, literacies that spring from rural contexts appear as either deficit models or as quaintly out of date.[1]

Composition readers that ask students to interrogate particular issues, although they increasingly address the topic of globalization, still represent rural America, if at all, in ways that subscribe to the problematic rhetorics we have discussed in this book. Diana George and John Trimbur's *Reading Culture: Contexts for Critical Reading and Writing*, in its chapter on "Public Space," features specifically urban and suburban locales: malls, Los Angeles, Atlanta, Ground Zero in New York City, city streets and sidewalks. The only exception is Barry Lopez's "Borders," an excerpt from *Crossing Open Ground*, describing the largely unpopulated border between Alaska and the Yukon Territory in evocative images of vast, open, empty, forbidding space. The only "culture" here is that of arctic foxes, tundra swans, and a single abandoned Eskimo house.

In its first edition, *Speculations: Readings in Culture, Identity, and Values* (Schuster and Van Pelt) contains in a section on "Work and Wealth" an essay by Lee Smith titled "The Face of Rural Poverty." In it, Smith subscribes to standard preservationist and abandonment rhetorics. He references *Let Us Now Praise Famous Men* and argues that "the world that Agee and Evans uncovered endures" (qtd. in Schuster and Van Pelt 621). He suggests that "the best thing the government could do would be to persuade residents to migrate to . . . promising small cities" (627) and concludes his essay by describing incentives the government could offer rural residents to move. This essay is the only one in the anthology that addresses the problems of rural areas, and it does so without establishing any kind of connection between its presumably urban and suburban student readership and the rural people it describes. It represents a missed opportunity to get a student audience to genuinely connect with rural people, and it promotes the idea that rural problems are not problems for city-dwellers. Similarly, the Longman special topics reader *Reading City Life* (Bruch and Marback) includes essays on suburban life but nowhere mentions the rural. While rural themes were not the focus of these texts, our sampling highlights the ways the absence or problematic depictions of rural lives and literacies are repeatedly reinforced to students. The composition classroom offers an excellent space to demonstrate to students that issues that seem at first glance to be only about farming or ecology are tapped into a complex global system and that rural, urban, and suburban life are deeply intertwined.

In this chapter, we describe a number of ways compositionists can bring a new understanding of rural literacies to this space and to the communities in which they reside. What follows are descriptions of three different first-year composition courses, each built around a different topical focus that engages rural literacies: media representation, food politics, and place. In each, we offer extended examples of how understanding aspects of rural literacies can enhance our work with students and provide a much-needed critical perspective on rural literacies. The units build on the research described in the preceding three chapters and address the economic, social, and political facets of rural literacies. Each unit can be utilized independently for a particular assignment or together for a whole course that takes as its focus rural literacies. Individually and collectively, these sites represent for us features of rural literacies that invite connections among students and teachers from a variety of positions. We encourage writing teachers to adapt these course models to their own university contexts and to consider how the places where their universities are located call to mind different assumptions, texts, and contexts for rural literacies.

Responding to Henry Giroux's call for a pedagogy that is wholly public in its nature, we also provide examples of how a critical, public pedagogy can be enacted through various organizations, groups, and projects that sponsor rural literacies. Like many scholars in composition studies, we envision the work of composition teachers and scholars as having a public dimension beyond the classroom. Cushman, Mortensen, and Weisser have called for compositionists to play a role as public intellectuals or activist intellectuals. While the definition and idea of public and activist intellectualism has been hotly debated across a variety of disciplines (see Weisser 117–27 for a useful summary), Christian Weisser has offered a tempered and useful view of how compositionists might engage in activist intellectual work in their communities. In Weisser's view, activist intellectuals are "individuals who work through, around, and beside our academic occupations to bring about social reform on local levels" (123). He envisions activist intellectual work as a practice that intersects across teaching, scholarship, and community life. We find his concept of activist intellectualism particularly useful for our own work as scholar-teachers interested in addressing rural literacies. It is our hope that this chapter provides models for how writing teachers can engage in activist intellectual work across the various arenas of our lives—teaching, scholarship, and community life—to affect change in the ways rural literacies are perceived, represented, practiced, and enacted.

## Designing a Media Representation Unit for a College Composition Course

Part of public pedagogy, according to Giroux, requires acknowledging the critical role of culture in shaping our ideas of ourselves and our relationships with others. In college composition classrooms, a number of first-year courses have been developed that train students to analyze cultural artifacts from sources such as print media, visual media, television, film, and advertising.[2] In *Rhetorics, Poetics, and Cultures: Refiguring College English Studies*, James Berlin describes the goal of many of these types of courses:

> Our main concern is the relation of current signifying practices to the structuring of subjectivities—of race, class, sexual orientation, age, ethnic, and gender formations, for example—in our students and ourselves. The effort is to make students aware of cultural codes, the competing discourses that influence their positioning as students of experience. Our

larger purpose is to encourage students to negotiate and resist those codes—these hegemonic discourses—to bring about more democratic and personally humane economic, social, and political arrangements. From our perspective, only in this way can students become genuinely competent writers and readers.

We thus guide students to locate in their experience the points at which they are now, engaging in negotiation and resistance with the cultural codes they daily encounter. These are then used as avenues of departure for a dialogue. (116)

The first-year composition course described here is the first of a two-semester sequence at the University of North Dakota and takes as its topical focus popular and media representations of rural people and rural literacies. Its goal is to use these materials and classroom dialogue and writing about such materials to foster an analysis of "the structuring of subjectivities . . . in our students and ourselves" based on our identifications as rural, urban, or suburban. This course description is not intended as a model for first-year composition with rural college students; instead, its purpose is to show how the potentially problematic relationships between academic literacy sponsors and rural students, and among rural, urban, and suburban students, can be addressed.

## Rationale

Even when our intentions are good, rural students may misinterpret our desire to genuinely connect with them. When Kim's husband, a native New Yorker, taught his first class at Berea College in rural Kentucky, he confessed to his students that he was nervous about his ability to communicate well with them as this was his first time teaching outside the northeastern United States. Later, a student told him that this had made a very bad first impression, as she and other students interpreted his remarks as, "I don't know how to talk to you people, because I'm from the center of culture and you're all stupid."

His intention had been to communicate something very different, but, given the cycles of stereotyping and counter-stereotyping that have long affected the relationship between Appalachian people and academic literacy sponsors, it was, perhaps, inevitable that his remarks would be interpreted in this way.

The academic job market lands many of us far from home, at institutions that may serve students from communities with which we are unfamiliar. Many of us teach at places that predominantly serve rural students, and we therefore must be prepared for the attitudes these students may bring to the classroom. First, regardless of their teachers' own origins or attitudes toward rural places and people, rural students may presume that their professors bring to the classroom a mindset that rural students are uncultured and subliterate and have little to contribute in the way of knowledge. Also, as described in chapter 2, rural students may devalue their own knowledge and previous education, assuming, in the words of one of Kim's students, that "my country teachers didn't teach me right."

Taking media representations of rural areas as a topic for a composition course addresses these problems in several ways. First, such a topic can promote a model of mutual inquiry in the classroom, in which both teachers and students engage in a genuine investigation of both the topic and their own assumptions about it.[3] Second, careful sequencing of the type of media representations considered, from the more blatantly stereotypical to the more subtle, can allow students and teachers to explore what they themselves believe about rural places and how this affects their relationships to one another, to the media, and to academic literacy. Third, this topic lets teachers and students assess the affective filters students bring to the composition classroom that shape their relationship with academic literacies. Getting these out on the table and exploring the distinctive features of academic literacy can encourage students to take an appropriative stance toward incorporating some features of academic literacy into their own literacies. As an additional benefit, this topic provides fertile ground for teaching the basics of argument and rhetorical analysis, as students are motivated to be critical of readings that they perceive to be critical of them.

## Readings

The course begins with an analysis of a reading that students are likely to find most objectionable: Bill Bryson's "Fat Girls in Des Moines." In the course of the essay, Bryson indulges in several stereotypes that coastal urban-dwellers hold about the Midwest. The title refers to what is, for many students, the most objectionable of all the images in the essay:

> Iowa women are almost always sensationally overweight.
> . . . [But] it's a strange, strange thing—the teenaged daughters of these fat women are always utterly delectable, as soft and gloriously rounded and naturally fresh-smelling as a basket of fruit. . . . It must be awful to marry one of these nubile cuties knowing that there is a time bomb ticking away in her that will at some unknown date make her bloat out into something huge and grotesque, presumably all of a sudden and without much notice, like a self-inflating raft from which the stopper has been abruptly jerked. (204–5)

The essay also discusses Iowans' literacy. Bryson is careful to say that Iowans are not "mentally deficient"; rather, they are "decidedly intelligent and sensible people" with the highest adult literacy rate in the country—99.5 percent, according to Bryson (206). He goes on, though, to describe them as "a tad slow . . . not because they're incapable of high-speed mental activity . . . [but because] there's not much call for it. Their wits are dulled by simple, wholesome faith in God and the soil and their fellow man" (207).

Such passages are ripe for argument analysis, rhetorical analysis, and a general discussion of the stereotypes urbanites hold about those who live in "flyover land." As a piece of humor, written by a Des Moines native, the essay fosters discussions of genre. Students disagree on how seriously readers are supposed to take Bryson's claims but on the whole feel that he sells out his hometown to get laughs from an urbane, cosmopolitan audience. (The piece originally appeared in *Granta*, a travel magazine primarily for urban audiences.) In its outrageous take on standard clichés, the essay allows for a discussion of the sources of these images. Bryson manages to dish out all the typical stereotypes about rural America in a short space here, from the noble, simple tillers of the soil referenced above to images of depravity reminiscent of both *Deliverance* and Erskine Caldwell, of an "old man" in "some no-hope town with a name like Draino, Indiana," who "would almost certainly have only one leg and probably one other truly arresting deficiency, like no nose or a caved-in forehead" (210).

Once Bryson's more explosive statements have been dealt with, the essay also encourages discussion of students' own relationships to their hometowns. At the end, after unleashing the full force of his wit against Des Moines, Bryson becomes seized with "nostalgia" for the place. Many students, especially those who have happily left very small towns for college in the small city of Grand Forks, have similarly ambiguous relationships with their hometowns at this particular stage of their lives. This is a delicate subject that is rarely initiated by the students themselves; however, if it is brought up by the reading or by the teacher's own musings on her or his relationship with home, students can have much to say on this topic. Bryson's essay also allows for discussion of other important topics, such as others' (and our own) desires to consume such caricatures of midwestern places. Do we find the essay funny? If so, why? What is the appeal of such images for rural, urban, and suburban people? What political goals does the promotion of such images serve? What is gained by dichotomizing people according to place in this fashion?

The class's work with the Bryson essay offers a model for the kinds of discussion that need to happen to open up the possibility of students and teachers renegotiating their senses of the rural, urban, and suburban and the relationships among them. A brief discussion of the other readings in the course shows how the class moves from issues of rural, urban, and suburban identities into an engagement with academic literacy.

Bryson's essay provides a segue into the subject of the next reading: different notions of "intelligence," "culture," and "literacy." Kathleen Norris's essay "Status: Or, Should Farmers Read Plato?" from *Dakota: A Spiritual Geography* introduces this topic. Mixing descriptions of uncultured, uneducated rural people with images of farmers reading Plato and waitresses reading *Anna Karenina*, Norris explores Dakotans' complicated relationship with "book learning": they seem both drawn to it and suspicious of it. Because it is difficult to isolate the exact nature of Norris's claims in this essay, it provokes a nuanced discussion of the complex relationship between status, education, and cultural literacy. This helps the class begin to describe the differing notions of "knowledge" and "literacy" held by different groups and the reasons for these distinctions. It also initiates an exploration of what counts as knowledge and literacy in the composition classroom. Norris's essay lets the class make the critical move into an explicit discussion of different ways of valuing and practicing literacy and of the benefits and stigmas that can accrue from such methods.

The other two central readings in the course both address the periodic movement to change the name of North Dakota to "Dakota" to promote tourism and investment in the state. The first, by Mark Singer, appeared in the *New Yorker* and offers a detailed analysis of the state's economic situation, quoting liberally from local leaders in ways that make them seem to be knowledgeable, canny people with a good deal of self-awareness. The second, a set of four humor columns by Dave Barry, takes a more satirical approach but also documents some of the realities of life in North Dakota and Grand Forks. Between the two sets of readings, the class begins to explore the realities that lie beneath the consumable images of the region that Barry exploits and Singer explores. This moves the class into the research segment of the course in which students are asked to investigate the deeper issues behind a particular rural image or stereotype.

There are many other possibilities for readings in a course such as this one; any cultural text that highlights the relationship between rural and nonrural people or communities would work well. Reality television, with its tendency to create drama by forcing dissimilar types to live together, offers many possibilities for analysis. Perhaps the best is the first season of *The Simple Life*, available on DVD, which features the antics of Paris Hilton (heir to the Hilton fortune) and Nicole Richie (daughter of Lionel Richie) after they are relocated to rural Arkansas to work on the Leding family farm. The controversial *Amish in the City* would be another example.

Given the media's obsession in the 2000 and 2004 presidential elections with dividing up America along red state/blue state lines, a productive course or unit could be developed around exploring the realities and rhetorical attractions of this concept. Barbara Kingsolver's essay "A Good Farmer," reprinted elsewhere as "The Good Farmer," could provide a good starting point for this discussion:

> Recently a national magazine asked me to write a commentary on the great divide between "the red and the blue"—imagery . . . suggesting a clear political difference between the rural heartland and urban coasts. Sorry, I replied to the magazine editors, but I'm the wrong person to ask: I live in red, tend to think blue and mostly vote green. If you're looking for oversimplification, skip the likes of me. Better yet, skip the whole idea. Recall that in many of those red states, just a razor's edge under half the voters likely pulled the blue lever, and vice versa—not to mention the greater numbers everywhere who didn't even show up at the polls. . . . Recall that farmers and hunters, historically, are more active environmentalists than many progressive, city-dwelling vegetarians. (And conversely, that some of the strongest land-conservation movements on the planet were born in the midst of cities.) Recall that we all have the same requirements for oxygen and drinking water, and that we all like them clean but relentlessly pollute them.

The point is that readings for such a course, and the discussions of those readings, must serve to complicate the easy media dichotomies that suggest that rural, urban, and suburban people have nothing to say to one another.

## Writing Assignments

The writing assignments for this class are designed to move students from argument analysis to rhetorical analysis to argument construction and research. In response to the Bryson essay, students identify a set of Bryson's claims, which they analyze for both logical and rhetorical effectiveness. With the Norris essay, students are similarly asked to sort out her claims, evidence, and rhetorical goals—essentially the same task as with the Bryson essay but practiced on a more difficult, nuanced piece of writing. The pairing of the Singer and Barry essays let students identify a claim or set of related claims used by Barry and use evidence collected by Singer to contest, support, or develop those claims.

The culminating assignment asks students to conduct independent research and bring their own knowledge of rural areas to the table. Students choose one issue raised by several of the essays they have read and construct their own argument about it, using as support firsthand knowledge as well as source material. In this way, students begin to see how their knowledge could be made compatible with academic standards. Even in a course with a focus such as this one, many students still have to be coaxed into believing that their firsthand knowledge "counts"—that, as in one case, a student's knowledge of the ways in which farm subsidies were awarded, attained by helping his father run the farm, could be made valid in an academic context if handled in a particular rhetorical fashion.

## Outcomes

Ultimately, this course has been successful at getting students to publicly work through some of the problematic relationships created by popular representations of rural regions for urban and suburban audiences. This topic is the explicit subject of much of the discussion and writing that takes place in the course. Students have also made some headway on negotiating their relationships with academic literacy and understanding how their experiences can count as knowledge in the composition classroom. Their writing has demonstrated steady progression in their abilities to analyze both arguments and rhetoric and to begin to work with sources to develop and complicate ideas. As they have in so many other cases, media materials provided accessible entry points for these first-year students to hone their analytical and rhetorical skills.

However, regardless of the cultural texts used as targets for analysis in a course such as this one, the relationship between rural students and academic literacy sponsors and the relationships among urban, suburban, and rural people will not be negotiated unless these topics are brought explicitly into classroom discussion and writing. It is easy enough to examine stereotypical images of rural America to teach the skills of argument and rhetorical analysis. But to use such material allows both teachers and students to negotiate the tensions among rural, urban, suburban, and academic literacies and requires certain pedagogical moves.

First, the idea that there are different systems of defining, valuing, and practicing literacy must become a central concept of the composition classroom. Kim begins her first-year composition courses by giving students a quick overview of Shirley Brice Heath's work in *Ways with Words*, emphasizing that each of us learns from our home communities and experiences outside of school particular ways of using and producing texts that may or may not match up with the ways of using and producing texts privileged by schools. Exploring what we've absorbed in the past about how and why to read and write and then comparing that with the messages we get about what counts as literacy in the university allow us to deal directly with the choices we must make about how much, or whether, to incorporate academic literacy practices into our own, or vice versa.

Second, the course must focus on a mutual exploration of both teachers' and students' assumptions about the differences among rural, urban, and suburban lifestyles and literacies. Teachers must be willing to first offer up their own assumptions about life in places dissimilar to their own hometowns as test cases for analysis to determine the origins, accuracy, and rhetorical appeal of those assumptions before asking students to submit their own assumptions to similar public scrutiny. Since identifying and questioning assumptions is a core skill of academic literacy, this move is particularly appropriate in the first-year composition classroom.

Third, it is the relationship among rural, urban, and suburban people that must be the ultimate topical focus of this course or unit, not an attempt to pin down the "reality" of some monolithic notion of "rural places" or an essentialized group known as "rural people." What readings such as the ones discussed here reveal is what different groups seem to want rural America to be. As such, they allow for input from all students and teachers—rural, urban, and suburban—and encourage them to investigate, as either subjects or consumers of these images, or both, the rhetorical constraints that such media representations have placed on our ability to relate to one another. Such a goal is particularly important in a space such as the first-year composition classroom at the University of North Dakota, in which a student from a town of fifty might find herself sitting next to an aviation major from New York City, each of them dealing with their adjustment to the relative size of Grand Forks compared to what they are used to.

## The Public Role of the Composition Professional in Addressing Media Representations

We compositionists can extend the goals of a course such as this one by offering public commentary and critique on media representations of the rural, urban, and suburban "divides" and on general rural issues. We can also speak out to contextualize research on rural literacy and education that gets reported in the media in misleading or exaggerated ways—for example, by tempering the "failing schools" label that gets assigned to rural districts that do not meet the adequate yearly progress guidelines of No Child Left Behind. University communities often provide many outlets for such activism. In Grand Forks, local and area newspapers often feature letters and guest editorials by faculty, and North Dakota Public Radio solicits opinion pieces that air statewide. The university itself provides a site for public activism on a number of topics that affect rural constituencies, such as the controversy over UND's "Fighting Sioux" sports team name and logo. An understanding of the prevalence and rhetorical consequences of the preservationist, modernizing, and abandonment metaphors and of the possibilities of the sustainability metaphor gives us a starting point for our analyses and activities on these issues.

There is much in the media that needs public critique. During the first half of 2001, the Center for Media and Public Affairs analyzed 337 news stories about rural America that had appeared in major newspapers, in news magazines, or on television networks. Their study suggests that, although the preservationist metaphor is waning in terms of offering a positive representation of rural life, "the media frequently use the term 'rural' to describe areas facing urbanization and trying to preserve a rural past or atmosphere." Also, "'rural' was frequently used as a kind of 'boutique' term to conjure up an idyllic vision, rather than as a mark of real places that have a rural lifestyle" ("What Do the Media Really Say"). The study also reports that 78 percent of the television news stories it surveyed focused on rising crime in rural areas, with particular attention to the rise in methamphetamine use, production, and distribution. Any sense of the viewer's or reader's connection to what is happening, or could happen, in these rural communities is downplayed. What happens in rural places, these representations suggest, is a result of unstoppable forces. It is unfortunate, but there is nothing anyone can do. This narrative of rural decline participates in the tragedy rhetoric that is critiqued in chapter 3 and promotes a lack of scrutiny of the public policies that have led to the economic destruction and decline of these areas.

By emphasizing differences and conflicts between rural and urban America and by adhering to preservationist, modernizing, and abandonment rhetorics, media portrayals of rural issues can inhibit any sense of urgency that political action can and should be taken to improve the conditions of rural life. They suggest that the ills of rural communities are idiosyncratic and cultural, denying the role that public policy, economic realities, and social complexities play in shaping the conditions of rural life and the circumstances for rural literacies. As public intellectuals, as community activists, and in the ways we ourselves choose to understand rural places, compositionists are ideally situated to resist such damaging rhetorics of representation and to offer more productive ones in their place. We can do this in a number of ways: through tried-and-true strategies of writing editorials; through publishing reviews of books, films, and television shows that address rural issues; and through direct advocacy work in our communities.[4] One concrete way we may choose to intervene in debates over the rural is to intervene in how our food system is constituted—an issue that the next unit takes up in its exploration of food politics.

## Designing a Food Politics Unit for a College Composition Course
### Rationale

As Eileen argues in chapter 3, although much has been written about the farm crisis, few commentators have approached the issue of food and farming as a fundamental issue involving critical literacy. Many Americans find farm issues so confusing and so utterly remote from their experiences of living and working in urban or suburban areas that they can't imagine or don't want to imagine how food arrives at the grocery store. Food comes in packages, boxes, and plastic wrappers; food is simply there, and it is relatively cheap compared to other commodities like gasoline or new technologies. Since it's cheap and easy to find—unless you are one of the nation's thousands who go hungry every day—why worry about how it is produced and distributed? Indeed, with obesity as the nation's number two preventable health problem (smoking is number one), most middle-class consumers of food are more likely to worry about whether or not they are eating too much or not exercising enough rather than where their food comes from.

Food's cheapness, abundance, and accessibility for many Americans make it one of the most taken-for-granted, although essential, commodities that directly affects our health and the health of the environment. At the same time that we have a relatively abundant and cheap food supply, we have an increasing loss of small family farms and, as chapter 3 shows, an increasing lack of awareness among the general American public about how their food is grown, marketed, distributed, and sold through the food industrial complex. Since we all have a stake in agriculture, we also have a vested interest in better informing ourselves and helping others become better informed about where our food comes from and how its production and consumption affect us and our environment.

Public interest in this topic is keen given the recent explosion of high profile books and documentaries addressing food and farm issues (for example, see Cook, Nestle, Manning, Schlosser, and Spurlock, to name only a few). Morgan Spurlock's film *Super Size Me*, an excellent companion piece to Eric Schlosser's *Fast Food Nation*, analyzes the obesity epidemic against the backdrop of Spurlock himself surviving on nothing but fast food from McDonald's for a month. Along the way, he examines American's eating habits and their health consequences, dramatically demonstrating how his health problems multiplied when he ate nothing but fast food. Even conservative columnist George Will jumped on the bandwagon in 2005 with a surprising editorial, "What We Owe What We Eat," in *Newsweek*, which urges conservatives to read Matthew Scully's critique of the ethics of factory farming, *Dominion: The Power of Man, the Suffering of Animals, and the Call to Mercy*. With increasing public scrutiny of factory farming, fast food industries, the obesity epidemic, and the loss of small family farms, a unit on food politics provides college students with the opportunity to study, analyze, and debate an issue of great public concern.

Teachers of writing courses have a particularly interesting vantage point from which to pursue critical literacy work on issues of the food industrial complex. First, our courses reach most of the students in our colleges and universities. In addition, many large composition programs are situated in land-grant institutions where students majoring in agriculture, agricultural economics, and food science make up a considerable portion of the student population. Even if such issues are introduced at urban colleges and universities and liberal arts institutions where agriculture or food science is not a subject of study, they are significant issues to address as they raise questions of public interest, environmental health, personal and societal health, and contemporary politics. Second, a focus on food politics fits in well with the focus in many introductory composition courses on critical analysis and argument. With the significant public attention given to issues of food politics in public essays, editorials, book-length studies, and documentaries, there is plenty of written material for students to assess, analyze, and debate. Third, a focus on food politics complements efforts in our field to raise questions of the environment and ecocomposition (Dobrin and Weisser, Weisser), place-based education (Brooke, Hogg in this book), and sustainability (Owens). Derek Owens argues in *Composition and Sustainability* that knowledge of sustainable agriculture and forestry are basic understandings that students should leave the university with if they are to be environmentally aware citizens: "It stands to reason that sustainable culture cannot exist unless sustainability features prominently throughout the curriculum" (28).

Owens is not alone in arguing that sustainability should be an important part of the university curriculum and of writing courses and English courses. Many colleges and universities have instituted required courses that address sustainability. Some campuses have drawn up and enacted plans to make their campuses more "sustainable" or "green." As the editors of *Sustainability on Campus: Stories and Strategies for Change* argue: "Campuses across the United States alone represent an enormous investment in buildings and land, and therefore how we maintain and build our physical plant, engage in buying practices, dispose of waste, and consume energy is critically important to the environmental health of the broader society" (Barlett and Chase 5). A number of such green campus initiatives also include efforts to promote local foods in campus dining facilities and involve the development of curricula related to food politics.

Although ecocomposition, sustainability, and place-based issues have become an increasingly strong emphasis in writing courses and in research on writing, there has been little or no published scholarship documenting writing courses that address food politics issues, even though there is a rich tradition of such courses being taught in the social sciences. There is evidence, though, that the field of composition studies is beginning to take up this issue. Notably, a panel at the 2004 Conference on College Composition and Communication offered perspectives on teaching Schlosser's *Fast Food Nation* in first-year composition classes, and it is likely the case that a number of courses across the country are taking up these issues, although the scholarship in the field is slow to reflect this change. Eileen has engaged the concept of sustainability in her writing courses by asking students to examine consumerism, the food industrial complex, and issues of globalization. More specifically, the second unit of her

Writing 205 course, a sophomore-level research and writing class that she teaches at Syracuse University, is devoted to asking students to research and write about the food industrial complex. Other instructors at Syracuse University also focus their sections of Writing 205 on this topic, although each instructor designs the unit according to his or her expertise and interests.

## Readings

The main text Eileen assigns to introduce debates and issues in the food industry is Schlosser's *New York Times* best-seller *Fast Food Nation*, a book that persuasively guides students through the history of the rise of fast food as an American institution and systematically unpacks its political, social, environmental, and global consequences. A number of chapters in the book focus on the American agricultural system: on corporate consolidation in agribusiness, on the loss of small cattle ranches and the rise of large Concentrated Animal Feeding Operations, the exploitation of slaughterhouse workers, and other topics, all of which connect back to the burgers and fries that many Americans consume on a daily basis. While it could be argued that Schlosser's book participates in the tragedy and smart diversification narratives of the farm crisis critiqued in chapter 3, the key difference is that he sketches the economic and political realities that lead to these commonplace narratives. As Schlosser narrates the tragic story of Hank, the Colorado rancher who committed suicide in the wake of tough times on his ranch, we also learn of the suburbanization of Colorado ranch lands and the global economic pressures and policies that Hank and other small ranchers face. As Schlosser puts it:

> It would be wrong to say that Hank's death was caused by the consolidating and homogenizing influence of the fast food chains, by monopoly power in the meatpacking industry, by depressed prices in the cattle market, by the economic forces bankrupting independent ranches, by the tax laws that favor wealthy ranchers, by the unrelenting push of Colorado's real estate developers. But it would not be entirely wrong. (146)

In short, *Fast Food Nation* highlights the systemic and structural issues with the human costs, allowing for the sort of integrated global analysis that Naomi Klein calls for in *Fences and Windows*, her analysis of alternative globalization movements. Klein argues that understanding the concept of global linkages is "about recognizing that every piece of our high-gloss consumer culture comes from somewhere. It's about following the webs of contracted factories, shell-game subsidiaries, and outsourced labor to find out where all the pieces are manufactured, under what conditions, which lobby groups wrote the rules of the game and which politicians were bought off along the way" (30). While Klein's comments about understanding "global linkages" address the manufacture of consumer goods specifically, her comments can be applied to the food industrial complex as well and offer an interesting commentary upon Schlosser's analysis.

To round out Schlosser's book with multimedia texts, Eileen shows three films that help students visualize how the food industrial complex affects workers, consumers, and the environment. The first is *Fast Food Women*, which provides an analysis of the lives and working conditions of women in eastern Kentucky working in four fast food outlets. The second is Spurlock's *Super Size Me*, and the final film is *The Meatrix*, a flash film that humorously but compellingly describes the rise of factory farms. Mimicking the plot and characters of the cult classic *The Matrix*, *The Meatrix* details the hidden truth about our food supply: that the idyllic small family farms of our national unconscious have been replaced by factory farms run by large agribusiness corporations. The film is interesting not only for its content but also for its quick-moving style and its spoof of popular culture. In conjunction with showing this film, Eileen discusses with her students the potential of new media as a tool for educating and persuading the public about food and farm issues, especially the Internet generation.

To round out the discussion of food and farm issues, Eileen also assigns supplemental readings on issues of globalization to open up questions of global trade, labor, and the role of the international community in addressing issues of agriculture and fair trade. Assigned chapters of Klein's book *No Logo* introduce students to debates over globalization, multinational corporate branding, and consumerism. Excerpts from Klein's more recent *Fences and Windows* detail her observations about the alternative globalization movements and their fight for fair trade, not just free trade. Visits to the on-line archive of the World Trade Organization History Project at the University of Washington also provide students with a glimpse into the protests that took place on November 29–December 3, 1999, in Seattle, Washington, at the WTO Third Ministerial Meeting. Students have the opportunity to view and analyze protest announcements, fliers, pamphlets, interviews, and other organizing and informational literature that was distributed before and during the protests. These readings and films combine to help students gain increasing insight into how citizen-activist movements have responded to questions of food politics and globalization.

## Writing Assignments

The writing assignments that accompany this unit include weekly two- to three-page responses to the assigned readings as well as a formal essay that involves students in collectively researching and writing a "research anthology" on a particular topic of concern that arose from their reading of *Fast Food Nation*, the other assigned readings, and the films. Although the anthology is a collective assignment, with students collaboratively authoring an introduction and conclusion and composing a cover, each student contributes an analytical essay of six to seven pages that introduces a specific issue appropriate to his or her anthology topic and provides informed perspectives on that issue. The group also gives a presentation on their anthology at the end of the unit, offering their ideas for discussion and critique.

In the course, Eileen's students have composed anthologies that investigate a number of agriculturally related topics, including a comparative analysis of factory farming of beef cattle versus organically raised range-fed beef, the rise of mad cow disease in light of contaminated feed and lapsed food safety inspection standards, French farmer Jose Bove's nationalistic resistance to McDonald's, President Bush's immigration policies and their impact on Mexican farm workers, and the conditions of banana workers in Costa Rica in light of free trade agreements. One of the chief advantages of this assignment is that students constantly move back and forth from their individual essay writing and research to thinking about the collective project as a whole. This mix of collective and individual research efforts challenges students' preconceived notions about writing and research as a single-minded enterprise and helps them figure out how to consider a topic from multiple angles.

## Outcomes

Interestingly, few of Eileen's students are from rural backgrounds, even fewer are from farming communities, and few coming into the course are initially aware of the issues raised in Schlosser's book, the other readings, and the films. The unit on food politics, however, helps students think through the food industrial complex in a way they may never have thought about it before. A unit on food politics, in Schlosser's words, encourages students to "think about where the food came from, about how and where it was made, and about what is set in motion by every fast food purchase" (270). While a number of Eileen's students say they won't stop eating fast food, they are thinking about it differently, and others maintain that the class unit has caused them to go further in seeking alternatives to fast food and convenience foods. Indeed, Eileen spends part of one class session talking with her students about "eat local" campaigns, farmers' markets, farm-to-cafeteria programs, and the international movement founded by Italian Carlo Petrini called "Slow Food," which opposes fast food culture and promotes the eating of local foods, sustainability, and biodiversity ("All About"). Some of Eileen's students go on to visit the local food co-op for the first time and seek out alternative places to eat and buy their groceries, since many of them live off-campus in apartments.

Eileen's students' desire to find out about alternative food sources encouraged her to plan a community linking project for a future version of the course. In this potential community linking project, she plans to create a speakers' bureau of community leaders in the area of sustainable agriculture and sustainable living. She plans to invite farmers and representatives from a local community supported agriculture organization, the Real Food Cooperative (the local organic food co-op), the Northeast Organic Farmers' Association, the Eastern Farm Workers Association, the USDA, and other local groups who will help students think of alternatives and socially just responses to the food industrial complex. She also will create opportunities for students to get involved in the work of these organizations and address how to bring opportunities to the university campus for students to buy and eat local foods. On a neighboring campus of the State University of New York College of Environmental Science and Forestry, student activists have set up an organic food stand. She plans to invite students in her course to dialogue with the founding members of this food stand and to consider and evaluate the university's dining services' use—or lack thereof—of local food sources.

The work Eileen's students are doing in this class is not so much a corrective to the rhetorics of the farm crisis critiqued in chapter 3 but a set of different narratives altogether—more specifically, ones that allow them to work toward understanding a network of community and global linkages and toward realizing an alternative agrarian literacy. Critical literacy work on the food industrial complex provides students with a way to understand the network of community and global linkages that currently shape our lives as food consumers and can help them begin to consider practices that will make those linkages more sustainable and equitable.

## Food Politics and Public Pedagogy

The work of addressing food politics and the food industrial complex, though, should not be limited to the college campus and the college writing classroom, although those are important spaces; it can be part of a broader platform for public pedagogy within communities concerned with community food security, food sovereignty, and support of small family farmers, whether the citizens of those communities are living in rural areas or in suburban and urban areas. The discussion of Farm Aid in chapter 3 provides an in-depth analysis of how one nonprofit organization has worked to educate the public about the significance of family farmed food and the plight of small family farmers as it has simultaneously provided aid and advice to

small family farmers. Farm Aid, however, is only one of many organizations devoted to fostering a public pedagogy about food issues.
Such food politics advocacy groups are numerous and wide-ranging,
spanning a variety of local nonprofits to national and international
organizations whose mission is to improve food sovereignty, such as
the Community Food Security Coalition. The CFSC, like Farm Aid,
strives to provide the public with the critical literacy skills necessary to make sustainable choices about the food system for families,
communities, and institutions. As a literacy sponsor for groups and
individuals, the CFSC provides publications in the form of how-to
booklets, reports, newsletters, assessment materials, and conferences
that help community members increase food sovereignty through a
range of measures, for example, setting up farm-to-cafeteria programs
in schools, linking farms with food banks, and increasing local food
access for low-income, transit-dependent residents.

In a recent position paper, "Education for Change," posted on the
CFSC Web site, local food activist Mark Winne argues that educators,
parents, and activists can be a force for change in promoting an alternative agrarian literacy that will change the face of America's obesity
epidemic and promote sustainable food in every community:

> It should be a matter of national educational policy that every
> child understands how and where their food is produced, and
> that they have the requisite skills to critique those systems
> of production. As Jim Hightower has warned, "Our kids are
> growing up thinking that a chicken has six legs because that's
> how many come in a package." Maybe, in fact, students should
> be required to read Jim Hightower as well as Joan Gussow,
> Frances Moore Lappe, Marion Nestle, Eric Schlosser, Wendell
> Berry, Walt Whitman and, God forbid, Marx and Engels.

Although Winne's call is largely focused on K–12 educators, he includes public educators in his manifesto:

> I would argue, however, that any attempt to reform our ap-
> proach to food and nutrition education must be comprehen-

sive and saturate every fiber of our public education institutions. We should not succumb to the temptation to limit our endeavors to isolated and discrete projects, as worthy as they may be. Unfortunately, it is simply not enough to yank the soda machines out of the schools, run a school garden for a few weeks, ban irradiated food, establish a school breakfast program here and there, install an organic salad bar in the school cafeteria. Yes, we need those projects and they must be multiplied a thousand fold. But we have to also worm, no, not worm, and bust our way into the circles of power, nationally as well as locally. We must make our schools the breeding ground for millions of food competent, healthy, and happy children who retain those attributes as adults and become demanding, knowledgeable food consumers, voters, and, in some cases, farmers, nutritionists, chefs, policymakers, and members of the local school boards that control the curricula.

His manifesto against agricultural illiteracy is a call not only to educate young people but also to provide food education for all levels of society: "Food learning must extend from the classroom to the cafeteria to the school garden to the local farms and markets, and include the larger social, economic, and cultural context of each community."

Winne's vision of food learning extending "from the classroom to the cafeteria to the school garden to the local farms and markets" has been realized at the CFSC-sponsored yearly "Farm to Cafeteria" conferences. At the second annual Farm to Cafeteria Conference (June 16–18, 2005) at Kenyon College in Ohio, hundreds of farmers, non-profit agencies, food and farm activists, farmers' market directors, USDA employees, community gardeners, public school teachers, college and university professors, and college students gathered to discuss processes and models for bringing local, family farmed food into their hospitals, K–12 schools, colleges and universities, and prisons. At a number of these sessions, college faculty and K–12 teachers across the disciplines shared syllabi and assignments that addressed food, farm, and sustainability issues. At several sessions as well, college student activists spoke with great vigor about how they have set up local food projects on their campuses. In addition, K–12 teachers and farmers addressed how they have used provisions in the federal school lunch program to bring locally farmed food to school cafeterias through salad bars featuring local produce or at school fund-raisers or special events ("Second"). The 2005 Farm to Cafeteria Conference made it clear that there is a nationwide movement to feature local foods and to teach and discuss food and farm issues across the disciplines. Indeed, CFSC's organizing and networking efforts through the national Farm to Cafeteria conferences provide an excellent model for creating partnerships between farmers, educators, parents, dining services personnel, and food and farm activists—partnerships that move communities closer toward Jacqueline Edmondson's notion of alternative agrarian literacy as addressed in chapter 3 and that allow communities to enact sustainable food systems.

Addressing food politics allows students and community members alike the opportunity to intervene in and change the food system in a way that benefits their health and the health of the environment. Food politics also creates in students and community members a renewed interest and loyalty to a sense of place: to buying local and connecting to the local while realizing the global connections that link our food system to the environmental health of the planet. In the next unit on designing a place-based unit for a composition course, the idea of place is developed more broadly as a site from which to address an understanding of rural literacies that is not necessarily bound to issues of food and farming.

### *Designing a Place-Based Unit for a College Composition Course*
**Rationale**

Certainly place has already been a part of writing classrooms through efforts in ecocomposition and place-based writing. Compositionists have combined critical pedagogies with place in the writing classroom. Owens writes of asking his urban students to "make written and photographic portraits of where they live" as an exercise leading toward sustainability (36). In Bruce McComiskey and Cynthia Ryan's collection, *City Comp: Identities, Spaces, Practices*, contributors describe how students write and analyze their urban contexts. At DePaul University in Chicago, students are invited to "Discover and Explore Chicago" through a week-long immersion experience and a course that uses Chicago as the site of inquiry. These are just a few examples of provocative models that are critically engaging in place, but their urban contexts reinforce the ways critical work and rural contexts have not been brought together in composition classrooms, nor have fixed place-based identities been challenged.[5]

At the same time, it might seem unremarkable to put together writing about place with rural literacies; in fact, it seems a commonplace practice among rural educators and rural students. The idea of writing about place can bring to mind notions of rendering one's place descriptively, creating a "sense of place" on the page, and this work can either be preservationist or dismissive of rural experiences. In such work, "place" often connotes only the literal physical space rather than other cultural, social, and material realities experienced within a place, and as a consequence, place-based identities become tethered to the physical locale. A critical pedagogy of place, however, described in chapter 4, disrupts this tendency by embracing the best of critical (with its focus on urban and social) and place-based (with its focus on rural and ecological) pedagogies. According to David Gruenewald, this fusion can be achieved by decolonization ("unlearning much of what dominant culture and schooling teaches") and reinhabitation ("learning to live-in-place in an area that has been disrupted and injured through past exploitation") (Gruenewald 9). Such a pedagogy first asks that students challenge not only dominant ideologies about their place but also their investment in and identification with these ideologies.

In a beginning composition class in Nebraska, Charlotte began this work by seeking to give students a glimpse of shifting and malleable identities, rather than fixed identities of rural or urban, to help them engage with place as a site for inquiry. While gearing up to read Teresa Jordan's memoir about Wyoming ranch life, *Riding the White Horse Home*, some students from Omaha said they could in no way relate to her discussion of being a "hick" because they identified themselves as urban (though from their writing they seemed to inhabit a suburban place and context). In an effort to help them move toward mutual identification as a class, Charlotte asked them instead to think of the class as a regional collective. She employed an idea from Iris Marion Young's *Justice and the Politics of Difference* where Young makes reference to the concept of regions in order to address some of the shortcomings of her discussion of cities. She explains:

> I conceive a region as both an economic unit and a territory that people identify as their living space. A region is the space across which people commonly travel to work, shop, play, visit their friends, and take the children on errands, the span of a day trip. It is the range of television and radio transmission. The expanse of a region thus varies with culture, geography, economic base, and primary modes of transportation. Regions usually have a city or cluster of cities as a focus of their activity and identity, but include less densely populated suburban and rural areas. While hardly economically self-sufficient, regions nevertheless count as units of economic interdependence, the geographical territory in which people both live and work, in which major distribution occurs, much of it of products made in the region. (252)

Just as geographers have reclaimed "region" as a tool for local inquiry in addition to a physical locale, allowing for a vision of place that moves beyond landscape to encompass varied aspects of culture within that place (see Glen Lich, Terry Jordan, and others), Young forwards the idea of region as a concept that encompasses rather than divides rural and urban. Keeping this framework in mind, Charlotte then asked students in the class how they are regarded when they visit Los Angeles or New York and mention in casual conversation that they are from Omaha, Nebraska. One student described an encounter with a nonrural person while standing in line at Disneyland; when the student revealed she was from Omaha, the person assumed it was a one-horse town and not a city of over 500,000. A shift in the classroom conversation occurred, and Charlotte realized the exchange began to be about a collective "we" among members of the class—not collective in the sense of the same but in the sense of seeing the malleability of how "we" define ourselves within a location and how others define us. This doesn't mean that Omaha students rid themselves of their assumptions of students from Venango, Nebraska, but that the physical boundaries of place were transcended by understanding locale as a shifting concept and also as an interdependent part of a whole region rather than as a self-contained town or city. This awareness and revision of how they are perceived and how they perceive others began a conversation about other kinds of interconnectedness between spaces that are usually viewed dichotomously.

The work begun in this classroom moment was a start to the kind of critical pedagogy of place Gruenewald calls for as students are asked to wrestle with comfortable and accepted assumptions about local places and their positionality within and against these assumptions. In asking students to research and write about a region, all students— and the instructor—can in some way locate themselves. This approach invites multiple perspectives but also mutual identification. From this orientation, and drawing from place-based experiential knowledge, discussions, and research, the class is then poised to critically engage and work toward decolonization and reinhabitation of a place.

### Integrating Issues of Place in a First-Year Composition Course

Charlotte now teaches in Texas, a state with a distinctive sense of place quite different from the rest of the plains states. Also unlike the other plains states, Texas encompasses a diverse range of topographies (in fact, only a portion of the state is truly a part of the Great Plains) and population differences, claiming three of the top-ten populated cities in the United States along with suburban and rural spaces ("Top 50 Cities"). Texas is also more ethnically diverse. Overall politically conservative, however, Texas handily fits in with its rural Great Plains counterparts to the north.

The state of Texas is also laden with stereotypes and images, some of which are revered and promoted by Texans and some that are problematic in the ways Kim describes in chapter 2 (for example, MTV's *Real World* reality series, set in Austin in 2005, shows cattle in the opening credits, despite the fact that Austin's population is nearly

700,000). Faced with this intriguing ideology of place, Charlotte developed a course, "Messin' with Texas: Writing about Place." When raising such issues of place, she begins with the assumption that everyone in the class is temporarily a Texan, since they are attending school and living at least part of the year in Texas. For students from Houston, Fort Worth embodies its nickname, "Cowtown," and is seen as a small city at best. For students from rural communities, Fort Worth, population 600,000, can be (as it was for Charlotte) the largest metropolitan area in which they've lived. Again, Charlotte first strives for a sense of mutual identification—not to mask or diminish important differences among members of the class but to build a coalition among students who have a common investment in their current local place.

## Readings

Keeping in mind what she learned from Paxton women about a sense of place, Charlotte defines place as expansively as possible and encourages the students to define for themselves what embodies a sense of place for them. Not surprisingly, she assigns writing about Texas (though, interestingly, given its mythic sense of statehood, while Texas hosts a slew of wonderful writers, place-identified authors and texts are not as prevalent as in other regions like Montana or Mississippi). Teachers anywhere, though, can seek out writing about the place their institution calls home, even if there are not many established memoirs in the area. Local authors are particularly important for this kind of work: the point is for students to hear from voices who don't write about a certain place from a distant vantage point. Students can be encouraged to seek resources from their home places or from their new campus space. Who wrote the local histories of the place they are writing about, and what assumptions are embedded in the kinds of histories they constructed? In what ways has public memory been formed and contested at the local level?

Asking students to write in memoir form about the tensions that exist within their local place, Charlotte assigns Molly Ivins's "Texas Women: True Grit and All the Rest," in which Ivins both embraces and challenges womanhood in Texas: "Please understand I'm not whining when I point out that Texas sexism is of an especially rank and noxious variety—this is more a Texas brag. It is my belief that it is virulence of Texas sexism that accounts for the strength of Texas women. It's what we have to overcome that makes us formidable survivors, say I with some complacency" (699). In this brief essay, Ivins remarks on a variety of Texas stereotypes that students collectively mark, knowing from growing up in the state. Despite the laughter as the class begins to talk about Ivins's text and the images familiar to them, students either love or hate this essay (and usually the split falls down gender lines). First, the class listens and unpacks why most of the women in the room feel an affinity for the piece and why many of the men don't. Then Charlotte asks what isn't familiar to them about the essay, and many first name the fact that "as late as 1969, married women did not have full property rights" (702).

From reading and discussion to writing, students' own nonfiction pieces require them to wrestle with the kind of tension Ivins exhibits in her essay: "It may be possible for a little girl to grow to womanhood in this state entirely sheltered from the rampant sexism all around her—but it's damned difficult. The result is that Texas women tend to know how to cope" (703). Often students' first drafts either glorify or dismiss their home place and fall into binary thinking, but often there is even one line that complicates this notion, and this is what is examined, the underbelly of the essay. As Kim describes above, first-year students are poised to examine the tensions of their home place as they adjust to leaving home. For rural students who have been encouraged to dismiss their dying hometown but may feel otherwise, this assignment can be particularly productive; for rural, suburban, and urban students who glorify their home place, this assignment asks them to consider what they might have overlooked as they construct their place.

## Writing Assignments

As the course progresses, other kinds of assignments in addition to the place-based memoir continue to ask students to examine Texas not just as a physical or ecological place but also as a social, cultural, economic, and political place. Since the beginning composition course at Texas Christian University requires students to use source material and to write in a number of different genres, exploratory essays and position papers allow students to incorporate both research and their experiential knowledge. As the class continues to unpack the Texas region and students select areas with which to focus their research, they can be provided with—and also provide—information that invites further investigation. For example, employing the Rural School and Community Trust Web site and its fact sheet on Texas can put rurality in context for the state:

> More rural people live in Texas than in any other state, but they are a small demographic minority nonetheless, accounting for less than one-fifth of the population. But rural child poverty and minority rates are high, making rural education especially important in Texas. Despite low spending on school administration and transportation, moderate school size, and no better than average teacher salaries, the proportion of school spending that gets into the classroom is quite low. ("Why Rural Matters")

In a move toward thinking about sustainability, the focus for discussion and writing in connection to such material is again on mutual identification—why facts that seem decidedly "a rural issue" are also state, national, and global issues. The discussion can begin by asking students questions such as Why is this a significant statistic? How does it compare with urban statistics on education in Texas? Discussions like these raise issues like the so-called Robin Hood Law, in which wealthier school districts in Texas must share their tax revenue with poorer districts. While not expressly a rural/urban issue, it provides a springboard to study the situation in terms of what is at stake for various parties involved in this controversial law, as well as what assumptions emerge in the ways different contingents are described. Or the class might discuss the ways current issues are connected to Texas, such as the fact that Clear Channel Communications is a Texas-based company that donated money to President Bush and also pulled the Dixie Chicks (a Texas band) from its radio stations after lead singer Natalie Maines made comments against Bush at a concert in London in 2003. Place, then, is the site for their investigations and writing, not just a descriptive and unexamined marker of identity.

Some students, new to Fort Worth and the campus of TCU, write about topics of great significance in their home place that have less importance in their new place. One student from Portland, Oregon, wrote about the disparity in attitudes about recycling, something she assumed was a given in U.S. culture until she came to TCU and saw the lackluster recycling programs for faculty, staff, and students alike. Another student who had used a bike as a mode of transportation before moving to campus noticed that few students rode bikes and seemed very dependent on cars (often SUVs at that), not unlike the situation in the city of Fort Worth. He first noted this as a passing comment on his way into class, and Charlotte asked him if he knew that Arlington, the city just east of Fort Worth, was the largest city in the United States without a public transportation system. The class talked informally about this for a few moments, and his paper advocating biking on campus to decrease car reliance by students built from there. In these instances, students could transfer their knowledge of one place in an effort to reinhabit another.

## Outcomes

The goal of such assignments is first to help students become better writers, in part by challenging them to revise in ways that make more complex their controlling ideas and their prose itself. The objectives of a themed course on place do not sacrifice the emphases on drafting and revising to create complex prose in which a controlling idea dominates, and they are particularly conducive to helping students understand rhetorical analysis and sensitivity. This work is aided by critical discussions in class that seek to explore the interdependence of places within—and beyond—a certain region. These pedagogical descriptions of place-based thinking and writing employ the three tenets of negotiation Kim demonstrates with media analysis: consideration of the ways literacy can be utilized and valued, exploration of both teacher and student assumptions, and the relationship among rural, suburban, and rural people.

It would be presumptuous to suggest that the two aspects of a critical pedagogy of place—decolonization and reinhabitation—can be achieved in a semester-long composition course, but opportunities for them arise through the ingredients of mutual identification, critical research and writing, and encouragement to neither dismiss nor glorify the place. Students, prompted by other students with both similar and different experiences of the same region, examine, perhaps, what the term "oil" connotes to someone from an oil-drilling town like Odessa or to someone from the wealthy Woodlands suburb of Houston whose parent is a manager at Texaco and are then encouraged to research a variety of opinions on Texas oil in the global economy. The objective is to help students invite critical analysis, argument, and experiential knowledge into their writing by both valuing and challenging what they and others say about their place.

## Public Pedagogies of Place beyond the Classroom

The need for public pedagogies to complicate place-based identities feels particularly great since the media, fueled by political strategists, classifies citizens as "red state" or "blue state," as though the state one lives in defines her or his personality. Thinking more critically about one's identification with place, and places themselves, should be an integral part of critical, public pedagogies that seek to help rural and nonrural citizens alike both celebrate and critique their place as well as gain a greater understanding of the interdependence of their place to regional, national, and global culture. In the conclusion to chapter 4, Charlotte describes how literacy work by rural women can move toward critical, public pedagogies by incorporating their meaning-making of local place more squarely into conversations and programs on place. In their hometowns and in on-line communities, these women create possibilities for or are already enacting decolonization and reinhabitation components of a critical pedagogy of place.

These kinds of work being done by rural women are a crucial part of rural literacies that get overlooked when celebration of place relies too heavily on preservationist thinking. Some kinds of place-based education being done in rural areas fall into such thinking, but at the same time, place-based education programs have much to contribute to the ways rural literacies are imagined in college settings and outside the classroom. As mentioned in chapter 4, many of the motivations for place-based education are conducive to the kinds of citizen participation we call for with critical, public pedagogies. Currently, place-based programs are primarily located in K–12 institutions, and the best of these programs deploy a critical, public pedagogy of place to effect change in their local communities. College educators as activist intellectuals, who have opportunities to partner with K–12 education, can help ensure that place-based programs employ a critical model.

The Llano Grande Center for Research and Development, located fifteen miles from the Texas-Mexico border in the Rio Grande Valley, is one such program. Students connected to the center hail from two of Texas's poorest districts, where 91 percent of families have an annual income of less than $10,000 (Higgins Null). According to its Web site, "The Center was formalized in 1997 with the assistance of the Annenberg Rural Challenge with the intent to bridge the gap between communities and schools by developing pedagogy of place curricula," though local residents had been talking about rural development before the center was official ("Llano Grande Center"). The center's work encompasses what one typically imagines for place-based education—oral history projects—but its Web site describes an active movement from story to action:

> Together, Llano Grande researchers and informants are constructing the unrecorded social history of their economically depressed but culturally vibrant communities. [The stories of] older residents . . . have been recorded, transcribed, and archived by students . . . usually in Spanish. Students have also translated and edited the transcriptions into narratives for publication in both English and Spanish. They are now

being studied and used by children at all grade levels who
have reworked them into fiction, artistic depictions, and even
a television documentary which Edcouch-Elsa High School
students produced for the local PBS station. (Higgins Null)

Students go through an extensive methodological process to gather
this information in which the older residents are interviewed, establishing connections and confidences. A bilingual journal helped
community members envision the project, and eventually community members were volunteering for the project. Most impressive,
though, is the way the stories led to programs that make meaning of
a significant cultural moment through literate acts. As described on
their Web site:

> Students, teachers, and community members . . . held a con-
> ference for those who had witnessed or taken part in a walk-
> out at Edcouch-Elsa High School in the spring of 1968. This
> pivotal event, protesting discriminatory practices throughout
> the local school system, hastened the end of "Anglo" domi-
> nance in local politics and local schools. The Anglo minority,
> who had occupied most positions of authority, moved away
> from the area over the next few years, creating new leadership
> opportunities for residents of Mexican descent. . . . Sharing
> reminiscences with other area residents as well as with a new,
> curious, and caring generation has been a way of increasing
> positive exchanges between communities inside and outside
> the school walls. (Higgins Null)

The center recognizes and values the importance of oral histories
and narratives on how life used to be, and if it stopped there, it would
be recognizable through the preservation metaphor, where the ideas
and stories raised seem fixed in the past. What marks the center's activities as a critical, public pedagogy that moves toward sustainability
is the way in which the collection of oral histories is not the end of
the literacy endeavor but the beginning. Economically, the program
has developed partnerships in order to create job opportunities, one

of which is transcribing oral history records on a contract basis for various Texas universities and historical sites. It has also produced a strong alumni network, used, among other ways, to foster mentor relationships and other contacts. The center asks rural people to use literacy to appreciate and cultivate their community while also working toward awareness and change; for Llano Grande students and facilitators, residents may stay or return to their home or they may leave and teach others of their home place. The center has also been highlighted by the Rural School and Community Trust, a nonprofit organization that works to help communities and schools gain strength together by working "with a network of schools and community groups striving to improve the quality of education and community life and to improve state education policies" ("About the Rural School and Community Trust"). The program is an excellent example of public pedagogies as local residents play a key role in the development and enactment of the work being done.[6]

The work of the Llano Grande Center provides a model for the ways a community can integrate a critical pedagogy of place into its school system, valuing local knowledge and public memory work. Creating liaisons among such K–12 programs, colleges and universities, and communities like the center fosters openings for all constituents to contribute to education about local place and the ways place affects and is affected by others; compositionists are primed to cultivate such opportunities. By situating themselves in their local place as activist intellectuals in the ways we've described—participating in public media critiques, becoming involved in networks and conferences involving food politics, and seeking out partnership programs such as the Llano Grande Center—compositionists can revise perceptions of rural literacies. A number of community-linking opportunities such as these could be pursued to encourage a connection to and familiarity with the organizations and groups that perpetuate rural literacies associated with sustainability. Students could also be asked to participate in on-line or face-to-face discussions with community leaders, workers, and advocacy organizations associated with rural development and urban-rural partnerships such as the Rural Womyn Zone or the CFSC.

## Working toward a Multiplicity of Rural Literacies

In the three pedagogical examples we delineate above, our goal is to provide generative rather than prescriptive course plans that can be shaped depending on local and academic contexts so that classes can analyze and investigate rural literacies and issues of sustainability from the vantage point of a critical, public pedagogy. Exploring and renegotiating the relationships among rural, urban, and suburban people as members of a global citizenry is a key component of critical, public pedagogies within and outside a classroom that lead toward sustainability. As we cite in chapter 1, "Public pedagogy . . . becomes part of a critical practice designed to understand the social context of everyday life as lived relations of power" (Giroux, "Public Pedagogy" 355). In each of our examples, rural literacies, rather than discrete content to learn about, serve as a site of inquiry about broader issues of literacy and power that lie at the heart of critical, public pedagogies. Furthermore, we point toward models of critical, public pedagogy that have been initiated outside the classroom by advocacy organizations and other citizen groups.

Throughout this volume, we have analyzed the social, political, and material issues that shape rural literacies. In doing so, we have worked to initiate a broader dialogue within the field of rhetoric and composition studies about the context, issues, and literacies of rural residents and communities—literacies that connect across geographic, economic, social, and cultural boundaries. We hope the questions that we have posed will be useful to literacy researchers, rhetoricians, writing program administrators, and teachers of writing as they consider how to design research projects, curricula, courses, and community engagement projects that represent a range of literate action and experiences in multiple contexts: rural, suburban, and urban.

Our ultimate wish for readers of this book is that the phrase "rural literacies" will come to have a rich and nuanced set of associations for you, informed by certain demonstrable realities about the state of rural America. "Rural literacies" should conjure images not of an abandoned one-room schoolhouse on a featureless plain or of a news special on the failures of rural education. While we have provided alternate images—of a woman opening a resource center, of a Web site fostering social change, of a discussion of *Fast Food Nation* in a composition course—we actively resisted simply replacing one set of specific images with another. Our goal is to work toward realities of rural literacies that are multiple and that encourage mutual identification among rural, urban, and suburban citizens. Indeed, the phrase "rural literacies" should suggest reading and writing as social action that supports and sustains diverse communities trying to cope with complex, often interlinked economic, social, cultural, and environmental issues. Addressing these interconnected issues through literate action and sponsorship of literate action is the responsibility of us all.

# Appendix
## Selected Bibliography on Rural Issues and Rural Literacies

Below is a selected bibliography categorized by background readings on rural life and experience, rural literacies and education, and memoirs and essays on rural life and experience. It is thorough but by no means exhaustive. An additional bibliography of rural books can be found at <eagle.clarion.edu/~grads/rural_source/ruralbooksinfo.htm>.

### Background Readings on Rural Life and Experience

Baker, Richard. *Los Dos Mundos: Rural Mexican Americans, Another America.* Logan: Utah State UP, 1995.

Batteau, Allen. *The Invention of Appalachia.* Tucson: U of Arizona P, 1990.

Comer, Krista. *Landscapes of the New West: Gender and Geography in Contemporary Women's Writing.* Chapel Hill: U of North Carolina P, 1999.

Commission on Country Life. *Report of the Commission on Country Life.* New York: Sturgis and Walton, 1911.

Davidson, Osha Gray. *Broken Heartland: The Rise of America's Rural Ghetto.* Iowa City: U of Iowa P, 1996.

Fink, Deborah. *Agrarian Women: Wives and Mothers in Rural Nebraska, 1880–1940.* Chapel Hill: U of North Carolina P, 1992.

———. *Cutting into the Meatpacking Line: Workers and Change in the Rural Midwest.* Chapel Hill: U of North Carolina P, 1998.

———. *Open Country, Iowa: Rural Women, Tradition, and Change.* Albany: State U of New York P, 1986.

Jackson, Wes, and William Vitek, eds. *Rooted in the Land: Essays on Community and Place.* New Haven, CT: Yale UP, 1996.

Popper, Deborah, and Frank Popper. "The Buffalo Commons: Metaphor as Method." *Geographical Review* 89.4 (1999): 491–510.

———. "The Great Plains: From Dust to Dust." *Planning* 53.12 (1987): 12–18.

Sayer, Karen. *Women of the Fields: Representations of Rural Women in the Nineteenth Century.* New York: Manchester UP, 1995.

Schlosser, Eric. *Fast Food Nation: The Dark Side of the All-American Meal.* New York: Perennial, 2002.

Shapiro, Henry. *Appalachia on Our Mind: The Southern Mountains and Mountaineers in the American Consciousness, 1870–1920*. Chapel Hill: U of North Carolina P, 1978.

Whisnant, David. *All That Is Native and Fine: The Politics of Culture in an American Region*. Chapel Hill: U of North Carolina P, 1983.

Williamson, J. W. *Hillbillyland: What the Movies Did to the Mountains and What the Mountains Did to the Movies*. Chapel Hill: U of North Carolina P, 1995.

W. K. Kellogg Foundation. "Perceptions of Rural America." 1 Nov. 2001. Downloaded PDF file. 31 July 2003 <http://www.wkkf.org/Pubs/FoodRur/Pub2973.pdf>.

———. "Perceptions of Rural America: Congressional Perspectives." 1 May 2002. Downloaded PDF file. 31 July 2003 <http://www.wkkf.org/Pubs/FoodRur/Pub3699.pdf>.

## Rural Literacies

Benally, Elaine R., Jack T. Cole, and Manuela Quezada-Aragon. *Issues in American Indian Education, Mexican American Education, Migrant Education, Outdoor Education, Rural Education, and Small Schools*. Las Cruces, NM.: ERIC Clearinghouse on Rural Education and Small Schools, 1987.

Brandt, Deborah. *Literacy in American Lives*. Cambridge: Cambridge UP, 2001.

Chlebowska, Krystyna. *Literacy for Rural Women in the Third World*. Lanham, MD: Bernan, 1990.

Edmondson, Jacqueline. *Prairie Town: Redefining Rural Life in the Age of Globalization*. Lanham, MD: Rowman, 2003.

Fishman, Andrea. *Amish Literacy: What and How It Means*. Portsmouth, NH: Heinemann, 1988.

Hautecoeur, Jean-Paul. *Alpha 94: Literacy and Cultural Development Strategies in Rural Areas*. Toronto: Culture Concepts, 1994.

Heath, Shirley Brice. *Ways with Words: Language, Life, and Work in Communities and Classrooms*. New York: Cambridge UP, 1983.

Horsman, Jennifer. *Something in My Mind Besides the Everyday: Women and Literacy*. Toronto: Women's Press, 1990.

Kett, Joseph. *The Pursuit of Knowledge under Difficulties: From Self-Improvement to Adult Education in America, 1750–1990*. Stanford, CA: Stanford UP, 1994.

Kruse, Martha. "From Village to College: Writing the Rural Experience." Diss. U of Nebraska–Lincoln, 1995.

Lofty, John. *Time to Write: The Influence of Time and Culture on Learning to Write*. Albany: State U of New York P, 1992.

Moffett, James. *Storm in the Mountains: A Case Study of Censorship, Conflict, and Consciousness*. Carbondale: Southern Illinois UP, 1989.

Mortensen, Peter. "Representations of Literacy and Region: Narrating 'Another America.'" *Pedagogy in the Age of Politics: Writing and Reading (in) the Academy*. Ed. Patricia Sullivan and Donna Qualley. Urbana, IL: NCTE, 1994. 100–120.

Petrosky, Anthony. "Rural Poverty and Literacy in the Mississippi Delta: Dilemmas, Paradoxes, and Conundrums." *The Right to Literacy*. Ed. Andrea Lunsford and James Slevin. New York: MLA, 1990.

Purcell-Gates, Victoria. *Other People's Words: The Cycle of Low Literacy*. Cambridge: Harvard UP, 1995.

Sohn, Katherine Kelleher. *Whistlin' and Crowin' Women of Appalachia: Literacy Practices since College*. Carbondale: Southern Illinois UP, 2006.

## Rural Education and Place-Based Education

Brooke, Robert, ed. *Place-Conscious Education and the Teaching of Writing*. New York: Teachers College P, 2003.

Haas, Toni, and Paul Nachtigal. *Place Value: An Educators' Guide to Good Literature on Rural Lifeways, Environments, and Purposes of Education*. Charleston, WV: ERIC Clearinghouse on Rural Education and Small Schools, 1998.

Howley, Craig B., and John M. Eckman, eds. *Sustainable Small Schools: A Handbook for Rural Communities*. Charleston, WV: ERIC Clearinghouse on Rural Education and Small Schools, 1997.

Miller, Bruce, and Karen J. Hahn. *Finding Their Own Place: Youth from Three Small Rural Communities Take Part in Instructive School-to-Work Experiences*. Charleston, WV: ERIC Clearinghouse on Rural Education and Small Schools, 1997.

Nachtigal, Paul, ed. *Rural Education: In Search of a Better Way*. Boulder, CO: Westview Press, 1982.

Sobel, David. *Mapmaking with Children: Sense of Place Education for the Elementary Years*. Portsmouth, NH: Heinemann, 1998.

———. *Place-Based Education: Connecting Classrooms and Communities*. Nature Literacy Series 4. Great Barrington, MA: Orion Society, 2004.

Theobald, Paul. *Call School: Rural Education in the Midwest to 1918*. Carbondale: Southern Illinois UP, 1995.

———. *Teaching the Commons: Place, Pride, and the Renewal of Community*. Boulder, CO: Westview Press, 1997.

Walker, Clare Leslie, John Tallmadge, Tom Wessels, and Ann Zwinger. *Into the Field: A Guide to Locally Focused Teaching*. Nature Literacy Series 3. Great Barrington, MA: Orion Society, 1999.

Webb, Clark D., Larry K. Shumway, and R. Wayne Shute. *Local Schools of Thought: A Search for Purpose in Rural Education*. Charleston, WV: ERIC Clearinghouse on Rural Education and Small Schools, 1996.

## Contemporary Memoirs and Essays on Rural Life

Barnes, Kim. *In the Wilderness: Coming of Age in Unknown Country*. New York: Bantam, 1996.

Bass, Rick. *The Book of Yaak*. Boston: Mariner, 1997.

Berry, Wendell. *The Art of the Commonplace: The Agrarian Essays of Wendell Berry*. Ed. Norman Wirzba. Washington, DC: Counterpoint, 2002.

———.*The Gift of Good Land: Further Essays Cultural and Agricultural*. San Francisco: North Point, 1981.

———. *The Unsettling of America: Culture and Agriculture*. San Francisco: Sierra Club, 1977.

Blew, Mary Clearman. *All but the Waltz: A Memoir of Five Generations in the Life of a Montana Family*. New York: Penguin, 1991.

———. *Balsamroot*. New York: Penguin, 1994.

———. *Bone Deep in the Landscape: Reading, Writing, and Place*. Norman: U of Oklahoma P, 1999.

Blunt, Judy. *Breaking Clean*. New York: Knopf, 2002.

Butala, Sharon. *Perfection of the Morning: A Woman's Awakening in Nature*. St. Paul: Hungry Mind Press, 1994.

Campbell, Maria. *Halfbreed*. Lincoln: U of Nebraska P, 1973.

Carter, Jimmy. *An Hour before Daylight: Memoirs of a Rural Boyhood*. New York: Simon, 2001.

Cook-Lynn, Elizabeth. *Why I Can't Read Wallace Stegner and Other Essays: A Tribal Voice*. Madison: U of Wisconsin P, 1996.

Ehrlich, Gretel. *The Solace of Open Spaces*. New York: Penguin, 1986.

Frazier, Ian. *Great Plains*. New York: Farrar, 1989.

Gilfillan, Merrill. *Magpie Rising: Sketches from the Great Plains*. Lincoln: U of Nebraska P, 2003.

Graves, John. *Hardscrabble: Observations on a Patch of Land*. Dallas: Southern Methodist UP, 2003.

Gruchow, Paul. *Grass Roots: The Universe of Home*. Minneapolis: Milkweed, 1995.

———. *The Necessity of Empty Places*. New York. St. Martin's, 1988.

Hasselstrom, Linda. *Between Grass and Sky*. Reno: U of Nevada P, 2002.

———. *Feels Like Far: A Rancher's Life on the Great Plains*. Boston: Houghton, 2001.

———. *Going Over East: Reflections of a Woman Rancher*. Golden, CO: Fulcrum, 1993.

———. *Land Circle: Writings Collected from the Land*. Golden, CO: Fulcrum, 1991.

Hasselstrom, Linda, Gaydell Collier, and Nancy Curtis, eds. *Crazy Woman Creek: Women Rewrite the American West*. Boston: Mariner, 2004.

———. *Leaning into the Wind: Women Write from the Heart of the West*. Boston: Houghton, 1997.

————. *Woven on the Wind: Women Write about Friendship in the Sagebrush West.* Boston: Houghton, 2001.

Jenkinson, Clay S. *Message on the Wind: A Spiritual Odyssey on the Northern Plains.* Reno: Marmarth, 2002.

Jordan, Teresa. *Riding the White Horse Home.* New York: Vintage Departures, 1993.

Kittredge, William. *Hole in the Sky.* New York: Knopf, 1992.

Klinkenborg, Verlyn. *The Rural Life.* New York: Little, 2002.

Kooser, Ted. *Local Wonders: Seasons in the Bohemian Alps.* Lincoln: U of Nebraska P, 2002.

Norris, Kathleen. *Dakota: A Spiritual Geography.* Boston: Houghton, 1993.

Norton, Lisa Dale. *Hawk Flies Above: Journey to the Heart of the Sandhills.* New York: Picador, 1996.

Quantic, Diane D., and P. Jane Hafen, eds. *A Great Plains Reader.* Lincoln: U of Nebraska P, 2003.

Richter, Robert. *Homefield: Sonata in Rural Voice.* Omaha: Backwaters Press, 2001.

Spence, Polly. *Moving Out: A Nebraska Woman's Life.* Lincoln: U of Nebraska P, 2002.

Spragg, Mark. *Where Rivers Change Direction.* New York: Riverhead, 2000.

Stegner, Wallace. *The American West as Living Space.* Ann Arbor: U of Michigan P, 1987.

————. *Marking the Sparrow's Fall: The Making of the American West.* New York: Owl Books, 1998.

————. *Where the Bluebird Sings to the Lemonade Springs.* New York: Random, 1992.

————. *Wolf Willow: A History, a Story, and a Memory of the Last Plains Frontier.* New York: Penguin, 2000.

# Notes

## 1. Constructing Rural Literacies: Moving Beyond the Rhetorics of Lack, Lag, and the Rosy Past

1. See Corby Kummer's "Principled Pork" in the September 2004 *Atlantic Monthly* and "The Unsustainability of Sustainability" by Bill Devall at <http://www.culturechange.org/issue19/unsustainability.htm>.

2. The President's Council on Sustainable Development goals read as follows:

Goal 1: Health and the Environment. Ensure that every person enjoys the benefits of clean air, clean water, and a healthy environment at home, at work, and at play.

Goal 2: Economic Prosperity. Sustain a healthy U.S. economy that grows sufficiently to create meaningful jobs, reduce poverty, and provide the opportunity for a high quality of life for all in an increasingly competitive world.

Goal 3: Equity. Ensure that all Americans are afforded justice and have the opportunity to achieve economic, environmental, and social well-being.

Goal 4: Conservation of Nature. Use, conserve, protect, and restore natural resources—land, air, water, and biodiversity—in ways that help ensure long-term social, economic, and environmental benefits for ourselves and future generations.

Goal 5: Stewardship. Create a widely held ethic of stewardship that strongly encourages individuals, institutions, and corporations to take full responsibility for the economic, environmental, and social consequences of their actions.

Goal 6: Sustainable Communities. Encourage people to work together to create healthy communities where natural and historic resources are preserved, jobs are available, sprawl is contained, neighborhoods are secure, education is lifelong, transportation and health care are accessible, and all citizens have opportunities to improve the quality of their lives.

Goal 7: Civic Engagement. Create full opportunity for citizens, businesses, and communities to participate in and influence the natural resource, environmental, and economic decisions that affect them.

Goal 8: Population. Move toward stabilization of U.S. population.

Goal 9: International Responsibility. Take a leadership role in the development and implementation of global sustainable development policies, standards of conduct, and trade and foreign policies that further the achievement of sustainability.

Goal 10: Education. Ensure that all Americans have equal access to education and lifelong learning opportunities that will prepare them for meaningful work, a high quality of life, and an understanding of the concepts involved in sustainable development.

3. It is worth noting that Owens's definition of sustainability takes aim at the consumerist culture typical of urban and suburban lifestyles, not traditional rural lifestyles where small farmers or others living close to the land engage in sustainable practices that come from long-established intergenerational land stewardship practices. However, Owens's definition is still a powerful one, as many rural areas have fallen into or embraced the kinds of consumerist lifestyles and unsustainable farming practices endorsed by neoliberal rhetorics of economic development.

4. The relationship between "norm" and "ideal" is important; in the case of literacy, both concepts have been used to categorize those who either lie outside the norm or fall woefully short of the ideal. Davis writes that the "norm," as statistically identified, can itself become a kind of wished-for ideal. In addition, reaching for high ideals is seen as a mechanism to elevate further the "norm."

5. This quote is attributed to Captain Richard Henry Pratt, who founded one of the first boarding schools, Carlisle Indian School, in Pennsylvania in 1879.

6. This quote is attributed to Commissioner of Indian Affairs T. J. Morgan.

7. For a discussion of problems specific to implementing NCLB in rural schools, see Cynthia Reeves's "Implementing the No Child Left Behind Act: Implications for Rural Schools and Districts," published on the Web site of the North Central Regional Educational Laboratory, <http://www.ncrel.org/policy/pubs/html/implicate>.

## 2. Rhetorics and Realities: The History and Effects of Stereotypes about Rural Literacies

1. Appalachian English as some sort of semi-preserved Elizabethan English and as one unified dialect has long since been disproved. See Michael Montgomery's essay "In the Appalachians They Speak Like Shakespeare."

2. According to the National Center for Education Statistics, between 1870 and 1900, the overall illiteracy rate in the United States, defined as the "percentage of persons 14 years old and over who were . . . unable to read or write in any language," was nearly halved, from 20.0 to 10.7 percent. Most of this improvement came from the education of newly freed blacks and others identified as "non-white" (79.9 percent to 44.5 percent). The real issue in raising literacy

rates at this time was the education of freed blacks instead of literacy missions to largely white Appalachia (U.S. Department of Commerce, *Historical Statistics* and *Ancestry and Language in the United States*).

3. Shapiro attributes Harney's essay in *Lippincott's Magazine*, "A Strange Land and a Peculiar People," with largely initiating the "othering" of Appalachia by local color writers. Mortensen describes the contributions of Fox and Allen to identifying the Kentucky mountains as a distinct, uncivilized space from Bluegrass Kentucky. Fox's novel *The Little Shepherd of Kingdom Come* describes a deserving mountain boy who comes down from the hills to be "civilized" by the effects of town life. Murfree's collection of stories *In the Tennessee Mountains* offers itself as a detailed study of the nature of mountain people, though the time Murfree actually spent in the Tennessee mountains was limited to brief sojourns there as a tourist.

4. In addition, economic policies such as outsourcing and the combination of factors that caused the farm crisis have genuinely isolated many rural Americans.

5. Mission school curricula documented by Kim Donehower in interviews with school alumnae.

6. An interesting analysis of the spread of Appalachian stereotypes to other rural areas in popular media is J. W. Williamson's *Hillbillyland: What the Movies Did to the Mountains and What the Mountains Did to the Movies.* Williamson argues that the film industry lifted the "hillbilly" stereotype out of its mountain context to form a code through which American moviegoers understand rural types. He analyzes "hillbilly" characters, from the mountain barbarians in *Deliverance* to Kurt Russell's slovenly rural Oregonian in *Overboard.* The uncivilized nature of these rural brutes can be terrifying, as in *Deliverance,* or humorous, as in the much-publicized *New Beverly Hillbillies,* a reality television show in development by CBS before protests halted production. The show aimed to plunk down a rural family in a community such as Beverly Hills, where they would be expected to demonstrate their ignorance of the jet-set lifestyle in amusing ways.

7. In contrast with George Vincent's commentary on the mountaineer is that of British folklorist Cecil Sharpe, who collected folksongs in the region in 1916. Sharpe commented, "That the illiterate may nevertheless reach a high level of culture will surprise those only who imagine that education and cultivation are convertible terms" (qtd. in Whisnant 117).

8. An approximate 22 percent illiteracy rate was reported in mountain counties; 18 percent in the Kentucky Bluegrass region.

9. In the writings of Fox and other local color writers, mountaineers were often portrayed as being of loose morals—all the more justification for missionary efforts to the mountains.

10. As rural regions in the United States are still seen by many as being predominantly white, despite the presence of significant Hispanic and American

Indian populations, a similar racial motivation can be seen in attempts to preserve "our common heritage" in rural places.

11. A good bibliography on diversity in Appalachia, put together by the Rentschler Library at Miami University, Hamilton, may be accessed at <www. ham.muohio.edu/library/pubs/appalachia.htm>. For general information on diversity in Appalachia, see Patricia Beaver and Helen Lewis, "Uncovering the Trail of Ethnic Denial: Ethnicity in Appalachia." Wayne Winkler's book *Walking toward Sunset: The Melungeons of Appalachia* is a good starting point for information on Melungeons, an Appalachian people whose heritage has been speculated to be a mix of northern European, American Indian, Portuguese, and Spanish.

12. Moffett's conclusions stand in sharp contrast to the transcripts of his Kanawha County interviews, in which, despite his sometimes heavy-handed Socratic questioning, he treats his informants with a good deal of respect. His relationship to them is more complex than a simple matter of arrogant academic and resentful locals, which makes his final conclusions all the more striking.

13. This is a much-simplified version of William H. Jansen's notions of esoteric and exoteric lore, later developed by Ellen Stekert. According to Jansen, "Esoteric applies to what one group thinks of itself and what it supposes others think of it. The exoteric is what one group thinks of another and what it thinks that other group thinks it thinks" (46). In my understanding of these terms, esoteric lore defines the group from within, asserting, in essence, "This is us." Exoteric lore defines the group in contradistinction to another entity "outside" the group; "This is them and we are not them." This chapter combines Jansen's ideas with Noyes's work on the role of performance in marking group identity. Noyes argues that it is only in the moment of performance that we can glimpse any sort of fixed identity on the part of a group.

14. All place and personal names are pseudonyms.

15. Analysis of Haines Gap informants' choices about literacy in light of the outside literacy sponsors in the community appears in Donehower, "Literacy Choices in an Appalachian Community."

16. Parts of the analysis of the literacy of the women of Haines Gap, especially this discussion of the function of Ida's literacy practices, were first written about in Donehower, "Reconsidering Power, Privilege, and the Public/Private Distinction in the Literacy of Rural Women."

17. Rural people are not the only ones facing a cultural illiteracy stigma in the United States. Public commentary over "Ebonics" movements show that rural people are just one of many groups tagged as subliterate by the mainstream culture.

18. See Katherine Kelleher Sohn, "Whistlin' and Crowin' Women of Appalachia: Literacy Practices since College" and in book-length form in Southern Illinois University Press's Studies in Writing and Rhetoric Series. Sohn studied nontraditional female college graduates to consider how their literacies affected their lives, careers, communities, and children after college. Martha Kruse's dis-

sertation, "From Village to College: Writing the Rural Experience," follows college students who hail from rural areas and "seeks to facilitate an understanding of the ways in which a rural upbringing may enhance, subvert, and complicate the acquisition of literate behaviors" (14). Adrienne Lamberti's dissertation on technical communication, "Eminent Domain: Documents of Coordination in Agriculture," uses a cultural studies methodology, personal interviews, and participant-observation to describe and analyze the development, writing, and publication of an agricultural nonprofit agency's "documents of coordination." Edmondson's *Prairie Town* assesses the changing nature of rural literacies through an ethnographic study of a rural Minnesota community.

## 3. The Rhetorics of the Farm Crisis: Toward Alternative Agrarian Literacies in a Globalized World

1. The definition of what constitutes a family farm is not self-evident. In fact, the U.S. Department of Agriculture has a specific formula for calculating which farms are family farms and has shifted their definition and criteria over time according to size and the amount of revenue generated. My definition of a family farm is drawn from the National Family Farm Coalition, which works to guarantee a sustainable livelihood for family farmers: "A family farm is not defined by size, but rather by the fact that the family provides the vast majority of the labor and management decisions. . . . The common goal of family farmers is farm sustainability—both economically and environmentally. On a family farm, the family takes the risks, makes the decisions and should receive the economic gains" ("What Is a Family Farm?"). It should be added to this definition that those gains should not be at the expense of agricultural workers, the environment, and the rural communities near the farm.

2. The expression "farm crisis" is not a historically accurate one as it implies a short-range economic problem when, in actuality, the "farm crisis" is cyclical and the current modern "farm crisis" is over three decades old. Nevertheless, the expression is deployed throughout this chapter, although I argue that it is a questionable term. My reason for continuing to use the term "farm crisis" is that it has become a shorthand terminology for understanding the economic shifts that are underway in rural America and in other parts of the globe where agricultural life and work for rural people has served as the dominant mode of production.

3. See Catherine McNicol Stock's *Rural Radicals: Righteous Rage in the American Grain*, a historical analysis of how rural radicalism has played out in two dominant forms: producerism, which has involved movements for social justice and egalitarianism, and "vigilantism," which has played out in reactive movements against immigrants and groups that rural people see as "outsiders." Stock argues that five contexts inform these movements: "frontier life, class, race, gender, and evangelism" (7).

4. Nixon-era secretary of agriculture Earl Butz used the phrase "get bigger or get out" to encourage farmers to expand their acreage and plant "fence-row to fence-row." The end result was that after the era of unchecked agricultural expansion, interest rates skyrocketed. Most farmers could not pay back their loans, and farm foreclosures became a frequent feature of rural life in farming communities throughout the 1980s.

5. For a readable analysis of how farm and food policy and nutritional information is influenced by food industry lobbying, see Marion Nestle's *Food Politics: How the Food Industry Influences Nutrition and Health.*

6. The literature on farm subsidies is wide-ranging, including historical analyses, ideological analyses, and partisan reports. A few sources are noteworthy and forecast the future of farm subsidies. The collection "A Food and Agriculture Policy for the 21st Century," edited by Michael Stumo, includes presentations and materials that resulted from the Organization for Competitive Markets' Food Policy Retreat convened April 29 to May 1, 2000, in Parkville, Missouri. The retreat addressed "widespread dissatisfaction with the current status of agricultural policy and market structure; the increasing consumer concern about the quality of their food and how food is produced; and the belief that progress must come from an approach that considers a wider range of stakeholders than merely agribusiness." The papers offer interesting solutions to our current food and farm policy situation.

7. For a critical assessment of the Freedom to Farm bill, see a report of the Environmental Working Group, *Freedom to Farm: An Analysis of Payments to Large Agribusiness Operations, Big City Residents, and the USDA Bureaucracy.* For a different take on the Freedom to Farm bill, see "Freedom to Farm Bill Has Not Hurt Agriculture—Yet," which offers a more sanguine view of Freedom to Farm from Dwight Aakre, North Dakota State University extension farm management economist.

8. For more on this situation, see the June 22, 2003, *60 Minutes* segment "Pork Power" on corporate hog farms in North Carolina, which spotlights rural residents who are fighting back against the environmental damage caused by this industry.

9. Food democracy is also an issue inextricably tied to human rights, women's rights, and questions of social and racial justice. As Shiva points out, "The vast majority of the world's people—70 percent—earn their livelihoods by producing food. The majority of these farmers are women" (7). In the United States and other European nations, farming has been an occupation dominated by white men and by white men who run agribusiness corporations. Overt racism is an issue for many black farmers in the United States. Black farmers have been subject to agricultural racism and to discrimination in obtaining loans and financing for their farm operations ("Agricultural Racism"). More recently, these farmers have fought back through the court system to gain fair consideration in the lending process, but for many black farmers, it is too late ("Obstruction of Justice"). One

interesting and encouraging trend is that a rising number of small farmers in the United States are women and of Hispanic heritage (Green). While women have often been involved in farming, they are usually not listed or counted as farm operators (they are often seen as "helpers"); their husbands or other male family members or partners are acknowledged as farmers. Changing attitudes and patterns of agriculture have led to an increase in female farmers: women are inheriting farmland from their husbands and are focusing on different types of farming, such as producing specialty crops and engaging in organic farming. In addition, a renaissance of farmers' markets has led to local distribution sites that women entrepreneurs are capitalizing upon. Even as trends such as these among small farmers portend possibilities, there is still the overwhelming dominance of the world's food production by large agribusiness firms, which are key manifestations of capitalist patriarchy.

10. For more on the social and economic conflicts of the orchard industry in eastern Washington State, see David Guterson's article "The Kingdom of Apples: Washington State" from *Harper's Magazine* and the documentary *Broken Limbs: Apples, Agriculture, and the New American Farmer*, a story of the orchard industry in the Wenatchee Valley told by the son of an orchardist.

11. Past versions of the Farm Aid Web site, including the July 2004 version of the Web site that is examined here, can be accessed through the Internet archive called the WayBack Machine, which shows Web pages dating back to 1998. I thank Mary Queen for calling my attention to this Web-based archival resource.

12. CFSC is a nonprofit 501(c)(3) North American organization "dedicated to building strong, sustainable, local and regional food systems that ensure access to affordable, nutritious, and culturally appropriate food for all people at all times. They seek to develop self-reliance among all communities in obtaining their food and to create a system of growing, manufacturing, processing, making available, and selling food that is regionally based and grounded in the principles of justice, democracy, and sustainability" (Community).

13. For more on the protests, see the digital archive "WTO: Seattle Collection."

14. It is worth noting here that many farmers, even those deemed successful, often work off-the-farm jobs to generate income to keep their farming operations afloat—a fact often not mentioned in farming success narratives. As I learned from attending the 2005 Farm to Cafeteria Conference, Ed Snavely, one of the featured farmers on the Farm Aid Web site, is one such farmer, working an off-the-farm job of forty hours per week.

## 4. Beyond Agrarianism: Toward a Critical Pedagogy of Place

1. A variety of writers and philosophers address the agrarian lifestyle, many of whom have produced critical texts for thinking about environmental

and social justice issues. For example, Wallace Stegner, known by some as the "grandfather of western literature," is also known for having "shaped the discourse of western public history so that its lessons encouraged environmental conservation over maximum use" (Comer 39, 42). Krista Comer contends that Western writers with a "Stegnerian bent," such as Ivan Doig, Norman McLean, or James Welch, to name a few, "come at western landscapes with fresh minds and political intentions" and thus don't necessarily reinscribe white patriarchal visions of Western spaces (101–2). Of course, Stegner—like so many white writers of the plains and the West—is problematic in other racial and gendered ways; see Elizabeth Cook-Lynn's *Why I Can't Read Wallace Stegner and Other Essays* as one example of this perspective.

2. For a more in-depth examination of these literacies, see my larger book project involving this research, *From the Garden Club: Rural Women Writing Community* (University of Nebraksa Press, 2006). Additional work with this research can be found in "The Space between Public and Private: Rural Nebraska Women's Literacy"; "'Private' Lives and 'Public' Writing: Rhetorical Practices of Western Nebraska Women"; and "'Settling Down' in Western Nebraska: Grounding Local History in Memoir."

3. Except for women whose writing is cited, all names are pseudonyms.

4. Books on ordinary writing, such as *The Extraordinary Work of Ordinary Writing: Annie Ray's Diary* by Jennifer Sinor and *Read This Only to Yourself: The Private Writings of Midwestern Women, 1880–1910* by Elizabeth Hampsten, focus on diaries, and while I gained much insight about the Paxton women's writings from these texts, I don't think the local writings I describe fit in with their diary analyses. As I argue in *From the Garden Club*, the ordinary writing done by the Paxton women does not seem to fall into the category of "private" writing, not meant for sharing, nor does it exactly fit into the more "public" kinds of "private" writing (and here I mean writing done in private form but with the intent to be seen by an audience, such as Eleanor Pruitt Stewart's *Letters of a Woman Homesteader*). Rather, their texts fall between the space of what's traditionally considered public and private—they were written for others, but the sense of audience was a very local readership, most likely their peers. Even if they had a sense that future generations or strangers would read them, they were not written with the intent to publish, but neither were they written for only themselves.

5. See *From the Garden Club* for more on class in Paxton.

## 5. Toward a Sustainable Citizenship and Pedagogy

1. The Amish have become a favorite symbol to mark the "ultra-rural" in American consciousness, as we see from such endeavors as the reality television show *Amish in the City*, which imagines that the greatest contrast and conflict possible would arise between urban and Amish youth. (The documentary *Devil's*

*Playground,* in contrast, shows that contemporary American adolescent culture has seeped deeply into Amish consciousness and that the imagined differences between Amish adolescents and their urban and suburban counterparts are fewer than we might think.) When the Amish occupy the "most rural" node on the urban-rural spectrum, "rural" comes to be associated with isolation, fundamentalist religious practices, "backward" or out-of-date ways of doing things, and a stubborn refusal to join the "modern" world.

2. Diana George and John Trimbur's textbook, *Reading Culture: Contexts for Critical Reading and Writing,* is perhaps the most widely used example of such a course model.

3. Marilyn Cooper, Diana George, and Dennis Lynch describe a model of an argument-based, mutual-inquiry-centered composition course in "Moments of Argument: Agonistic Inquiry and Confrontational Cooperation."

4. There are national opportunities for rural advocacy as well. One of the most promising is the 80-55 Coalition. Founded in 2003, it is a broad nonpartisan group working to gain rural America its proper representation in the political process. The coalition dispels myths about rural Americans, spurs "the public, the media and subject matter experts to take action and participate in substantive discussion" on rural issues, and acknowledges the contributions of rural Americans to our nation's livelihood ("About Us"). Its Web site, <www.8055.org>, provides resources on rural topics and opportunities to volunteer as part of the coalition's political and community organizing activities.

5. See Robert Brooke's edited collection, *Rural Voices: Place-Conscious Education and the Teaching of Writing,* described in chapter 2, for examples of rural writing on place in K–12 classrooms. See also Nedra Reynolds's *Geographies of Writing.*

6. Not surprisingly, these programs are not attempted without obstacles, the dominant one being the limits of standardized tests to quantifying this kind of interdisciplinary learning.

# Works Cited

"About Ruralwomyn." *The Rural Womyn Zone.* 21 July 2005 <http://ruralwomyn. net/mailman/listinfo/ruralwomyn_ruralwomyn.net>.

"About the Rural School and Community Trust." *Rural School and Community Trust.* 1 Sept. 2004 <http://www.ruraledu.org/about/rt_what.htm>.

"About Us." *80–55 Coalition for Rural America.* 15 Sept. 2004 <http://www.8055. org/aboutus.html>.

Adler, Mortimer, and Charles Van Doren. *How to Read a Book.* New York: Touchstone, 1972.

Adler-Kassner, Linda, ed. *Considering Literacy.* New York: Longman, 2006.

"Agricultural Racism: Bitter Harvest for Blacks." *Philadelphia Inquirer* 10 Aug. 2004. 29 Aug. 2004 <http://www.ewg.org/news/story.php?id=2992>.

"All About Slow Food." *Slow Food.* 3 Mar. 2006 <http://www.slowfood.com/eng/ sf_cose/sf_cose.lasso>.

Allen, James Lane. *The Blue-grass Region of Kentucky and Other Kentucky Articles.* New York: Harper and Brothers, 1892.

*Amish in the City.* Prod. Steven Cantor, Jon Kroll, Daniel Laikind, et al. UPN, 2004.

Andrzejewski, Julie, and John Alessio. "Education for Global Citizenship and Social Responsibility." *Progressive Perspectives* 1.2 (Spring 1999): 1–23. 25 Sept. 2004 <http://www.uvm.edu/~dewey/monographs/glomono.html# Education%20for%20Global%20Citizenship%20and%20Social>.

The Annenberg Challenge. "What Rural Schools Can Teach Urban Systems." *Challenge Journal.* 17 Dec. 2003 <http://www.annenbergchallenge.org/pubs/ cj/v1n2/pg4.html>.

Aristotle. *On Rhetoric: A Theory of Civic Discourse.* Trans. George Kennedy. New York: Oxford UP, 1991.

"Arts and Cultural Heritage." *Rural School and Community Trust.* 8 Feb. 2004 <http://www.ruraledu.org/topics/artcult.htm>.

Barlett, Peggy F., and Geoffrey W. Chase, eds. *Sustainability on Campus: Stories and Strategies for Change.* Cambridge: MIT P, 2004.

Barry, Dave. "Buffalo Jerky to Catfish Seminars: It's the Grand Cities." *Miami Herald* 11 Nov. 2001.

———. "From Ice Fishing to Stuff Suspended in Jell-O: A Good Time." *Miami Herald* 3 Mar. 2002.

———. "Grand Illusions." *Boston Globe,* 26 Aug. 2001.

———. "OK, They're Brrr-y, Brrr-y Nice Up There in North Dakota." *Miami Herald* 24 Feb. 2002.

Batteau, Allen. *The Invention of Appalachia.* Tucson: U of Arizona P, 1990.

Beaver, Patricia, and Helen Lewis. "Uncovering the Trail of Ethnic Denial: Ethnicity in Appalachia." *Cultural Diversity in the U.S. South: Anthropological Contributions to a Region in Transition.* Ed. Carole Hill and Patricia Beaver. Athens: U of Georgia P, 1988. 51–68.

"The Beginning . . ." *Farm Aid.* 4 June 2004 <http://www.farmaid.org/site/PageServer?pagename=aboutus_history>.

Belasco, Susan, ed. *Constructing Literacies.* Boston: Heinle and Heinle, 2001.

Berlin, James A. *Rhetorics, Poetics, and Cultures: Refiguring College English Studies.* Urbana, IL: NCTE, 1996.

Berry, Wendell. "Conserving Communities." *Rooted in the Land: Essays on Community and Place.* Ed. Wes Jackson and William Vitek. New Haven, CT: Yale UP, 1996. 76–84.

———. *The Unsettling of America: Culture and Agriculture.* San Francisco: Sierra Club, 1977.

Blackburn, Tom. "The Ballad of Davy Crockett." Music by George Bruns. Performed by Bill Hayes. *The Top Pops.* RCA/Victor, 1956.

Blew, Mary Clearman. *All but the Waltz: A Memoir of Five Generations in the Life of a Montana Family.* New York: Penguin, 1991.

Bonacich, Edna. Interview. "Is Wal-Mart Good for America?" *Frontline.* PBS. 3 Mar. 2006 <http://www.pbs.org/wgbh/pages/frontline/shows/walmart/interviews/bonacich.html>.

Brandt, Deborah. *Literacy in American Lives.* Cambridge: Cambridge UP, 2001.

———. "Sponsors of Literacy." *College Composition and Communication* 49.2 (1998): 165–85.

"A Brief History of the Central Nebraska Public Power and Irrigation District." *The Central Nebraska Public Power and Irrigation District.* 21 July 2005 <http://www.cnppid.com/History_Central_P2.htm>.

*Broken Limbs: Apples, Agriculture, and the New American Farmer.* Dir. Jamie Howell and Guy Evans. Documentary film. 57 minutes. Bullfrog Films, 2004.

Brooke, Robert, ed. *Rural Voices: Place-Conscious Education and the Teaching of Writing.* New York: Teachers College P, 2003.

Bruch, Patrick, and Richard Marback, eds. *Reading City Life.* New York: Longman, 2005.

Bryson, Bill. "Fat Girls in Des Moines." *The Best of Granta Travel.* Ed. Bill Buford. London: Penguin, 1991. 203–11.

Burke, Kenneth. *A Rhetoric of Motives.* New York: Prentice Hall, 1950.

"A Call for a New Farm and Trade Policy." *Farm Aid.* 17 Sept. 2004 <http://www.farmaid.org/site/News2?page=NewsArticle&id=5284&news_iv_ctrl=-1>.

Carlson, Paul. *The Plains Indians.* College Station: Texas A&M UP, 1998.

"Census 2000 Urban and Rural Classification." *U.S. Census Bureau.* 25 Sept. 2004 <http://www.census.gov/geo/www/ua/ua_2k.html>.

Christensen, Fae. "Cemetery Record of Paxton Resident from Here to Eternity." Unpublished essay, n.d.

———. "How Old Is Paxton?" Unpublished essay, n.d.

Columbo, Gary, Robert Cullen, and Bonnie Lisle, eds. *Rereading America: Cultural Contexts for Critical Thinking and Writing.* 5th ed. Boston: Bedford/St. Martin's, 2001.

Comer, Krista. *Landscapes of the New West: Gender and Geography in Contemporary Women's Writing.* Chapel Hill: U of North Carolina P, 1999.

Commission on Country Life. *Report of the Commission on Country Life.* New York: Sturgis and Walton, 1911.

*Community Food Security Coalition.* 28 June 2005 <http://www.foodsecurity.org/>.

Cook, Christopher D. *Diet for a Dead Planet: How the Food Industry Is Killing Us.* New York: New Press, 2004.

Cook-Lynn, Elizabeth. *Why I Can't Read Wallace Stegner and Other Essays: A Tribal Voice.* Madison: U of Wisconsin P, 1996.

Cooper, Marilyn, Diana George, and Dennis Lynch. "Moments of Argument: Agonistic Inquiry and Confrontational Cooperation." *College Composition and Communication* 48.1 (1997): 61–85.

Cushman, Ellen. "The Public Intellectual, Activist Research, and Service-Learning." *College English* 61.1 (1999): 68–76.

———. "Rhetorician as an Agent of Social Change." *College Composition and Communication* 47.1 (1996): 7–28.

Davidson, Osha Gray. *Broken Heartland: The Rise of America's Rural Ghetto.* Iowa City: U of Iowa P, 1996.

Davis, Dee, and Tim Marema. "A Rural Perspective." *Center for Rural Strategies.* 2 Sept. 2004 <http://www.ruralstrategies.org/issues/perspective2.html>.

Davis, Lennard. *Enforcing Normalcy: Disability, Deafness, and the Body.* New York: Verso, 1995.

"Dear Friend." *Farm Aid.* 4 June 2004 <http://www.farmaid.org/site/PageServer?pagename=info_help>.

*Deliverance.* Dir. John Boorman. Screenplay by James Dickey. Warner Brothers, 1972.

*Devil's Playground.* Dir. Lucy Walker. Cinemax, 2002.

Dickey, James. *Deliverance.* Boston: Houghton, 1970.

Dobrin, Sidney L., and Christian Weisser, eds. *Ecocomposition: Theoretical and Pedagogical Approaches.* Albany: State U of New York P, 2001.

Donehower, Kim. "Literacy Choices in an Appalachian Community." *Journal of Appalachian Studies* 9.2 (2003): 341–62.

———. "Reconsidering Power, Privilege, and the Public/Private Distinction in the Literacy of Rural Women." *Women and Literacy: Inquiries for a New*

*Century*. Ed. Beth Daniell and Peter Mortensen. Urbana, IL: LEA/NCTE, 2007. 91–108.

Edmondson, Jacqueline. *Prairie Town: Redefining Rural Life in the Age of Globalization*. Lanham, MD: Rowman, 2003.

Education Commission of the States. "Distance Education Overcomes Isolation." *State Education Leader* 19.1 (2001). 2 July 2003 <http://www.ecs.org/clearinghouse/24/10/2410.htm>.

Environmental Working Group. *Freedom to Farm: An Analysis of Payments to Large Agribusiness Operations, Big City Residents, and the USDA Bureaucracy*. 27 Feb. 1996. 20 July 2005 <http://www.ewg.org/reports/FTFWeb/ftfcontents.html>.

"Factory Farms." *Farm Aid*. 4 June 2004 <http://www.farmaid.org/PageServer?pagename=info_facts_factory>.

"Fair Prices: Time Is Running Out for Family Farms and Rural Communities." *Farm Crisis*. 21 Mar. 2004 <http://www.farmcrisis.org/>.

Faleide, Lisa Swanson. "Narrative for Prairie Commons Center for Women Program and Curriculum Development." Unpublished essay, n.d.

"Family Farmers: Struggling to Stay on the Land." *Farm Aid*. 15 Sept. 2004 <http://www.farmaid.org/site/PageServer?pagename=info_facts_help>.

"Farm Aid and YOU Saved a Family Farm." *Farm Aid*. 17 Sept. 2004 <http://www.farmaid.org/site/News2?page=NewsArticle&id=5681>.

"Farm Aid FAQs." *Farm Aid*. 24 Jan. 2002. WayBack Machine Internet Archive. 20 Sept. 2004 <http://web.archive.org/web/20020611013808/www.farmaid.org/event/info/faq.asp>.

"Farm Aid Home Page." *Farm Aid*. 5 July 2004. WayBack Machine Internet Archive. 20 June 2006 <http://web.archive.org/web/20040705051134/www.farmaid.org/site/PageServer>.

"The Farm Aid Mission Statement." *Farm Aid*. 4 June 2004 <http://www.farmaid.org/site/PageServer?pagename=aboutus_mission>.

"Farm Facts." *Farm Aid*. 24 Jan 2002. WayBack Machine Internet Archive. 20 Sept. 2004 <http://web.archive.org/web/20020611012826/www.farmaid.org/event/info/facts.asp>.

*Fast Food Women*. Dir. and prod. Anne Lewis Johnson. Appalshop Film and Video, 1991.

Fink, Deborah. *Agrarian Women: Wives and Mothers in Rural Nebraska, 1880–1940*. Chapel Hill: U of North Carolina P, 1992.

———. *Cutting into the Meatpacking Line: Workers and Change in the Rural Midwest*. Chapel Hill: U of North Carolina P, 1998.

———. *Open Country, Iowa: Rural Women, Tradition, and Change*. Albany: State U of New York P, 1986.

"First Chance Project." *The Rural Womyn Zone*. 21 July 2005 <http://www.ruralwomyn.net/firstchance.html>.

Fishman, Andrea. *Amish Literacy: What and How It Means.* Portsmouth, NH: Heinemann, 1988.

Fox, John. *The Kentuckians.* New York: Harper and Brothers, 1898.

———. *The Little Shepherd of Kingdom Come.* New York: Scribner's, 1903.

———. *The Trail of the Lonesome Pine.* New York: Scribner's, 1908.

Frazier, Ian. *Great Plains.* New York: Farrar, 1989.

"Freedom to Farm Bill Has Not Hurt Agriculture—Yet." *Prairie Grain* 15 (Sept.– Oct. 1998). 19 July 2005 <http://www.smallgrains.org/Springwh/sep98/farmbill.htm>.

Freire, Paulo. *Pedagogy in Process: The Letters to Guinea Bissau.* New York: Seabury, 1978.

———. *Pedagogy of Hope: Reliving Pedagogy of the Oppressed.* New York: Continuum, 1995.

———. *Pedagogy of the Oppressed.* Harmondsworth, Eng.: Penguin, 1972.

Friend, Christy. "From the Contact Zone to the City: Iris Marion Young and Composition Theory." *JAC: Journal of Advanced Composition* 19.4 (Winter 1999): 657–76.

George, Diana, and John Trimbur, eds. *Reading Culture: Contexts for Critical Reading and Writing.* 5th ed. New York: Longman, 2004.

Giroux, Henry A. "Cultural Studies, Public Pedagogy, and the Responsibility of Intellectuals." *Communication and Critical/Cultural Studies* 1.1 (2004): 59–79.

———. "Public Pedagogy and the Politics of Neo-liberalism: Making the Political More Pedagogical." *Policy Futures in Education* 2.3–4 (2004): 494–503.

———. "Public Pedagogy as Cultural Politics: Stuart Hall and the 'Crisis' of Culture." *Cultural Studies* 14.2 (2000): 341–60.

"The Global Free Trade of Food: Trading Away Family Farms and Consumer Choice." *Farm Aid.* 20 Mar. 2004 <http://www.farmaid.org/site/PageServer?pagename=info_facts_global>.

Goffman, Erving. *Stigma: Notes on the Management of Spoiled Identity.* 1963. New York: Touchstone, 1986.

Green, Marcus. "Women in Agriculture: The Number of Females Operating Farms Continues to Climb." *Courier Journal* 30 May 2004. 12 Sept. 2004 <http://www.courier-journal.com/business/news2004/05/30/E3-farm30–9921.html>.

Greider, William. "The Last Farm Crisis." *The Nation* 20 Nov. 2000. 20 Mar. 2004 <http://www.thenation.com/docprint.mhtml?i=20001120&s=greider>.

Gruchow, Paul. *The Necessity of Empty Places.* New York: St. Martin's, 1988.

Gruenewald, David. "The Best of Both Worlds: A Critical Pedagogy of Place." *Educational Researcher* 32.4 (May 2003): 3–12.

Guterson, David. "The Kingdom of Apples: Washington State." *Harper's Magazine* Oct. 1999: 1–9. 24 Sept. 2004 <http://www.wkkf.org/Programming/ResourceOverview.aspx?CID=4&ID=2973>.

Hampsten, Elizabeth. *Read This Only to Yourself: The Private Writings of Midwestern Women, 1880–1910.* Bloomington: Indiana UP, 1982.

Harney, Will Wallace. "A Strange Land and a Peculiar People." *Lippincott's Magazine* 12 (1873): 429–38.

Hasselstrom, Linda, Gaydell Collier, and Nancy Curtis, eds. *Leaning into the Wind: Women Write from the Heart of the West.* Boston: Houghton, 1997.

Hawken, Paul. "A Report from the WTO/Seattle Conference." *Global Vision: Communicating Sustainability.* 6 Jan. 2000. 8 Jan. 2007 <http://www.global-vision.org/misc/hawken1.html>.

Heath, Shirley Brice. *Ways with Words: Language, Life, and Work in Communities and Classrooms.* New York: Cambridge UP, 1983.

Higgins Null, Elisabeth. "Llano Grande Center's Oral History Project Sparks Cultural and Economic Renewal in Texas's Rio Grande Valley." *Rural School and Community Trust* 2003. 3 Aug. 2004 <http://www.ruraledu.org/projects/project0400.html>.

Himley, Margaret, Kelly L. Fave, Allen Larson, Susan Yadlon, and the Political Moments Study Group. *Political Moments in the Classroom.* Portsmouth, NH: Heinemann, 1997.

Hogg, Charlotte. *From the Garden Club: Rural Women Writing Community.* Lincoln: U of Nebraska P, 2006.

———. "'Private' Lives and 'Public' Writing: Rhetorical Practices of Western Nebraska Women." *Great Plains Quarterly* 22.3 (Summer 2002): 183–98.

———. "'Settling Down' in Western Nebraska: Grounding Local History in Memoir." *Western American Literature* 37.2 (Fall 2002): 223–40.

———. "The Space between Public and Private: Rural Nebraska Women's Literacy." *Multiple Literacies for the Twenty-first Century.* Ed. Brian Huot, Charles Bazerman, and Beth Stroble. Cresskill, NJ: Hampton Press, 2004. 75–90.

Hogg, Dorlis Osborn. "Dorlis Osborn Hogg." *Keith County Pioneer Centennial Queen Pageant.* Ogallala, NE: Campbell Printing, 1973. 6–7.

———. Untitled essay. *Early Paxton.* Ed. Joyce Lierley. Unpublished anthology, 1982. 59–102.

Ivins, Molly. "Texas Women: True Grit and All the Rest." *Lone Star Literature: From the Red River to the Rio Grande: A Texas Anthology.* Ed. Don Graham. New York: Norton, 2003. 698–703.

Jackson, Wes, and William Vitek, eds. *Rooted in the Land: Essays on Community and Place.* New Haven, CT: Yale UP, 1996.

Jansen, William H. "The Esoteric-Exoteric Factor in Folklore. *The Study of Folklore.* Ed. Alan Dundes. Englewood Cliffs, NJ: Prentice-Hall, 1965. 43–51.

Jefferson, Thomas. *Notes on the State of Virginia.* Ed. Merrill D. Peterson. New York: Library of America, Literary Classics of the United States, 1984. Electronic Text Center. Charlottesville, VA: University of Virginia Library, 1993. 8 Jan. 2007 <http://etext.lib.virginia.edu/etcbin/toccer-new2?id=Jef Virg.

sgm&images=images/modeng&data=/texts/english/modeng/parsed&tag
=public&part=all>.

Jordan, Teresa. *Riding the White Horse Home.* New York: Vintage Departures, 1993.

Jordan, Terry G. "The Concept and Method." *Regional Studies: The Interplay of Land and People.* Ed. Glen E. Lich. College Station: Texas A&M UP, 1992. 8–24.

"Kentucky Adult Literacy Survey." *Kentucky Adult Education.* 30 June 2004 <http://adulted.state.ky.us/kals_survey.htm>.

Kingsolver, Barbara. "A Good Farmer." *The Nation* 3 Nov. 2003.

Klein, Naomi. *Fences and Windows: Dispatches from the Frontlines of the Anti-globalization Debates.* New York: Picador, 2002.

———. *No Logo: No Space, No Choice, No Jobs.* New York: Picador, 2002.

Kruse, Martha. "From Village to College: Writing the Rural Experience." Diss. U of Nebraska–Lincoln, 1995.

Lakoff, George, and Mark Johnson. *Metaphors We Live By.* Chicago: U of Chicago P, 1980.

Lamb, Russell L. "The New Farm Economy." *Regulation* 2003–04: 10–15. 25 June 2005 <http://www.cato.org/pubs/regulation/regv26n4/v26n4-1.pdf>.

Lamberti, Adrienne. "Eminent Domain: Documents of Coordination in Agriculture." Diss. University of Iowa, 2003.

Levine, Lawrence. *Highbrow/Lowbrow: The Emergence of Cultural Hierarchy in America.* Cambridge: Harvard UP, 1988.

Lich, Glen E. Preface. *Regional Studies: The Interplay of Land and People.* Ed. Glen E. Lich. College Station: Texas A&M UP, 1992.

Lierley, Joyce Miank. *Affectionately Yours: Three Immigrants, the American Civil War, and a Michigan Family Saga.* Omaha: Making History, 1998.

Lilliston, Ben, and Niel Ritchie. "Freedom to Fail: How U.S. Farming Policies Have Helped Agribusiness and Pushed Family Farmers toward Extinction." *Multinational Monitor* 21.7–8 (July–Aug. 2000). 22 Mar. 2004 <http://multinationalmonitor.org/mm2000/00july-aug/lilliston.html>.

"The Llano Grande Center." *The Llano Grande Center for Research and Development.* 3 Aug. 2004 <http://www.llanogrande.org/>.

Lofty, John. *Time to Write: The Influence of Time and Culture on Learning to Write.* Albany: State U of New York P, 1992.

Lyson, Thomas A. "What Does a School Mean to a Community? Assessing the Social and Economic Benefits of Schools to Rural Villages in New York." *Journal of Research in Rural Education* 17.3 (2002): 131–37.

MacDaniels, Carol, with Robert Brooke. "Developing School/Community Connections: The Nebraska Writing Project's Rural Institute Program." Ed. Robert Brooke. *Rural Voices: Place-Conscious Education and the Teaching of Writing.* New York: Teachers College P, 2003. 154–70.

Manning, Richard. *Against the Grain: How Agriculture Has Hijacked Civilization.* New York: North Point Press, 2005.

Mathieu, Paula, George Grattan, Tim Lindgren, and Staci Schultz, eds. *Writing Places*. New York: Longman, 2006.

McComiskey, Bruce, and Cynthia Ryan, eds. *City Comp: Identities, Spaces, Practices*. Albany: State U of New York P, 2003.

McGuire, Jana. "School at the Center Program is 'Education without Walls.'" *UNL News Releases* July 1999. 17 Dec. 2003 <http://www.unl.edu/pr/1999/799/7299enews.html>.

*The Meatrix*. Dir. Louis Fox. Animated film. FreeRange Graphics in conjunction with Sustainable Table, 2003. Internet Flash film. 8 Jan. 2007 <http://www.themeatrix1.com/>.

Miller, Bruce. "The Role of Rural Schools in Community Development: Policy Issues and Implications." *Northwest Regional Educational Laboratory* 1995. 26 Sept. 2004 <http://www.nwrel.org/ruraled/role.html>.

Moffett, James. *Storm in the Mountains: A Case Study of Censorship, Conflict, and Consciousness*. Carbondale: Southern Illinois UP, 1989.

Montgomery, Michael. "In the Appalachians They Speak Like Shakespeare." *Language Myths*. Ed. L. Bauer and P. Trudgill. London: Penguin, 1998. 66–76.

Morris, Charles E., III, and Stephen H. Browne, eds. *Readings on the Rhetoric of Social Protest*. State College, PA: Strata Publishing, 2001.

Mortensen, Peter. "Going Public." *College Composition and Communication* 50 (1998): 182–205.

———. "Representations of Literacy and Region: Narrating 'Another America.'" *Pedagogy in the Age of Politics: Writing and Reading (in) the Academy*. Ed. Patricia Sullivan and Donna Qualley. Urbana, IL: NCTE, 1994. 100–120.

Murfree, Mary Noalles. *In the Tennessee Mountains*. Boston: Houghton, 1884.

Nachtigal, Paul, ed. *Rural Education: In Search of a Better Way*. Boulder, CO: Westview Press, 1982.

———. "Rural School Improvement Efforts: An Interpretive History." *Rural Education: In Search of a Better Way*. Ed. Paul Nachtigal. Boulder, CO: Westview Press, 1982. 15–26.

National Center for Education Statistics. *Literacy from 1870 to 1979: Illiteracy*. 2 Sept. 2005 <http://nces.ed.gov/naal/historicaldata/illiteracy.asp>.

National Education Association. *Rural Education*. 2 July 2003 <http://www.nea.org/schools/rural/>.

"National Issues." *Appalachia Educational Laboratory*. 2 July 2003 <http://www.ael.org/rel/rural/rurlabot.htm>.

"Nebraska Quick Facts." *U.S. Census Bureau*. 12 Sept. 2004 <http://quickfacts.census.gov/qfd/states/31000.html>.

Nestle, Marion. *Food Politics: How the Food Industry Influences Nutrition and Health*. Berkeley: U of California P, 2002.

Norberg-Hodge, Helena, and Steven Gorelick. "Bringing the Food Economy Home." *International Society for Ecology and Culture*. 25 Sept. 2004 <http://www.isec.org.uk/articles/bringing.html>.

Norris, Kathleen. "Status: Or, Should Farmers Read Plato?" *Dakota: A Spiritual Geography*. New York: Houghton, 1993. 136–41.

"Not Your Average Pigs: Curly Tail Organic Farm." *Farm Aid*. 17 Sept. 2004 <http://www.farmaid.org/site/News2?page=NewsArticle&id=5683& news_iv_ctrl=-1>.

Noyes, Dorothy. "Group." *Journal of American Folklore* 108 (1995): 449–78.

"Obstruction of Justice: USDA Undermines Historic Civil Rights Settlement with Black Farmers." *Environmental Working Group*. 29 Aug. 2004 <http://www. ewg.org/reports/blackfarmers/execsumm.php>.

"Out of This World Milk: Milky Way Dairy." *Farm Aid*. 17 Sept. 2004 <http://www. farmaid.org/site/News2?page=NewsArticle&id=5685&news_iv_ctrl=-1>.

Owens, Derek. *Composition and Sustainability: Teaching for a Threatened Generation*. Urbana, IL: NCTE, 2001.

Pepperdine, Sharon. "Social Indicators of Rural Community Sustainability: An Example from the Woady Yaloak Catchment." *First National Conference on the Future of Australia's Country Towns*. 15 Dec. 2004 <http://www.regional. org.au/au/countrytowns/strategies/pepperdine.hym>.

Popper, Deborah, and Frank Popper. "The Buffalo Commons: Metaphor as Method." *Geographical Review* 89.4 (1999): 491–510.

———. "The Great Plains: From Dust to Dust." *Planning* 53.12 (1987): 12–18.

"Pork Power: Are Pork Farmers Creating a Waste Hazard?" *60 Minutes*, 22 June 2003. 11 Dec. 2006 <http://www.foodsecurity.org/f2cconf2005.html>.

President's Council on Sustainable Development. "National Goals toward Sustainable Development." *Sustainable America: A New Consensus for the Prosperity, Opportunity and a Healthy Environment for the Future*. 30 Aug. 2004 <http:// clinton2.nara.gov/PCSD/Publications/TF_Reports/amer-chap1.html>.

Reitz, Rosa. Untitled essay. *Early Paxton*. Ed. Joyce Lierley. Unpublished anthology, 1982. 59–102.

"Rethinking 'Save the Family Farm.'" *ActionMedia*. 20 Mar. 2004 <http://www. turnonthenews.com/Farm%20Crisis.htm>.

Reynolds, Nedra. "Composition's Imagined Geographies: The Politics of Space in the Frontier, City, and Cyberspace." *College Composition and Communication* 50.1 (1998): 12–35.

———. *Geographies of Writing: Inhabiting Places and Encountering Difference*. Carbondale: Southern Illinois UP, 2004.

"Rural Voices, Country Schools." *National Writing Project*. 12 Sept. 2004 <http:// www.writingproject.org/Programs/rvcs/>.

*The Rural Womyn Zone*. 21 July 2005 <http://www.ruralwomyn.net/>.

Sassen, Saskia. "The Global City: Strategic Site/New Frontier." *IndiaSeminar.com* 503 (July 2001). 8 Jan. 2007 <http://www.india-seminar.com/2001/503/ 503%20saskia%20sassen.htm>.

Schlosser, Eric. *Fast Food Nation: The Dark Side of the All-American Meal*. New York: Perennial, 2002.

Schultz, Lucille. *The Young Composers: Composition's Beginnings in Nineteenth-Century Schools*. Carbondale: Southern Illinois UP, 1999.

Schuster, Charles, and William Van Pelt, eds. *Speculations: Readings in Culture, Identity, and Values*. Englewood Cliffs, NJ: Prentice, 1993.

Schwartz, Dona. "Introduction." *Waucoma Twilight: Generations of the Farm*. Washington, DC: Smithsonian Institution Press, 1992. 4 Mar. 2003 <http://sjmc. cla.umn.edu/faculty/schwartz/contents/Waucoma_Twilight/waucoma_twilight. html>.

Scully, Matthew. *Dominion: The Power of Man, the Suffering of Animals, and the Call to Mercy*. New York: St. Martin's/Griffin, 2003.

"Second National Farm to Cafeteria Conference: Putting Local Food on the Table: Farms and Food Service in Partnership." *Community Food Security Coalition*. 7 Dec. 2006 <http://www.foodsecurity.org/f2cconf2005.html>.

Shapiro, Henry. *Appalachia on Our Mind: The Southern Mountains and Mountaineers in the American Consciousness, 1870–1920*. Chapel Hill: U of North Carolina P, 1978.

Shiva, Vandana. *Stolen Harvest: The Hijacking of the Global Food Supply*. Boston: South End Press, 1999.

Shor, Ira. *Critical Teaching and Everyday Life*. Chicago: U of Chicago P, 1987.

———. "What Is Critical Literacy?" *Journal for Pedagogy, Pluralism, and Praxis* 4.1 (Fall 1999). 15 Sept. 2004 <http://www.lesley.edu/journals/jppp/4/shor. html>.

Siegel, Bernie. *Love, Medicine, and Miracles: Lessons Learned about Self-Healing from a Surgeon's Experience with Exceptional Patients*. New York: Harper, 1988.

*The Simple Life*. Prod. Mary-Ellis Bunim, Jonathan Murray, et al. Fox, 2003.

Singer, Mark. "True North." *New Yorker* 18 and 25 Feb. 2002, 118–23.

Sinor, Jennifer. *The Extraordinary Work of Ordinary Writing: Annie Ray's Diary*. Iowa City: U of Iowa P, 2002.

Smith, Lee. "The Face of Rural Poverty." *Fortune* Dec. 1990: 100–110.

Sohn, Katherine Kelleher. "Whistlin' and Crowin' Women of Appalachia: Literacy Practices since College." *CCC* 54.3 (2003): 423–52.

———. *Whistlin' and Crowin' Women of Appalachia: Literacy Practices since College*. Carbondale: Southern Illinois UP, 2006.

Spurlock, Morgan. *Don't Eat This Book! Fast Food and the Supersizing of America*. New York: Putnam, 2005.

Stekert, Ellen J. Unpublished lectures. Minneapolis: University of Minnesota, 1995.

Stewart, Elinore Pruitt. *Letters of a Woman Homesteader*. 1914. New York: Mariner, 1998.

Stock, Catherine McNicol. *Rural Radicals: Righteous Rage in the American Grain*. Ithaca: Cornell UP, 1996.

Stuart, Jesse. *The Thread That Runs So True*. New York: Simon, 1949.

Stumo, Michael, ed. "A Food and Agriculture Policy for the 21st Century." The Organization for Competitive Markets. *The Agribusiness Accountability Initiative*. 1 Jan. 2000. 11 Dec. 2006 <http://www.agribusinessaccountability. org/bin/view.fpl/1198/cms_category/1700.html>.

*Super Size Me*. Dir. Morgan Spurlock. The Con, 2004.

"Support." *Farm Aid*. 12 July 2004 <http://www.farmaid.org/site/PageServer? pagename=support_SP04_p2#bottom>.

"Sustaining Rural Living." *The Rural Womyn Zone*. 21 July 2005 <http://www. ruralwomyn.net/sustain.html>.

Szeman, Imre. "Introduction: Learning to Learn from Seattle." *Review of Education, Pedagogy, and Cultural Studies* 24 (2002): 1–12.

Theobald, Paul. *Call School: Rural Education in the Midwest to 1918*. Carbondale: Southern Illinois UP, 1995.

———. "Rural Philosophy for Education: Wendell Berry's Tradition." *ERIC Digest Clearinghouse on Rural Education and Small Schools*. Jan. 1992. 22 July 2005 <http://www.eric.ed.gov/ERICDocs/data/ericdocs2/content_storage_ 01/0000000b/80/2a/16/b0.pdf>.

———. *Teaching the Commons: Place, Pride, and the Renewal of Community*. Boulder, CO: Westview Press, 1997.

"Think Rural: Perceptions of Rural America." *Center for Rural Strategies*. 25 Sept. 2004 <http://www.ruralstrategies.org/issues/perceptions.html>.

"A Time to Act: A Report on the USDA National Commission on Small Farms." *United States Department of Agriculture National Commission on Small Farms*, Jan. 1998. 20 Mar. 2004 <http://www.reeusda.gov/smallfarm/report.htm>.

"Top 50 Cities in the U.S. by Population and Rank." *Infoplease*. 8 Aug. 2005 <http://www.infoplease.com/ipa/A0763098.html>.

United Nations Conference on Environment and Development. *United Nations*. 30 Aug. 2004 <http://www.un.org/geninfo/bp/enviro.html>.

"The Urban Archipelago: It's the Cities, Stupid." *The Stranger* 11–14 Nov. 2004. 20 Jan. 2004 <http://www.thestranger.com/2004–11–11/feature.html>.

U.S. Department of Commerce. Bureau of the Census. Current Population Reports, Series P-23. *Ancestry and Language in the United States, November 1979*. Washington, DC: GPO, 1982.

———. Bureau of the Census. *Historical Statistics of the United States, Colonial Times to 1970*. Washington, DC: GPO, 1976.

Vincent, George. "A Retarded Frontier." *American Journal of Sociology* 4 (1898): 1–20.

Weisser, Christian. *Moving Beyond Academic Discourse: Composition Studies and the Public Sphere*. Carbondale: Southern Illinois UP, 2002.

"What Do the Media Really Say When They Talk about Rural?" *80–55 Coalition for Rural America*. 1 Sept. 2004 <http://www.8055.0rg/doc_media_about_rural. html>.

"What Is a Family Farm?" *National Family Farm Coalition.* 3 Mar. 2006 <http://www.nffc.net/what/familyfarm.html>.

"What Is Farm to School?" *National Farm to School Program.* 15 Aug. 2005 <www.farmtoschool.org>.

"What Is Rural?" *United States Department of Agriculture.* 2 Sept. 2004 <http://www.nal.usda.gov/ric/faqs/ruralfaq.htm>.

"What Is the CFSC?" *The Community Food Security Coalition.* 14 Aug. 2005 <http://www.foodsecurity.org/>.

Whisnant, David. *All That Is Native and Fine: The Politics of Culture in an American Region.* Chapel Hill: U of North Carolina P, 1983.

"Why Rural Matters in Texas." *The Rural School and Community Trust.* 8 Aug. 2005 <http://www.ruraledu.org>.

"Why RWZ Is Online." *The Rural Womyn Zone.* 21 July 2005 <http://www.ruralwomyn.net/>.

"WIC Farmers' Market Nutrition Program." *USDA Food and Nutrition Service.* 17 Sept. 2004 <http://www.fns.usda.gov/wic/FMNP/FMNPfaqs.htm#7>.

Wilentz, Sean. "It Wasn't Morality That Divided Bush and Kerry Voters—It Was . . ." *History News Network* 5 Nov. 2004. 20 Jan. 2004 <http://hnn.us/articles/8548.html>.

Will, George W. "What We Owe What We Eat." *Newsweek* 18 July 2005. 7 Aug 2005 <http://www.msnbc.msn.com/id/8525632/site/newsweek/>.

Williamson, J. W. *Hillbillyland: What the Movies Did to the Mountains and What the Mountains Did to the Movies.* Chapel Hill: U of North Carolina P, 1995.

Windels, Elsie Lenore Holmstedt. Untitled essay. *Early Paxton.* Ed. Joyce Lierley. Unpublished anthology, 1982. 220–33.

Winkler, Wayne. *Walking toward Sunset: The Melungeons of Appalachia.* Macon, GA: Mercer UP, 2004.

Winne, Mark. "Education for Change." *The Community Food Security Coalition.* 14 Aug. 2005 <http://www.foodsecurity.org/views_education.html >.

W. K. Kellogg Foundation. "Perceptions of Rural America." *W. K. Kellogg Foundation.* 1 Nov. 2001. 31 July 2003 <http://www.wkkf.org/Pubs/FoodRur/Pub2973.pdf >.

———. "Perceptions of Rural America: Congressional Perspectives." *W. K. Kellogg Foundation.* 1 May 2002. 31 July 2003 <http://www.wkkf.org/Pubs/FoodRur/Pub3699.pdf>.

Woodhouse, Janice L., and Clifford E. Knapp. "Place-Based Curriculum and Instruction: Outdoor and Environmental Education Approaches." *ERIC Digest Clearinghouse on Rural Education and Small Schools.* Dec. 2000. 21 July 2005 <http://www.eric.ed.gov/ERICDocs/data/ericdocs2/content_storage_01/0000000b/80/2a/32/4c.pdf>.

World Commission on Environment and Development (The Brundtland Commission). *Our Common Future.* Oxford: Oxford UP, 1987.

"The WTO History Project." *University of Washington.* 7 Dec. 2006 <http://depts.washington.edu/wtohist/index.htm>.

"The WTO in Brief: Part I. The Multilateral Trading System: Past, Present, and Future." *World Trade Organization.* 19 May 2004 <http://www.wto.org/english/thewto_e/whatis_e/inbrief_e/inbr01_e.htm>.

"The WTO in Brief: Part II. The Organization." *World Trade Organization.* 19 May 2004 <http://www.wto.org/english/thewto_e/whatis_e/inbrief_e/inbr02_e.htm>.

"WTO: Seattle Collection." *University of Washington Libraries Digital Collections.* 25 Sept. 2004 <http://content.lib.washington.edu/WTOweb/>.

Young, Iris Marion. *Justice and the Politics of Difference.* Princeton: Princeton UP, 1990.

# Index

Informants are indexed by first names; they are also indexed by last name if it has been provided in the text.

**Kim Donehower** is an assistant professor of English at the University of North Dakota, where she teaches courses in writing, pedagogy, and literature and directs the Red River Valley Writing Project. Her work on rural literacies has been published in the *Journal of Appalachian Studies* and in *Women and Literacy: Inquiries for a New Century.*

**Charlotte Hogg** is an assistant professor of English at Texas Christian University, where she teaches a variety of writing classes. Her work has been published in *Western American Literature, Great Plains Quarterly, Clackamas Literary Review, Sundog: The Southeast Review,* and elsewhere. She is the author of *From the Garden Club: Rural Women Writing Community.*

**Eileen E. Schell** is an associate professor of writing and rhetoric and a faculty affiliate in women's studies at Syracuse University, where she teaches undergraduate and graduate courses in writing and rhetoric and undergraduate courses and community writing workshops on memoir, autobiography, and place-based writing. She is the author of *Gypsy Academics and Mother-Teachers: Gender, Contingent Labor, and Writing Instruction* and coeditor with Patricia Lambert Stock of *Moving a Mountain: Transforming the Role of Contingent Faculty in Composition Studies and Higher Education,* which won the 2003 Conference on College Composition and Communication Best Book Award.

# Other Books in the Studies in Writing & Rhetoric Series